JULIA HORN

Active Reading

Continuum Literary Studies

Active Reading

Transformative Writing
in Literary Studies

BEN KNIGHTS AND
CHRIS THURGAR-DAWSON

continuum

Continuum
The Tower Building   80 Maiden Lane
11 York Road   Suite 704
London SE1 7NX   New York, NY 10038

British Library Cataloguing-in-Publication Data
A catalogue record for this book is available from the British Library.

ISBN: HB: 0–8264–8700–9

Library of Congress Cataloging-in-Publication Data
A catalog record for this book is available from the Library of Congress.

Typeset by YHT Ltd, London
Printed and bound in Great Britain by Biddles Ltd, King's Lynn, Norfolk

Contents

Acknowledgements

This book has incurred a large number of debts of gratitude. Its first perhaps is to colleagues in the Development of University English Teaching Project. We would particularly like to commemorate two friends and colleagues whose untimely deaths represent such a loss to the communities of teaching: Barry Palmer and Colin Evans. The National Teaching Fellowship Scheme enabled an experimental module to become a project. Thanks are due to Sally Brown who nurtured the early stages of the National Teaching Fellowship. We would like to thank Denis Calderon who first suggested that Ben Knights apply for a Fellowship and has generously supported him ever since. We feel it invidious to pick out individual colleagues from the University of Teesside School of Arts and Media, or from the Higher Education Academy English Subject Centre, but we want to thank you all. Above all we would like to thank all those Teesside students and all the other participants in workshops who have taken part in and helped develop the modules on which this book is based. In particular we would like to thank those who generously gave their permission for their words and extracts from their assignments to be reproduced here. Anna Sandeman and her colleagues at Continuum have been encouraging and helpful throughout. 'Places We Love' is taken from 'Ivan V. Lalić: A Rusty Needle', translated by Francis R. Jones. Published by Avril Press Poetry in 1996: thanks to Kit Yee Wong. And finally, we thank Christine and Pam who have supported each of us beyond all possibility of praise and acknowledgement.

Introduction

Active Reading tells and reflects upon the story of a project carried out at the University of Teesside in the UK from 2001 onwards. Like any story, this one contains elements of other stories, and draws upon and echoes yet others. And to explain it, we will have to tell other stories again. For example, the story behind DUET (the Development of University English Teaching Project), or that of the condition of English Studies in British universities at the beginning of the twenty-first century. We know that there is a growing number of other colleagues who are working along these or similar lines. So we are writing in the hope that our project will chime with the activities or aspirations of many of those who teach English literature. Our book is also, we hope, a contribution to a resurgent discussion of creativity in education.[1] At the same time we need to emphasize from the beginning that — while we see ourselves as helping to build bridges between Creative Writing and Literary Studies — our project is about helping students to become better (more resourceful, less easily defeated) readers. Along the way they may become better writers; they may even discover a propensity for writing. If so, that is a wonderful bonus, but it has never been our prime objective. Our promise to ourselves and to our students was that engagement with the kind of activities described here would enable them to engage with the written word as active and self-aware makers of meaning. As producers (even on a small scale) they might start to feel the domain of textuality was no longer strange and alien. And they would be building themselves a basis for a lifetime of learning, their subject meaning far more than a mass of information to be forgotten once the assessment was over.

Several years on, we are impressed and delighted by the provisional outcomes of this project and would like to share them with others. We note how difficult in many ways it has become for literary studies to talk about pleasure, and we hope to foster pleasure in learning without falling into either amateurishness, *belles lettres*, or a reified notion of desire. The activities which we advocate can perfectly well be aligned with the provision of a document which might in many ways seem the very antithesis of our own orientation towards education as a form of living, the Quality Assurance Agency (QAA) Subject Benchmark.[2] We are not aiming to replace or undermine serious forms of learning or scholarship;

rather we describe a process of enrichment: optional modules which enhance and complement the student experience. We aim to help students discover that both the collaborative space of the seminar/workshop and the act of writing are in themselves opportunities for learning, and not simply vehicles for reaching a pre-determined goal.

While this book represents a joint project, and a collaborative process of research and writing, we agreed at an early stage to take primary responsibility for writing different chapters. Ben Knights for the historical and theoretical chapters, 1–4, and the chapter on applications beyond English Studies, Chapter 8; and Chris Thurgar-Dawson for chapters 5–7 on the modules and their students. We take joint responsibility for the overall result. A broad overview of the book is as follows.

In offering a reading of the contemporary condition of English Studies in Higher Education (HE), Chapter 1 provides a context for the project and for the chapters that follow. Chapter 2 takes up another aspect of context in offering a history of the practice of creative/critical crossover, principally, though not exclusively, in HE. Chapter 3 explores the tradition of Literary Criticism, both in relation to the creation of imaginative literature and as an ambiguous form of writing in itself. Chapter 4 extends that argument chronologically in articulating the implications for writing of the embedding of Literary and Critical Theory in English programmes. The next three chapters comprise a case study of the project and the modules on which it is based. Chapter 5 explores the setting up and early stages of a verbal arts workshop within the modular framework. Chapters 6 and 7 respectively document and reflect upon the student experience of the development of the workshop process and the procedures of assessment. Chapter 8 steps outside the BA programme in exploring applications to lifelong learning, specifically taking up the potential role of recreative writing in forms of professional development. We hope that the mutual influence of the practically oriented chapters and those which are more historical or theoretical in nature will generate insights and connections which would not have been possible in a book that was simply oriented to one or the other pole.

Finally, we want to make our position clear. We hope to persuade. We believe that the related subjects that cluster under the umbrella terms 'English' or 'English Studies' are of immense social and cultural importance. But they are not subjects that lend themselves to vogue instrumentalism or to strategic learning. They require students to engage in what has widely come to be known as 'deep learning'. Like many others, we are troubled by the pressures that condense the curriculum to what Philip Davis once called 'reductive knowingness'. We want learners to engage in an active dialogue with a variety of cultural habitats. Such dialogue must involve risky but productive exposure to discourses and textual phenomena they themselves may regard as alien. Where contemporary technologies of learning are oriented towards success, we aim to create space and support for learning from failure. Hence the importance of drafting and, in social terms, of modelling a small-scale learning community which can foster tolerance of risk. As teachers we all have to help create and maintain a space outside the pressures either of professionalized learning imposed from above or conformist cool imposed by peers. We hope that this book will encourage teachers who share our belief, and add to their resources.

Part I

Pedagogic Context

1 Contexts

It is perhaps already evident that this book seeks to be more than a handbook or a manual on a particular teaching practice.[3] Naturally, we hope that readers will take from it stimulating ideas for teaching. But if those ideas are to have any valency (or indeed if they are to succeed as a stimulus), that process must take place within a larger argument about English Studies in Higher Education. This chapter will supply a context for the rest of the book by providing an analysis of the situation of the English-related disciplines at the end of the twentieth and the beginning of the twenty-first century – principally, though we hope not exclusively, in the United Kingdom – and will offer one kind of route map for the future. This is not to connive at a notion of a 'crisis' in English Studies. Shouts of 'crisis' can prove self-fulfilling, or provide cover for attempted capture of the subject from within. We would rather work with all the various energies of the subject than conjure into being another sect. We shall, however, argue that distortions brought about in large part by the continuing professionalization and specialization of research (reinforced by the Research Assessment Exercise) are distracting subject practitioners from thinking about teaching at the very moment when – for reasons we go on to outline – it is crucial that they engage in that thinking. The alternative could well be – at least for the literature domain – the fate of Classics in the mid-twentieth century: becoming a high cultural value subject for a very small elite of the privately-educated. It will also be necessary to use the chapter to do some ground clearing about the beliefs and practices surrounding 'active reading'. We make a case for reconfiguring English Studies, and we propose the value of drawing literature, language and creative writing into a mutually productive web through raising the profile of 'production' for both students and their teachers. To that extent, our suggestions converge with the argument developed over many years by Robert Scholes:

> In an age like ours, pastiche and parody are the natural way into our cultural heritage. We should make better use of this route in making this heritage available to students. (Scholes 1998: 161)

> As I hope I have made plain, by giving production a larger role in the discipline of English, I do not mean just allowing credit for traditional

courses in composition or creative writing ... I am asking for rethinking of what writing and other modes of linguistic production have to offer students and a reconstruction of the courses themselves. Those who teach students how to write poetry, fiction and drama have never expected all their students ... to become professional writers ... They have always believed, however ... that their students would become better readers of literature because of their attempts to write it. And they are right, I have no doubt. What is necessary, now, is for the discipline as a whole to accept this position and to rethink the role of writing in English studies with few preconceptions beyond the goal of producing the most literate students possible. (Scholes 1998: 162)[4]

Any debate about the curriculum and the subject matter is also a debate about the process in which that subject matter is enacted or realized. There is, we suggest, a close connection between promoting an exchange between critical and creative practice and raising the visibility of pedagogy.[5] Both have to do with the materiality of words and practices. Visibility is essential if as a profession we are to make our tacit knowledge about what we do into active knowledge capable of being shared, critiqued and developed. Throughout, we argue that the conventional critical/creative binary divide (while pragmatically functional) is profoundly unstable: that reading, critique, re-imagining, even doing literary criticism, are themselves already forms of re-making, which in the end take place in dialogues within what Stanley Fish calls 'interpretive communities' (Fish 1980). 'Textual production' potentially draws upon and feeds back into all branches of the subject.

Like any other discipline, English Studies represents an ongoing negotiation between a federation of teaching and research tribes.[6] Because of the widely available nature of its subject matters, it (more than many other disciplines) simultaneously represents a negotiation between the tribes of those who practise in universities, those who have responsibility for school education and a diverse lay public. In many ways the history of the subject over the past one hundred years can be read in terms of the successive phases of that ongoing negotiation. In a 'soft' subject (Becher and Trowler 2001), the knowledge transacted between lecturers and students is also to some degree open to negotiation between professionals (endowed with research standing) and those who pass through or who enter the discipline. English Studies exhibits 'low paradigm consensus'. In other words, the curriculum of an English Studies degree is only partially dictated by a communal standard about what knowledge, understanding and skills students should achieve.[7] To a greater or lesser degree (and naturally subject also to other factors like resource and staff availability) the curriculum is open to market forces and intellectual fashion, expressed through both undergraduate and postgraduate students. As we shall see later, the steady rise of Creative Writing, or modules in Gothic, Sci-Fi and Contemporary Fiction are examples of the subject changing in tune with changing demand. (Changes which, once cemented in the curriculum, in turn breed the next generation of research students.) Those who design English curricula have increasingly to enter into a persuasive dialogue with their market to promote strands or modules in, say, Medieval, Tudor or Eighteenth-Century literature.

Because the subject evolves from expectations and mental models entertained by students and reading publics as well as by writers and academic professionals the identity of the student learner is a fairly fluid construct (Knights 2005). Practically, as anyone who has run induction programmes for new undergraduates knows, this leads to considerable uncertainty on all sides about what new students are actually being inducted into. Students attempt to guess what is in their teachers' minds, or invent their own information-based construct. Even back in the days 'before theory' such tensions were generally lived out in a more or less overt tussle between the substantialist desires of students and the formalist propensities of their lecturers. Even Creative Writing – in the early days at all events – struggled to put over the apparently counter-intuitive imagist and avant-garde propositions on which its practice was based. Students tended to be more emotionally drawn to the aura of 'everyone has a novel in them' than to Ezra Pound's imagist injunction to simplify.[8] It is perhaps an irony that 'English Studies' has spent much of its institutional existence explaining to students that the interest they thought they had in their subject was the wrong one.

As teachers we could gain a lot from doing our own ethnography upon that meeting of tribes that takes place in the first year (see Green 2005). Behind that proposition lurks another: that could we but realize it, the English subject disciplines between them possess considerable if largely latent tools for pedagogic analysis and understanding.[9] There is a metacognitive possibility here: that the skills and conceptual equipment elaborated for reading texts might transfer (not in bulk, but at all events analogically) to generate heightened awareness of pedagogic process. The vocabularies of genre, style, narrative and metaphor are not only capable of pedagogic application, but, transferred to that field, are highly generative. In fact, profound pedagogic implications reside within all the debates English has been having with itself – whether concerning addressivity, dialogism, the reader, gender, the uncanny, power, 'the queer', the post-colonial, the construction of the subject, utopia or the use of linguistic corpora. The paradox is that, despite these debates, the day-to-day practice of the subject has (though with many exceptions) been largely carried on within traditional templates, protocols for interaction that long antedate the massive changes which have overtaken Higher Education since the early 1990s. In his *Who Killed Shakespeare?* Patrick

Brantlinger appeals to the humanities to take part in a collective rescue effort 'in the face of the catastrophes brought about by the alleged triumph of political liberalism and the free market' (2001: 200–1). It is a core part of our argument that if some variant of English Studies is to survive and take part in that necessary cultural resurgence then it cannot be at the level of ideas alone, however important those ideas might be. Change has to take place at the level of practice: the grammars that govern the interaction between teachers and students and students and each other; the protocols of notation and assessment, the collaborative nature of the productive processes in which both teachers and students engage. While, as even a half-baked 'learning and teaching strategy' can tell you, the goal is the autonomous learner, we cannot – if we ever could – go on working on the assumption that outside the classroom (or away from the virtual/learning environment (VLE)) students naturally and intuitively know what to do. While we should not patronize students, we have to collaborate with each other and with students in shaping structures for learning.

The rest of the chapter sketches this context. While it centres on English Studies, it attempts to take into account dynamics that originate from far outside that particular parish. The larger environment bears upon disciplines in different ways, and we can only understand the local dynamics of English within that larger environment. 'English', as we have pointed out, is very far from being a subject produced by or owned by scholars in universities. Nevertheless, the meaning of the subject to those who practise it professionally plays a major role in shaping the subject as it comes to be known by learners. Our hypothesis is that a major factor in bringing about change in the subject in universities has been the speeded up professionalization and specialization of the subject as researched and written. This specialization, we contend, has tended to squeeze out attention to pedagogy. The demands on lecturers are such that it is often simpler to fall back on conventional methods without noticing that they do not suit many of our students. On this hypothesis, we shall start with the supply side and then move on to demand. This will map the context for the chapters that follow.[10]

SPECIALIZATION, CURRICULUM AND PROFESSION

No variety of 'English' can evade the close study of language. Yet that remark, innocuous to the point of banality, has a very different weighting in different communities of the subject. While this book concentrates mostly on the symbiosis between the teaching of literature and the teaching of writing, we do not want to collude in an exclusion of English

Language teaching. It is a pedagogic tragedy that the theory revolution of the 1970s and 1980s was in general so temperamentally averse to empirical language study.[11] As one of Evans' respondents, a linguistician, remarked:

> There's no common cause with theory. They would say I ought to get my literary theory right, and I would say they ought to get their linguistics right. There's a conceptual boundary between me and my colleagues. I have to adopt their way of talking about texts. (Evans 1993: 171)

Of course, English departments in British universities from the early twentieth century were no strangers to the teaching of English language. But until the 1960s the process concerned was historical and philological, and its practitioners were (as to a lesser extent they still are) the departmental specialists in Anglo-Saxon, Old Norse and Middle English – simultaneously teachers of those languages and scholars of their respective literatures. Their position was stronger in some departments than others: weakest or even non-existent in those departments with least of an Oxford or London lineage. But practitioners of literature and culture as they were, and often living in a state of armed co-existence with their literary critical colleagues, language people in this sense were accepted as having a place in English departments. Joke as they might among themselves about the tediousness of medieval scholarship, modernists were usually willing to accept the guardian of 'The Seafarer', of Chaucer, or of the *Gawain* Poet as 'one of us'. With the rise in the 1960s and 1970s of the new structural linguistics this situation changed considerably. By the late 1970s a new breed of synchronic linguists had emerged. Often they had more in common with their colleagues in Modern Languages or indeed in Education or Psychology than they did with the teachers of Old Norse, and they were increasingly to be found within the newly formed departments of Linguistics. While some Stylisticians and Critical Linguists in the mould of Roger Fowler, Mick Short, Ron Carter or Robert Hodge engaged in a heroic attempt to hold together the study of literature, culture and language, the ensuing history was one where during the 1980s, and outside certain enclaves, the teaching of literature and of language grew apart. This situation was exacerbated by the deep distrust for linguistics entertained by most of the new schools of 'Theory'. With their roots in Parisian derivatives of Saussure, most theorists perceived language studies to be hopelessly empirical and agents of political amnesia. It was the students of English and the discipline itself that missed out as a result of this covert civil war.[12] Another of Evans' respondents, this time a student, remarked:

When you are doing language in a department where there is English
literature you do get marginalized. A lot of the English literature
lecturers look at us as if we're inferior ... (1993: 171)

One of our arguments for the textual production we advocate is that –
where students do not have access to the pedagogies of linguistics – it can
go some of the way towards an engagement with language as self-aware
practice. The decline in uptake of languages other than English in schools
and universities has exacerbated the problem. The loss among a majority
of students of even a modicum of external perspective on their language
and culture makes all the more necessary a project which opens a few
windows in the prison house of monolingualism.

The situation in Literature is not clear either. But for our purposes, and
at the cost of a good deal of simplification, certain trends may be identified. The dominant theme is professional specialization. To simplify,
across the middle decades of the twentieth century a university teacher of
English (unless he or she were a Medievalist) was expected to be able to
range widely across a broadly accepted canon. You might lecture in your
specialist area – the eighteenth century, say, or the Victorian novel
(though the expectation was that anyone should be able to lecture on
Shakespeare and probably Wordsworth as well). But for tutorial purposes, the understanding was that lecturers knew enough about Milton,
Hopkins, Conrad, James, Lawrence or Eliot to teach undergraduate or
even postgraduate students. While it has always been an ill-informed slur
that the Leavises and their followers were formalists, careless of history, it
was nevertheless the case that in pedagogic terms the grounding of the
subject in practical criticism could create this appearance. The core of the
discipline was seen to reside in a limited number of texts and authors, to
which the trained critical intelligence could be as successfully applied in
the classroom as in the professional conference. The task was criticism;
and in seeking to defend a particular version of continuity against the
dissipating energies of the contemporary, criticism demanded a close
personal encounter between articulate reader and text. This is a schematic
case, and certainly advertisements for lectureships still frequently specify
mixed expertise. Nevertheless, it remains broadly true that the generalist
set of expectations, and the rituals of debate and argumentation that went
with it, was on its way to becoming residual.[13]

If we stand back from local detail, the picture, as indicated above, is
one of an accelerated process of specialization. (See Gawthrope and Martin
2004 throughout, but especially 2.8 on 'coverage and aims'.) A number
of factors are involved. The professionalization of the research doctorate
coupled with intense competition for university posts results in a competitive edge for those postgraduates who can demonstrate marginal
advantage in terms of 'value added'. Above all, the Research Assessment

Exercise (RAE) has richly ambiguous outcomes. In national terms, English has in many ways benefited from its own extraordinary success. But the net effect has been analogous to dumping nitrate fertilizer on a complex eco-system. Some life forms have adapted and flourished, while denying light and moisture to others. And a massive distortion of the narrative of the teaching career has taken place as departments and universities struggle for competitive advantage. While most of us are prepared to make the best of an argument for 'research-led teaching', there is little point in denying that the effect for those departments that benefit from or expect to benefit from the RAE is an orientation of priorities where teaching and the administration of the degree assumes a relatively lowly position. The many lecturers who care deeply about their students and their teaching increasingly have to struggle (often at considerable personal cost) to reconcile their own and institutional priorities.

Specialization within the Ph.D. and the publishing of monographs and articles has other effects, too. There is, so to say, a convergence of the intellectual and the material. Thus one of the effects of the spread of forms of historicism has been to make English in some ways more like History. While many of us would applaud this trend, there are pedagogic side-effects, for example the sheer volume of immersed knowledge felt to be required before one can make significant statements about texts. While researchers revel in the popular cultures and publishing histories surrounding their chosen subject, becoming along the way authorities in aspects of medicine, anthropology or law, the effect of publicly flaunting this knowledge can be to reinforce in students the belief that the subject is actually information-based. The implication is that since you could never emulate your tutor's erudition, it is better to take assiduous notes and make a show of quasi-professional knowledge from two or three recommended extracts. Even the increased specialization of the Level 3 special topic – while valuably exposing students to knowledge in the process – can militate against wider reading and knowledge; the research predilections of a specific departmental community creating an oddly distorted idea of the subject. Given the ever-increasing gap between teacher knowledge and student knowledge, research trends (the Gothic; postcolonial studies; embodiment) can be experienced by students as forms of coercive orthodoxy. At the same time the teaching culture of departments has shifted towards a kind of imitative professionalism, a normative assumption that a BA programme exists to turn out researchers. Thus undergraduates (while they do of course find ways of resisting or subverting the process) are now regularly trained in searching, referencing and citation procedures that a generation ago would not normally have been achieved by a research student. Programme handbooks seek to inculcate the differential virtues of Harvard, MLA or Chicago. Supervisors entertain the (often fond) hope that the near-universal Level 3 dissertation will be carried out on the lines of an MA. Which is not to say that these are bad things, or that students ought not to learn some scholarly courtesies. But it is to suggest that the paradigmatic career of the research professional has exerted and daily exerts more pressure on narratives of teaching and learning.

Our account is not an attempt to write a contemporary history of the subject, but rather to identify salient aspects of that history in relation to the evolution (or stasis) of pedagogic practice. We are sympathetic to David Bleich's argument that most parts of the academy:

> by tradition and through its practices of classical values, have separated 'knowledge' of anything from the pedagogical practices that pass it on. (2001: 117)

And, like him, we believe that to assume 'the materiality of language would change many things that we take for granted in English studies' (2001: 130). That language cannot solely be identified with the language of the text, nor with that of literary criticism or critique. It is also the language of the classroom and its associated practices. It is a paradox that neither 'theory' nor the forms of historicism that have flourished more recently address the materiality of classroom language and practice.

THE STUDENT EXPERIENCE

Shifts in the professional community and research base of English Studies have left relatively intact a set of assumptions about the nature of the undergraduate experience. While, obviously, any teacher has their tale of contrary instances, the paradigm of undergraduate study is still one of socialization into an exclusive community. That induction is associated with forms of knowledge, activity, argumentation and assessment, above all the analytical essay.[14] While this paradigm is still held by those who see themselves as members of the 'subject community', it is, we shall argue, one which has grown progressively further from the actual phenomena of student experience. We do not want to become embroiled in generalizations about what 'students today' know or do not know. But a major influence on this book and its recommendations is the observation that very many – perhaps even the majority of – students of English literature do not feel at home in the 'imagined community' of the subject.[15] This sense of being a stranger in the world in which, to a considerable degree, English Literary Studies is still predicated is by no means confined to those groups to whom it might (for reasons of race, region or class) most obviously apply. It means that very many students adopt a relationship to English literature and culture which might not too fancifully be described as postcolonial. With that in mind, it is to the student experience we now turn.

The English disciplines have remained among the most popular. In round figures, UK single honours programmes recruit around 8,500 students each year (slightly more than History, and nearly double the number for Media Studies), and a similar number are enrolled on joint and combined honours programmes. In 2004–5, the Higher Education Statistical Agency lists 50,325 'home' English students (including postgraduates) (www.hesa.ac.uk/holisdocs/pubinfo/student/subject 0405. htm). (See also Sadie Williams, *Admissions Trends in Undergraduate English: Statistics and Attitudes*, English Subject Centre 2002.) But they have been only sporadically successful in responding to policies of access and widening participation. English (particularly in its literature variant) has had patchy success in overcoming its limited social reach in terms of gender, class and ethnicity. With a gender ratio that appears to be stuck at around 3:1 in favour of women, it is only a slight exaggeration to say that in broad terms (and with several prominent institutional exceptions) English Literature at BA level remains a white, middle class and female subject. Its immediate competitors, English Language, Media Studies, Journalism and, in the immediate past, Cultural Studies, have had slightly more success in extending their social reach. Debating the reasons is not the rationale of this book, but we have to assume that we are seeing far more than a collective failure on the part of departments and admissions tutors to reach out into the wider community. The reasons, let us speculate, are more profound and have to do variously with the reproduction and meaning of literacy within British society, with the differential ambitions and success of boys and girls as readers, and perhaps to some extent with class resentments over the cultural capital attached to 'high literacy'. Neither does it help this situation that relative numbers of mature and of part-time students are in decline (Williams 2002: 2.6 and figures). In this context, we simply want to argue for ways of making the processes and assessment of 'English' more various, especially in a context where English is competing with related subjects and where there may be considerable scope for creative hybrids along the boundaries, with Media Studies, Linguistics or Drama. Since the number of those studying English in joint or combined honours programmes far exceeds those studying single honours, it would in any case be in the interest of subject specialists to take advantage, intellectually and even economically, of the weakened boundaries with other disciplines which in any case characterize the research scene.

The recruitment of undergraduate students into English is, of course, subject to the same pressures and vagaries of public policy as is recruitment to other subjects. Nevertheless, the longer term changes experienced over recent years, from the massive university expansion of the early 1990s to the arrival of top-up fees and the planned increase of 'variable' fees in 2006 may bear on the English disciplines in particular ways. Fears of debt, alongside the Government and White Paper emphasis on 'employability' and the 'skills deficit', have created a situation where an apparently non-vocational subject is likely to be seen by many potential students and their parents and peers as an unwise choice. Attempting to trim their sails to the prevailing winds, university managements have engaged in major 're-profiling exercises', and to these, too, English subject groups have been vulnerable. In this context, then, there is all the more need for the English disciplines to highlight the skills and aptitudes acquired during the degree. But in the face of the steady drift towards 'marketization' the subject should not lose its nerve. Though public support for 'lifelong education' is largely rhetorical, the English community has powerful things to say about learning for life and about aspects of experience that are only tangentially attached to economic success. But we do need to be able to convey a coherent picture of the nature of the knowledge and praxis that characterize the formal study of the subject.

One more crucial set of forces shapes the student experience. As we have repeatedly noted, 'English', whether as a body of knowledge or as a constellation of practices, is not and never has been the exclusive property of the university community. But for most of its existence there has been fruitful two-way commerce between the subject as practised in schools and in universities. For reasons which we have space only to summarize here, during the period between (roughly) 1990 and the early 2000s that commerce ceased. English in schools and English in universities became tribes marooned on separate islands. On the school side of the divide, the major force was the National Curriculum, the succession of instruments and initiatives that followed and the rise of Ofsted. The assumption still widely made in the late 1980s that university teachers would at least influence the direction of change was rudely shattered when the Major Government effectively rejected the Cox Report and Ronald Carter's *Language in the National Curriculum* (Cox 1991, 1995). With university lecturers scarcely any longer represented on the examination boards, and teachers and teacher trainers battening down to cope with a storm of efforts to micro-manage the curriculum, formal contact with the universities was lost.

The situation on the university side of the divide was rather different. While from 1994 onwards university departments were learning to live with their own Quality Regime incarnated in the Teaching Quality Assessment, it was curriculum change rather than public policy initiatives that drove universities away from the norms of school English. Such change derived from the process of specialization outlined earlier: the continued separation out of language and literature, and the embedding of 'theory', increasingly packaged in 'readers', anthologies and guide-books for an undergraduate audience. Then in 2000 the reform of A-level had major implications for students. 'Curriculum 2000' brought in a revised two-year programme of Advanced Subsidiary (AS) and A2 (see Barlow in Green 2005). Whatever the virtues of this attempt to broaden and to modularize A-levels, many unintended consequences followed both from the squeezing out of free-ranging time in the first (AS) year, and the packaging of the curriculum into units governed by 'assessment objectives'.[16] The effect upon the experience and expectations of students has been profound and is as yet only partially understood (Green 2005; Hodgson and Spours 2003). While many university lecturers were erroneously inclined to blame the teachers (who found themselves in the position of 'teaching to the test'), the effect seems to have been that students entering university had internalized intellectual habits deeply antipathetic to those which their lecturers professed.

It is widely observed by teachers on both sides of the divide that the unitization and assessment objectives of Curriculum 2000 have fostered strategic, assessment-focused learning and reinforced the misunder-standing that knowledge can be equated with information. It is reported that – counter to the university aims of creating more independent, self-reliant students – those emerging from Curriculum 2000, and keenly conscious as consumers of the financial consequences of their degree, are showing symptoms of increased dependency: a desire, expressed both informally and in evaluations, for being given notes, a strategic con-centration on assessment, and an unwillingness to read more widely or to undertake any work that is not assessed.

This book is addressed to the situation sketched here. We make a dual claim. Firstly, that the influence of students in their new-found role as consumers should not simply be deplored. The subject must not abandon its own values, but has everything to gain from entering into a more informed dialogue with its students' expressed interests. Secondly, this is not the moment for 'more of the same'. That is to say that the subject must, as a matter of urgency, review its own teaching, learning and assessment practices. To that review, hybridizations along the boundaries of 'literature', 'language' and 'creative writing' could make a central contribution. Creative writing, while it has recently taken on the appearance of a kind of pastoral within the utilitarian regime, does not represent an educational utopia. But it is a domain which both engages powerful investments on the part of students and generates pedagogic and assessment processes from which the subject at large has much to learn.

CONVERGENCE AND THE RISE OF CREATIVE WRITING

In view of the argument about research specialization put forward earlier, we should also note elements of convergence: points where student and staff cultures have, to some degree, met and mutually influenced each other. Some of the most popular curriculum areas are domains such as Film Studies, the Gothic and Children's Fiction, where there is evidently a productive symbiosis between research activity and youth cultures. Such convergences suggest the need to elaborate a more sophisticated argument about the influence of the market. Thus – while this has not altogether been an alignment of perspectives – English lecturers have frequently sought to appeal to their students over a shared interest in the erotic. And the curriculum has always to some degree responded to its environment, whether we think of the Tragedy Paper in the 1920s Cambridge Tripos, or the rise of Holocaust Studies in the 1990s. Our final topic, at all events, represents an example of convergence between teacher and student cultures.

In moving towards the next chapter, the remaining element to discuss is the rise of Creative Writing. While Creative Writing has a long history in US Universities, as an educational programme it is a relatively recent development in Britain. The MA programme at the University of East Anglia was founded in 1970, and under the auspices of Malcolm Bradbury rapidly acquired prestige. In Adult and Continuing Education, Creative Writing enjoyed a boom in the late 1970s and to some extent became embedded thereafter (see O'Rourke 2005). Nevertheless, it was slow to take root in BA programmes. David Craig was teaching writing at Lancaster in the early 1970s. Sheffield City Polytechnic (later to become Sheffield Hallam University) offered modules from 1982 (see Monteith and Miles 1992). Nevertheless, it was only in the mid- to late 1990s and alongside a proliferation of writing fellowships and writer-in-residence schemes that Creative Writing took off in British universities. Though there a few examples of single honours programmes, in general Creative Writing is practised either in joint honours, or within strands of modules. A subject not taught in schools (where there is relatively little scope for verbally creative work after primary school), it has become massively successful in terms of recruitment. There seems to be a near insatiable demand, and many departments report pressure for dedicated or single-honours courses. At the same time, and while generally practised within English departments, the subject exists in a state of intellectual and material tension with its hosts. An animated debate exists over who should teach the subject, and this debate has been widely resolved into an orthodoxy that it should be taught by practitioners. In turn, the widespread appointment of published writers on short-term or part-time contracts has exaggerated inter-tribal conflict between self-employed writers and academics. Meanwhile, academics who identify with (and may indeed themselves practise as) writers often seek to mark themselves off from what they see as arid scholasticism. Despite these tensions, the presence of Creative Writing in close proximity to 'English' has opened the way for potential cross-fertilization of practices which 'English' still has to fully exploit. Such practices include running workshops as an alternative to the traditional seminar, and assessment by portfolio and reflective commentary. We shall return to this hybridization in the next chapter. But let us note that many teachers who cross the borders see a value for writing neither in terms of self-expression nor in terms of the making of future Booker Prize winners, but as itself an educational process that permits deeper engagement with the already written.[17]

> ... academically-based Creative Writing teaching cannot have as its determining force the conviction that fiction writing is merely, or even mostly, (a) therapy, (b) self-expression, (c) a training ground for the next batch of great writers, (d) a form of play or (e) a glorified form of literacy or study skills training.
>
> All of the above may be by-products of the process ... However, the primary purpose of an undergraduate Creative Writing course is (a) to develop a combined critical and writerly understanding of fictional genres and the imaginative possibilities of language, in order to be able to make informed choices; (b) to enhance all literacy skills; (c) to develop a critical literary intelligence leading to an informed critical vocabulary; (d) to create more hungry readers. (Michelene Wandor in Holland (ed.) 2003: 13)

We have now perhaps reached a point where English Studies might conceivably be reconfigured through its own pedagogy (McCurrie and Kilian 2004: 43–64). As part of a varied repertoire, that pedagogy should include, we argue, skills in the creative reformation and transformation of texts. Such a development would involve bringing together strengths derived from the teaching of language and creative writing, as well as literature. To that subject we turn in the chapters that follow.

NOTE that this chapter draws heavily on four reports by the English Subject Centre:

Williams, Sadie. 2002. *Admission Trends in Undergraduate English*.
Martin, Philip and Jane Gawthrope. 2003. *Survey of the English Curriculum and Teaching in UK Higher Education*.
Holland, Siobhan. 2003. *Creative Writing: A Good Practice Guide*.
Green, Andrew. 2005. *Four Perspectives on Transition: English Literature from Sixth Form to University*.

2 Literary Practice

[F]or one of the best responses to a poem is surely another poem. (Scholes 2001: 59)

... which texts would I consent to write (to re-write), to desire to put forth in this world of mine? What evaluation finds is precisely this value: what can be written (re-written) today: *the writerly*. Why is the writerly our value? Because the goal of literary work (of literature as work) is to make the reader no longer a consumer, but a producer of the text. Our literature is characterized by the pitiless divorce which the literary institution maintains between the producer of the text and its customer, between its author and its reader. (Barthes 1975: 4)

This setting apart of pupils' work as 'personal' or 'creative' suggests that it is somehow more rhapsodic and egocentric than other forms of writing. It is seen as a product of the child's mysterious affective processes, a matter of inspiration, inscrutable and ineducable.

Literature has been made respectable by lifting it out of this marshy emotional terrain, but the effect has been destructive. We do not think with one half of ourselves and feel with the other, but we synthesize the two: we think feelingly and feel intelligently. As we read, we think and feel in the same act. It is essential to take up methods of teaching literature which will mobilize the entire capacities of the pupil. Writing is a particularly fine instrument for harnessing the many layers of the reading response, because it is in the nature of language to connote and denote at the same time ... (Hackman 1987)

Pedagogic crossover between creative and critical activities is not a recent innovation. The history of such crossovers – within the broader history explored in the previous chapter – offers a context for the rest of the book. Let us begin by acknowledging that pedagogy and the development of curriculum are not simply driven by internal dynamics, but register at several removes the movements of public policy. Since the late 1980s, a continuous thread of British government policy has been to micro-manage education through a dizzying succession of initiatives and statutory implements. It is as though education has come to be seen as a domain of social control in the very moment of the triumph of free-market ideologies. Behind the rhetoric of markets and choice, behind the declared aim of rolling back the state, the education system and the universities along with it are required to exercise the discipline, the social control over cultural reproduction which the market itself has forsworn. Having unleashed hedonism as the social energy of progress, the state is searching for ways of inculcating morality and discipline. Economic deregulation finds its mirror image in the regulation of knowledge. So, in turn, the universities have themselves been opened up to a degree of surveillance by state and quasi-governmental agencies unimaginable only fifteen years ago (see, for example, Readings 1996).

These pressures bear on all disciplines. But as a subject that purported to be the custodian of the national language and culture, the domain of social meanings and of social dreaming, English experienced the effects of this agenda in highly specific ways. One of the effects of the perpetually shifting domain of educational institutions is to create amnesia, a kind of continuous present in which exacting initiatives loom up out of the fog. It is all the more necessary, therefore, to remain in touch with our collective memories. What follows is a brief history of the activities advocated by this book.

THEORY, PEDAGOGY, WRITING

No attempt to explore the role of writing and transformative writing in relation to English degree programmes can be made without locating the topic in the larger history of the subject. It may seem to be spelling out the obvious but, from its inception as a university subject, English Literature especially has found it necessary to manage its own relationship to writing. Its medium was its message, in a way that was not true for History, Sociology or Politics – or even for Philosophy. From the beginning, it sought to mark out its own intellectual territory by demonstrating its own value as a supplement to that which was already written: by what right should 'English', or literary criticism, intervene in the spontaneous relations between books and their readers? What could it add? These are the sort of questions which in our own time are said to concern 'added value'. What special sort of readers did it seek to create by evolving its own writing practices as an educational and publishable subject; or by establishing colonial relations between the domain of imagination and that of criticism? The very attempt to adjudicate on what writing mattered (thus establishing demarcation lines to mark off major writing from that whose significance was merely utilitarian, sociological or symptomatic) implied a simultaneous judgement on the value of kinds of reading and readers. In the course of its establishment as an educational subject, 'English' created a hierarchical succession of filters with major implications for learning processes as well as for literature itself. In short, an academic subject that took writing and creativity as its domain had from the start an ambivalent relation to its own praxis as writing – its severe commitment to standards a bulwark against playfulness or escapism.

In picking up the story around 1980, we have, at risk of simplification, to identify some of the forces that were bringing about change in the subject. New intellectual and tribal alliances were being formed among practitioners, leading to shifting configurations between on the one hand 'English' as the systematic study of privileged texts, and on the other, contemporary cultural studies, film, psychoanalysis, linguistics and philosophy. Fuelled by intellectual energies drawn from linguistics and anthropology, there was, as we have seen, a growing internal revolt within the profession against those who had appeared to be dominant in the subject: what we might conveniently see as the rise of 'theory' (see Chapter 4).

The process of creating and maintaining an academic subject necessitates exclusion, a drawing of boundaries to ward off all that the subject is not. Such patterns of exclusion filter down into the experience of students, and their understanding – or creative misunderstanding – of the performances that they are required to carry out (Knights 2005). Socialization into an academic subject requires students to internalize images of who they are *not* supposed to be, as well as the roles they are expected to imitate. In the process of turning itself into a scholarly discipline, one hegemonic form of English had pinned its colours to judgement, evaluation, scrutiny, discrimination, and in so doing adopted a highly selective orientation towards creativity. As Peter Abbs noted, 'there was a marked tendency in the early Cambridge school to elevate the act of criticism above the act of creation. The very word *Scrutiny* unambiguously proclaimed what kind of activity it most esteemed' (Abbs 1982:16).

Forty years on, university English (while admittedly fed by multiple streams) was broadly characterized by critical rituals of evaluation which effectively kept creative practice out of the curriculum. Whether a student identified with the stance or not, the effect of such unremitting severity of judgement was inevitably to inhibit public expression of creativity. The influence of such procedures also had the effect of enforcing an educational status hierarchy by which the further the young person moved up the school the more thoroughly imaginative writing was winnowed out from high-status critical activity. Broadly speaking, the further students progressed through school, the less they were expected to engage in messy, 'low-status' activity. It is still the case now that activity fostered in primary school is drying up by Key Stage 3. At

A-level (which until the small-scale emergence of A-level English Language in the mid-1980s was Literature only) literary criticism hybridized into 'informed personal response' (Barlow in Green 2005). Those students who went on to university recognized soon enough that imaginative writing (like poster paint, collages, printed handwriting and sugar paper) signified 'training college' or education department. The dominant form of 'English' in UK universities (as also, to an extent, those of the most prestigious North American institutions) positioned itself at a critical distance from the material embodiedness of production. It was in the very 'moment of theory' that Raymond Williams observed that the

> extraordinary neglect of the subject of production in modern academic literary thought . . . is attributable to the notion of literature as an object and as existing in the past. Interest in the active process of making is suppressed in favour of the more negotiable activity of responding to an object. Now I believe that the processes of production, the production of discourse in writing are always fundamental . . . I believe that the emphasis on practice is now crucial and that the neglect of practice is a contributory factor to our cultural crisis . . . (1977: 30)[18]

One way of understanding literary critical practice might be as a kind of secular puritanism calling the lax and polytheistic domain of letters to a stern, true order. The *Scrutiny* generation took its stand against what they saw as the belletristic habits of gentlemen amateurs and the self-admiration of Bloomsbury. Oddly enough, the new critical practice that followed the carnival years of 1968–73 turned out to be another and in some ways parallel bout of iconoclasm. Up and down the land the puritans of theory set about hammering icons out of niches, making bonfires of vestments and altar cloths, and handing down anathemas on the slovenly habits of a wilted Clerisy.[19] And yet what happened to university and polytechnic English in the years on either side of 1980 had mixed implications for writing as academic practice.

Institutionally, these were the years when in the polytechnics English BA programmes validated by the Council for National Academic Awards (CNAA) emerged out of interdisciplinary Humanities programmes. Generally speaking, these programmes sought to model themselves on those in the traditional universities. They nevertheless represented a considerable widening of the student base (Protherough 1989), the more so if we add into the context the work of the Open University and its innovative distance-learning English programmes championed by Graham Martin and his colleagues. Though classroom practice remained largely unaffected, numerous variants of 'theory' were becoming established in English departments, usually (though not invariably) championed by young, newly appointed, lecturers. As we saw in the previous chapter, the fragile hegemony that literary criticism had (in most, if not all, UK English departments) achieved over loose federations of medievalists, philologists and textual scholars started to break up. It found itself challenged by the new hegemony-in-waiting of 'theory'. Yet, perhaps predictably, many forms of theory inherited rather than challenged some of the deep-laid habits of the intellectual regime they sought to supplant. For our purposes here, one of the key features of much of the theory on the new left was its avowed 'anti-humanism'. Out of a blend of Althusserian Marxism and Lacanian Psychoanalysis (with a dash of the Barthes of 'Death of the Author' and *S/Z*) the insurgents concocted a mixture which was potent in terms of critique. Taken internally, this mixture excited those students who identified with the approach to all that 'pleasure of disillusioning' which had characterized their new critical predecessors. (For examples, see Evans 1993, Chapter 7.) Nevertheless, as we shall see in Chapter 4, there were many ways in which versions of theory could (and subsequently did) feed into practices of writing. That aspect of Barthes' work which linked up with reader response; 'French feminism'; the Marxist emphasis on production and the unity of theory and practice; variations on intertextuality – all these contained implications for the nature of educational practice. But, in relation to writing, all these tended to be trumped by a spreading suspicion of activities which appeared to derive from and reinforce an uncomplicated, essentialist relation to expression and the core of the expressive self.

This outline is not of course intended as a history of creative writing. But to understand the rise of writing practices that go beyond the analytical essay, we have to acknowledge that the early years of theory tended to privilege and give fresh life to this traditional form. Radical students aspired to the debunking rhetoric superlatively handled by a Catherine Belsey, a Terence Hawkes or a Terry Eagleton. Deep suspicions surrounded creativity as bourgeois imposture. At this distance it is nearly impossible to recapture the quasi-theological energy invested in the campaign to unmask what came to be known as 'liberal humanism'. Much of the reformation sketched above had the (possibly perverse) effect of reinforcing quite traditional ways of doing things in university Humanities departments: the lecture, the unstructured seminar (a free-for-all for the confident and articulate), and above all, in this connection, the critical essay. This was what Rob Pope was later to refer to as the 'often woeful gap between sublime theoretical possibilities and actual teaching practice' (Pope 1995: 10). The daily practice of theory spoke of the distance to be established between learner and subject matter if that learner were not to tumble down the slippery slope into ideological incorporation. In this world view, emotion, the aesthetic and the self were deeply suspect. Where *Scrutiny* had campaigned against sentimentality and addictive reading, post-structuralist theory went several stages further to campaign against the myth of foundations. Practitioners set about persuading their students that the subject they had chosen was the ideological agent of the capitalist state and that therefore the only intellectually reputable stance was one of constant suspicion. This privilege accorded to distantiation was an influential part of the context in which advocates of writing had to operate.

And yet there were ways – as we shall see – in which the spread of theory also foregrounded writing as a practice. Like any movement, it was itself heteroglossic. And the questions being posed were important ones. These challenges to the authenticity of both experience and expression cannot even now be lightly brushed aside. We have no intention here of creating a narrative that is 'anti-theory', or that sees English education in the twenty-first century finally returning to stereotypical Romantic values: imagination, unconstrained creativity, self, human nature, 'finding a voice'. Some proponents of creative writing in our own moment have serious questions to answer about their conventional Romanticism and their flirtation with the male sage. The anti-expressivist arguments merit being taken very seriously, especially, in the present context, in their bearing upon writing as educational practice.[20]

As suggested in the previous chapter, the history of a discipline is, among other things, a covert history of the relations between the culture of the staff tribe and that of the student tribe. It would be possible to argue that part of the appeal of the study of English literature (and, too, perhaps part of the Romantic inheritance of the subject) has been its licensing of inwardness and a language for the articulation of the self. People who choose to become students of English have been and still are attracted, let us suppose, by the promise of this licence, by a subject that not only sanctioned talking about emotions and relationships, but was premised on the significance and prodigality of inner space. In a post-Romantic culture, this propensity, we might continue, is even further developed in those who themselves sought to 'write' (in the heightened sense of writing poetry or art fiction). So the challenge being articulated within anti-essentialist 'theory' was indeed radical. From several different and superficially incompatible directions – from the Derridean critique of presence; from Barthes' giddying vision of culture as palimpsest of quotations, from the radical social constructionism which converged with Foucault, from the Machereyan alliance of Lacan and Althusser – could be drawn the inference that inner space (the supposed site of creativity as much as of a sense of stable selfhood) was an illusion. Naively, to treat that space as a reality was to be seduced into a false consciousness, paying tribute to the very essentialism from which theory was doing its best to rescue the student. As Macherey snootily summed up his own argument:

All speculation over man the creator is intended to eliminate a real knowledge: the 'creative process' is, precisely, not a process, a labour; it is a religious formula to be found on funeral monuments.

For the same reasons, all considerations of genius, of the subjectivity of the artist, of his soul, are on principle uninteresting.

You will understand why, in this book, the word 'creation' is suppressed and systematically replaced by 'production'. (Macherey, trans. Wall, 1978: 68)

Looking back now across the wasteland of subsequent educational politics, what strikes us most is how much this programme paradoxically had in common with that of its dialectical antitype: behaviourism. Now, at the beginning of the twenty-first century, it may have become necessary to recover an emancipatory understanding of privacy and the inward life. Even to assert with Richard Sennett that a degree of stable selfhood and inner space (so far from being a pernicious bourgeois myth) might actually constitute a terrain of resistance to the penetration of global capitalism (Sennett 1998).

CREATIVE CRITICISM

Writing Experiment, Durham, 1983

In the spring of 1983 a short evening course in the Durham University Department of Adult and Continuing Education was advertised as follows:

This is an invitation to a different sort of English course. This course will try to cross the usual line between 'appreciation' and 'writing'. We shall read and think about some short poems and passages. Then we shall try to extend our response by doing some writing ourselves. This is not a 'creative writing' course, and you won't be expected to be an accomplished writer – you may not even have tried to write before. If this course succeeds we should all find that we have developed a more vivid response to our reading – and more understanding of our own creative powers.

The rise of theory was one aspect of the intellectual and social turbulence of those years when the Thatcher project – the project of the Centre for Policy Studies and the Institute of Economic Affairs – was still new. But just as no one at the time could know which way the new political formation would go, the intellectual and educational shape of the new era was not at all obvious. It would be a mistake to assume that, pedagogically speaking, the new movements all pressed in a single direction. Several factors meant that islands of attention to pedagogic practice could be found within the discipline. These included the leakage across accepted disciplinary boundaries caused by the rise of Cultural Studies in proximity to English, and also the continuing existence of some commerce across the school–university divide. In this section we shall review those with most relevance to our larger theme.

When in the late 1960s John Broadbent moved from Cambridge to a chair at the new University of East Anglia, he left a world where the pedagogic norm was the tutorial and the seminar an innovation, for one where the seminar was the norm. But this proved a disappointment:

> Student power was crumbling and much with it: people came late to classes or not at all, hadn't read the books, did not participate or talked demotically, they did not know each other's names nor I theirs ... (Evans 1995: 18)

His response suggests a felt need to refresh university teaching by what, significantly, he refers to as 'regression'.

> In an effort to get out of this, I regressed to techniques used in primary schools – thematic topics, dramatic improvisation – and I cast responsibility for planning the course onto the students.

Working with a group of colleagues, and influenced by the Tavistock tradition in group-relations training and organizational behaviour, he subsequently went on to found the Development of University English Teaching Project (DUET), which held its first week-long working conference at Norwich in 1980. This was, so to speak, staff development *avant la lettre*. Above all, this was an action research project, with a larger aim of the hands-on exploration of the dynamics of teaching and learning.

Outcomes were sought not in terms of research papers but in the subsequent reflective practice of participants. The workshops were designed on the principle derived from the Tavistock Conferences: the creation of a bounded space within which the 'here and now' could be read for the light it threw on behaviour in groups and organizations. Academics who attended the conferences were invited to reflect on what they discovered about their own roles, about their relatedness to their subject, to their students and to authority, and then to carry the understandings they achieved back into their own place of work. In hybridizing Wilfred Bion's work on groups with Literary Studies, DUET proposed not only that the group could be read like a text, but also that such readings were the foundation for reinvigorated pedagogic practice. One 'strand' of the weave of which, from the beginning, DUET workshops were built was a sequence of small group sessions usually referred to as 'literary practice' – the seed of the project discussed here (see Palmer in Evans (ed.) 1995: 150–74; Knights 1992: 11–13).

As subsequently outlined in a mimeographed publication 'The Literary Practice Book', these sessions were built on the values of trust, cooperation and positive valuation – values all seen, by implication, to be lacking in the traditional seminar. The experience of these sessions was shaped by their juxtaposition with the other strands of the workshop.

> It should be borne in mind that the distinctive lightness and mutual trust of the Writing sessions is in part a function of their place within a larger programme in which other needs and preoccupations are being satisfied elsewhere. (Palmer in Evans 1995: 161)

DUET participants were always invited to explore parallels between the phenomena of the workshop and their professional life at their home institutions, and in this light we might note a parallel with writing modules within a student's BA programme. Activities were initially small-scale and cumulative, and worked in and out of existing texts. While in the early stages suggestions tended to come from the staff member leading the group, increasingly over the duration of the workshop suggestions and activities were initiated by members of the group and collaboratively conducted.

DUET: The Literary Practice Event

These sessions will be conducted separately in classes, with rooms and membership as for the Academic Development Event but with the addition of staff members. The methods used will vary but the common objective is to provide opportunities for participants to engage together in the practice of writing and the formation of a critical seminar.

The emphasis, then, will be on practical ways of forming a working group; and of eliciting imaginative or descriptive writing. The assumption is that these practices are related: that attention to people as members of a working group, and to their imaginative and expressive resources, may develop critical as well as writing skills.

There is no expectation of special skill or experience in creative writing. It is assumed that, given the right conditions, people find appropriate ability in themselves. The conditions, which will be offered as ground rules to start with, include:

absence of threat: only supportive comments will be asked for; achievable goals: structured exercises to start with; meaningfulness

> for the individual: attention to the problem of how individuals may take authority to write for themselves within a group.
> (*DUET Workshop Programme*)

In his vivid description of the writing event, Barry Palmer (Evans (ed.) 1995, Chapter 8) points specifically to the larger implications of what was often experienced as a quiet, reflective activity:

> From my own experience, it is the transitions between reading and writing that lead to insight. (Evans (ed.) 1995: 169)

> ...the DUET experiment with writing not only raises but *enacts* a fundamental question: what is the purpose of English literature courses in higher education? (171)

DUET's deliberate challenge to university teachers of English was to transcend their own dissatisfaction with the institutional world of teaching and find their way back to the sources of vigour within their subject. One such source was licensed play with words. In this the project was not alone – dissatisfaction with the teaching of English in universities and polytechnics was surfacing elsewhere. Teachers thus dissatisfied frequently turned towards *poiesis*. (It is not possible, without conducting an oral history, to reconstruct what students felt about teaching ten years on from 1968.) John Broadbent was not the only university teacher of English who was coming to question his role as a critic devoted to bringing up the next generation of critics. In 1984 Brian Cox (professor of English at the University of Manchester and founder of the *Critical Quarterly* and its summer schools) joined forces with the teacher-poet Anne Cluysenaar (then teaching at Sheffield City Polytechnic) to found the Verbal Arts Association. The fledgling organization held its first conference in Manchester the following year. The manifesto for the VAA deserves quoting at length.

> Other arts, such as music, painting, sculpture or drama, include practice as an essential component. In contrast, courses in literature usually concentrate on the understanding, descriptions and evaluation of texts, with some attention to critical method. Courses in language are mainly concerned to introduce students to the analysis of speech acts and to linguistic theory. Most literature and language courses do not require students to develop their skills in non-discursive modes of prose or in verse. This is an extraordinary situation.
>   Students of English at polytechnics and universities often write dull, second-hand discursive prose and are taught to do nothing else. This is particularly unfortunate because many of these students

privately attempt to develop creative abilities in language, and all must be counted among the most verbally gifted of their generation. English, as at present constituted, neither meets their needs nor, arguably, fulfils its duty to the community, to which verbal skills are so vitally necessary.

Practice in the verbal arts is valuable not only for its own sake, but because it helps students appreciate the achievement of writers of the past and take an informed interest in contemporary writing. It provides an intimate and practical insight into how language works, so acting as the ideal bridge between literary and linguistic concerns. Modern literary theory, too, is most easily understood by students who have made their own raids on the inarticulate.

During its short life, the Verbal Arts Association brought together in conferences teachers from both secondary and tertiary sectors with practising poets and writers. Its events were characterized by a mix of larger panel events and small groups dedicated to on-the-spot practice. Sessions would typically move from exercises suggested by the facilitator to activities suggested by members of the group. Readings and semi-formal presentations were part of the blend. Like DUET, the VAA sought to reform pedagogy (to start indeed by raising pedagogy to the level of visibility) but not in the first place by working directly with students. Its object was to bring together teachers in order to achieve a shared, communal understanding of practice and develop new habits.

We suggested earlier that one of the sources for an awakening sense of pedagogy was some degree of permeability between university and school English. While some leading figures were senior figures in the university subject community, it is notable that self-aware pedagogic practices often flourished on the margins of university English departments: in DUET workshops, in adult education or in teacher training. One major contributor was Peter Abbs of the Education Department at the University of Sussex, whose *English Within the Arts: A Radical Alternative for English and the Arts in the Curriculum* was published in 1982. English, he argued, was a 'creative discipline', which should 'now form strong philosophical, practical and political alliances with the undervalued disciplines of art, dance, drama, music and film' (1982: 7). Practical art-making meant not just self-expression but accepting the discipline of the medium of verbal art. The 'medium has its own inner propensities, its own laws, its own history. It allows and forbids. It invites and resists' (41). Trainee teachers and in turn their pupils should be tolerant of notes and jottings, of the unfinished, of 'living with poetry in process' (61). In advancing this argument, Abbs took issue both with the organicist literary critical tradition and the anti-humanism of theory. Thus he argued for the use of writers' notes, drafts and early versions:

this suggests one important approach to the study of literature which is often neglected, namely the examination of a poem in terms of its development, its growth from impulse, through immediate expression, through revision and elaboration to the realization of representative form. (1982: 59)

Generous response would be developed through the interaction of reading and writing.

Abbs was writing from the standpoint of teacher training, and it was this that gave his book its immediacy and detail. But he serves here as an important reminder, if any were needed, that creative/critical experiment was not confined to the universities and polytechnics. While our primary subject here is not English in schools, we must acknowledge, even if only briefly, the affinities between what we have been describing and related activities in secondary schools, especially at A-level. During the 1980s many teachers were adapting methods and procedures widely used lower down the education system to the more 'academic' domain of A-level.[21] Considerable enthusiasm was aroused from 1978 by the Associated Examining Board's alternative coursework syllabus (AEB 660), and many teachers and teacher organizations set about exploiting the opportunities thus created. Incited by PGCE tutors to explore the coursework element of A-level, and often inspired by Ted Hughes' *Poetry in the Making* (1967), many young teachers turned towards hybrids of critical and creative practice. Particularly active in the domain of creative criticism and transformative writing was a group of teachers associated with the National Association for the Teaching of English (NATE). NATE had itself been deeply influenced by the 'growth through English' movement associated with John Dixon and others (see *Growth Through English* (1969), the title of Dixon's account of the 1967 Dartmouth Seminar). NATE's annual conferences and publications consistently promoted a wealth of creative approaches to textual study and assessment. Examples include Susan Hackman's *Responding in Writing: The Use of Exploratory Writing in the Classroom* (1987), quoted at the head of this chapter. A year later, the NATE Post-14 Committee publication *English A-level in Practice* (1988) included 'An A–Z of Creative Exercises for A-level Literature'. Nearly a hundred creative activities on and around texts were assembled by John Parry who noted that an 'active engagement with words on the page means that the student literally makes something of the text' (42). Barbara Bleiman's *Activities for A-level English* (1991) draws on this tradition of work and suggests that in the period before the options started to close down there was widespread receptivity in sixth forms towards creative/critical approaches. To sum up: for a brief period in the 1980s it looked to many not only as though a reciprocity of practice across the tertiary–secondary line was possible, but also that, more specifically, critical/creative crossover would be a key element. Such an ambition is clearly visible in the Cox Report.

> We should transform our students from passive consumers to active makers. They would become members of a working community. They would look forward to next week, when they might publish a maga-zine or take part in a play or complete a piece of writing which they have discussed with friends. I think this transformation, already taking place in some institutions of higher education, is inevitable, and expect to see this quiet revolution in teaching practices triumphant throughout education in the 1990s. (Cox 1991: 154)

And it was in that hope that, for example, a group of us (in conjunction with Durham Local Education Authority) ran a succession of two- and three-day workshops for sixth-form teachers between 1984 and 1990. Teachers fell eagerly upon the writing workshops. External forces were, however, to prove too strong, and the hope for a trans-sector renewal of pedagogy was doomed to disappointment.

Before this chapter becomes merely a catalogue of initiatives and movements, it is time to take stock. To make the point again: it is not the object of this book, let alone this chapter, to achieve a history of creative writing in British Higher Education. Its concern, rather, is with the emergence within university English Studies of a pedagogic practice whose aim was to enable reciprocity between critical and creative activity. At this point, then, it seems useful to try to pin down some of the common features of the various elements of this emerging pedagogy. Chapter 4 will then take up the nature of the dialogic relation between creative/critical activity and 'theory'. Self-evidently, the initiatives instanced above have implications for the kind of writing practised in learning and assessment, above all for the traditional essay. All of them implied a loosening or redefinition of boundaries and hierarchies. This re-designing of the theatre of cultural and pedagogic performance in turn involved re-orientations along several different axes – between reader and text; teacher and taught; serious and playful; cognitive and affective; subjectivity and structure; solitary and collaborative; adult and child. Such re-orientations potentially redefined the pedagogic space and breached traditional hierarchic distinctions between that which was held to be appropriate in school and that which was appropriate in university (and by implication that which is appropriate in the traditional British borderland between the two: the sixth form).

In overcoming some accepted distinctions, such orientations insisted on teaching and learning as forms of dynamic activity, important in their own right rather than simply as vehicles for achievements beyond themselves. Thus John Broadbent was apt to quote John Dewey's 1897 essay *My Pedagogic Creed*:

> I believe that education which does not occur through forms of life, forms that are worth living for their own sake, is always a poor substitute for the genuine reality and tends to cramp and to deaden. (http://dewey.pragmatism.org/creed.htm)

Some of these resonances may be heard in the influential writings of Roland Barthes. In the course of articulating his seminal distinction between 'work' and 'text', Barthes (to whom we shall return in Chapter 4) located text in a field of activity. Effectively, he contrasted the passivity of mere consumption with the paradoxically demanding process of play.

> The Text ... decants the work ... from its consumption and recuperates it as play, task, production, practice. This means that the Text requires an attempt to abolish (or at least to diminish) the distance between writing and reading, not by intensifying the reader's projection into the work, but by linking the two together into one and the same signifying practice.

> Rhetoric ... taught *writing* ... In fact *reading*, in the sense of *consuming*, is not *playing* with the text. 'Playing' must be taken here in all the polysemy of the term: the text 'plays' ... and the reader plays twice over: he *plays at* the Text (ludic meaning), he seeks a practice which reproduces it; but, so that this practice is not reduced to a passive, interior mimesis (the Text being precisely what resists this reduction), he *plays* the Text ... (Barthes [1971] 1986: 62–3)

Barthes goes on to observe that 'we must not forget that *play* is also a musical term; the history of music (as practice, not as "art") is moreover, quite parallel to that of the Text ...' The relation to the unfolding critical/creative project is clear. Here, at least in potential, there seems to be a reaching out after a more democratic, participative cultural practice. The context of Barthes' essay was French higher education in the immediate aftermath of *les évènements* of 1968, but we need to understand what Barthes' British readership were searching for in his work. On the one hand educational radicals under the influence of Ivan Illich or Paulo Freire imagined the abolition of education systems; others, however, were willing to work from within to subvert the system. A programme that appeared to reconstitute the reader or student as a cultural actor had potent appeal, especially since it called into question accepted authority structures, whether the authority of the author, or of the text as cultural monument, the teacher, the learning institution and its hierarchy, or even of the rational ego of the self. Its latent implications for the actual life of the classroom remained to be explored.

Those who were most dissatisfied with the state of learning in English Studies were drawn towards practices which were inherently constructivist. Seeing a profound analogy between the process of writing and the process of learning, they were drawn towards accounts of learning which foregrounded the processes (intellectual, affective and social) in which students engage in order to learn. English it seems (while it had arrived by a different route) had converged with the new work on student learning which was simultaneously emerging in the late 1970s and early 1980s in the wake of Ference Marton and Roger Säljö's 1976 article 'On qualitative differences in learning'.[22] Central to educational psychology's new preoccupation with student learning styles and with the alignment (or lack of it) with the styles of their teachers, was an implication that teachers must attend not only to the body of scholarly knowledge but also to the design of learning environments. While it is improbable that in 1980 anyone in English Studies had heard of Marton's work, this convergence suggests a common environment of educational thinking, or perhaps more accurately a response to a common set of problems. There has, we suggest, always been a latent constructivist strand within English Studies. At certain historical moments this becomes more overt.

Whatever the (circa) 1968 ancestry of their ideas, most of those who adopted writing workshop approaches were not seeking to abolish or replace the established processes of analytic discussion. What they were claiming – implicitly or overtly – was that, firstly, the performance of literary criticism (oral or written) typically drew on and reinforced a narrow band of response, and, secondly, that even assuming its benefits, most (if not all) students needed more of what Bruner referred to as scaffolding. Part of the role of the teacher was therefore to support students in getting to the point where they could start to join in meaningful discussion.

In the view of Broadbent and his colleagues, students in seminars were typically inhibited, looking warily over their shoulders, nervously trying to read the signs. Many of the procedures mentioned in this chapter represented an attempt to re-orientate the student experience, and were designed to help students participate in seminar or class in a way that previously only the most confident or articulate had felt safe enough to do so. If a teacher could create the appropriate environment, verbal power would become more devolved. With this pedagogic premise, 'doing' the subject required more of tutors than the possession of scholarly knowledge or mastery of the appropriate discourse. Students needed to be initiated into the process of discussion as much as they needed reading lists or feedback on essays. It was, in fact, coming to be understood in these quarters that seminar speech was not a natural language, that the seminar was a cultural form, as difficult in its own way as a modernist poem. To swim in this medium required at the very least a few lessons with armbands if students were to learn to negotiate the cross-currents of peer pressure and tutor expectation, or to work productively with their individual or collective anxieties and projections. Such a pedagogic re-reading of the seminar demanded a re-alignment of the cognitive and the affective, a recognition that both text and seminar unlocked emotions which the traditional seminar (for reasons good as well as bad) was organized to side-step. To encourage risk-taking, the teacher not only had to create an environment of reasonable security, but also structure activity in such a way that students possessed of different kinds of intelligence and levels of prior experience could engage with the subject matter. Several years later the point was forcibly made by Rob Pope. After describing some of his own 'textual intervention' activities, he goes on to say:

> There is yet another fundamental and often overlooked *pedagogic* point in all this too, another lesson in learning. It relates to the often woeful gap between sublime theoretical possibilities and actual teaching practice. Put bluntly ... it is not enough simply to *tell* people that 'texts are plural' ... 'the product of an open series of intertextual and impersonal dialogue', and so on. (These are all potentially very valu-able terms ... *as long* as they are not merely parroted to echo a new critical orthodoxy.) Nor should it then be necessary ... simply to *tell* them that texts are also to some extent explainable and even pre-dictable as socio-historical constructs, that texts ... 'both reveal and attempt to conceal the site of their own inner contradictions ...' and so on. Again, these are all insights which if properly internalized ... can be very useful indeed. But again, as merely ritual gestures, the duti-fully delivered antiphonal responses to the revised liturgy of a new critical priesthood, they are worse than useless. They are dangerous – as are all unchallenged dogmas. (Pope 1995: 10–11)

For the ambassadors of creative/critical crossover, the subject matter is, in some measure, generated on the spot, moving in and out of poems or passages, and liberating the energies of students from bored or dutiful compliance. In this important tradition, the refreshment of the subject is seen as likely to be generated not simply, or even at all, from the scholarly generation of knowledge, but from the reinvigoration of the transactions between student, teacher and text.

THE FATE OF CRITICAL/CREATIVE PRACTICE

After this overview of critical/creative practice in the 1980s, it remains to summarize the story down to the present. In spite of the excited hopes which new pedagogies had aroused, the new forms of critical/creative pedagogy did not in fact become the norm. Where they continued, they flourished in the margins and in pockets. Indeed, the whole attempt to raise the visibility of English pedagogy remained patchy. Scattered alumni of DUET devised experimental, writing-based courses with titles like 'Creative Criticism' and 'Polemical Writing'. Occasional DUET-influenced works of criticism appeared where authors sought to leaven critical analysis with autobiographical insight into the experience of learning.[23] But although a large number of teachers were influenced by DUET and by other similar initiatives, on the whole they continued to work as individuals within their departments. As a broad generalization, the communal pedagogy of English was not reformed.

While generally impressed by the quality of teaching and learning support in English, the Overview of the Teaching Quality Assessment (TQA) of 1994–5 was not altogether complimentary.

> Other aspects in observed classes judged to require improvement included a lack of rigour and intellectual challenge, an absence of overall structure or a failure to clarify key points of learning, or a tendency for some students to lose interest. Some lecturers and tutors appeared to have difficulty making the most of two- and three-hour blocks of classwork, failing to vary teaching methods and duration of activity. In a number of observed seminars, students were given too few opportunities to contribute, and were consequently encouraged to become relatively passive. Generally, such classes also failed to stimulate appropriate expectations of further progression in other parts of the course. (*TQA Overview Report*, 1995)

More pointedly, a group of English academics who had acted as TQA visitors summed up their experience:

> We think that the Assessment Challenge did a great service in pointing up the potential prestige of university English teaching. We are inclined to think that the profession is not up to receiving this service. Inside the English departments how many meetings have been arranged to discuss what happened? How many of the assessors have talked to their colleagues and peers ... about what they saw and thought? We are morally sure that in the Engliterate the subject has been more or less dropped.

Yet the 'peer review mounted in the Assessment Challenge might have had some funny things about it, but it showed a way to go.' The authors conclude that it 'is imperative that lecturers in English place high value on and give thought to their mystery.' (Kate Fullbrook *et al.* 1996)

Let us try to account for this very partial spread of new practices, without going back in detail over the ground already covered in the previous chapter. A brief and tentative summary suggests that the adverse factors included the rapid absorption of theory into the bloodstream of the subject in HE (though not in secondary schools). More specifically, that the theory so absorbed was the subject of rapid commodification at the end of the 1980s and the beginning of the 1990s with the massive publication success of a spate of guides, anthologies and theory readers. The effects of theory thus commodified converged after 1992 with the rise of the Research Assessment Exercise (RAE) and a more professional but also more routinized approach to the activities of academic staff. Since, as we have seen, the revival of critical/creative practice and of attention to higher education pedagogy in the 1980s had been connected with a degree of cross-border fertilization between university/polytechnic and secondary sectors, the subsequent history of relations with the secondary sector is directly relevant. The abrupt separation between tertiary and secondary that occurred after 1989 dammed one fresh source of refreshed tertiary practice. Simultaneously, initial teaching training had to concentrate much harder on preparing trainee teachers for the new world of competencies and initiatives. And while the 1990s saw the rise of 'staff development' for academic staff (especially in the wake of the 'Enterprise in Higher Education' initiative), most of this was generic or discipline independent, and tended to reinforce old prejudices among discipline communities.

Yet we certainly should not paint a picture of overall decline in interest in pedagogy in general or transformative writing in particular. In some quarters critical/creative activity went on. While the week-long workshops came to be replaced by shorter events, DUET carried on into the new millennium, and indeed in 1996 bid for and obtained funding from the newly established Fund for the Development of Teaching and Learning (FDTL) which enabled it for the first time in its history to employ a paid administrator and embark on an ambitious new series of workshops. At Oxford Brookes University, Rob Pope had been experimenting with what he came to call 'Textual Intervention', and his ambitious and detailed book of that title was published (by Routledge) in 1995. At the University of Bangor, Graeme Harper embraced various adjacent strands in his project 'Reading to Write, Writing to be Read'. His summary report

suggests that students of Creative Writing feel strongly that their creative work impacts positively on their ability to operate as literary critics. Students also identified the positive role that critical approaches provide in helping them to evaluate and improve their creative writing. The report findings help to undermine negative stereotypes about the relationship between literature and creative writing courses. (www.english.heacademy.ac.uk/explore/projects/archive/creative/creative1.php)

And other, newer voices were heard as individual lecturers found their way towards creative/critical activities. Nick Everett from the University of Leicester:

> The first point – and one it now amazes me I did not make use of sooner – follows from the basic principle that, where possible, learning about something should include trying it oneself. (Everett 2005: 233)

> My ideal would be an English in which creative writing enhances and augments without in any way impeding or threatening traditional literary study. (241)

At around the same time, at St Edmund Hall, Oxford, Lucy Newlyn and her colleagues were embarking on a programme of writing workshops designed to complement students' literary studies. 'In the academic teaching of English', they argue,

> the rise of criticism may have gone so far that it has blotted out a full understanding of what the creative process entails. Only by writing poetry themselves can students fully appreciate the choices and processes that are involved. By bringing creative and critical writing so closely into conjunction through our workshops, we were all able to experience at first hand what it was like to be at once 'primary' and 'secondary'. Through a kind of internal role-play, we could grasp the implications of the collaborative/competitive dynamic which always pertains between creation and reception; and which is peculiarly alive in poet/critics. (Newlyn 2003 I: 83)

Alongside portfolios, learning logs and group assessment, creative/critical practice seemed to have acquired a presence in the mainstream. In 2000, the QAA English Subject Benchmark referred to

> awareness of the range and variety of approaches to literary study, which may include creative practice, performance, and extensive specialization in critical and/or linguistic theory . . .

Hybrid forms of writing also have a recognized place in the new English Language and Literature A-level specifications that emerged from Curriculum 2000, though it is perhaps symptomatic that many English Literature courses do not accept the new hybrid A-level as a qualification.

This whole book (and Chapters 5–7 specifically) is a case study of two teachers' response to the histories sketched here. We lay claim neither to uniqueness nor to having 'found the answer' to the growing gap between teacher and student expectations. We simply want to share an argument about pedagogic inventiveness. It was in 2000, the moment of the new modular A-level and of the English Subject Benchmark, that – aware of the effect on students' learning lives of the shifting forces charted in Chapter 1 – Ben Knights originally developed a new second-level module within the Teesside English Studies programme. The aim of the module, we told the first cohort of students to join in 2000, was 'to generate and sustain a form of activity which supplements "academic" writing in other modules'.

Writing for Reading

Welcome to a new and exciting module. Compared to subjects like Music or Art where students actually compose and create, the dominant mode of English Studies is cognitive and analytical. In the normal way, what you have to do is write critical and interpretative essays. The aim of this module on the other hand is to offer a secure space and encouragement for 'serious play'.

... the whole module will cross-fertilize work done in other modules by inviting a close but different kind of attention to written language, text and the demands of textuality. While most of the writing you do for your degree is critical and analytical (generally some variation on the 'essay'), the aim of this module is to help familiarize you with the processes and structures of the written language through the practice of formative and experimental writing. The module makes the assumption that it can be valuable to supplement the critical and historical study of texts with forms of productive activity.

Required to spell out objectives, Knights opted for the following. By the end of this module the student should, he said:

- have achieved an enhanced sense of the varieties and expressive resources of written English
- have developed a greater 'inwardness' with selected styles and forms of fiction and poetry

- have added to their skills in critical reading
- have enriched their sense of different genres and forms of address
- possess a greater facility in the use of sophisticated written registers.

The success of this module in its own circumstances led to a number of further developments, one of which was this present book. Chapters 5 to 7 will give a more detailed account of the modules concerned, their practices, students and assessment. But first we will turn to the relationship between writing and two modalities of English Studies, literary criticism (Chapter 3) and 'theory' (Chapter 4).

3 Writing and Literary Criticism

But is Criticism really a creative art?

GILBERT. Why should it not be? It works with materials, and puts them into a form that is at once new and delightful. What more can one say of poetry? Indeed, I would call criticism a creation within a creation. For just as the great artists, from Homer and Aeschylus, down to Shakespeare and Keats, did not go directly to life for their subject-matter, but sought for it in myth, and legend, and ancient tale, so the critic deals with materials that others have, as it were, purified for him, and to which imaginative form and colour have been already added. Nay, more, I would say that the highest Criticism, being the purest form of personal impression, is in its way more creative than creation, as it has least reference to any standard external to itself, and is, in fact, its own reason for existing, and, as the Greeks would put it, in itself, and to itself, an end. (Oscar Wilde, 'The Critic as Artist' in Oscar Wilde, *Plays, Prose Writings and Poems*, Everyman's Library 1930: 25)

In the middle of discussing his 'second type' of ambiguity, William Empson is examining the conversation between Pandarus and Criseyde when he gets to Pandarus' words: 'And elde daunteth daunger at the last.' After a paragraph spent unpicking this line he breaks off to anticipate the reader's objection:

The line is a straightforward ambiguity of the second type, and I hope the reader will not object that I have been making up a poem of my own. Mr. Eliot somewhere says that is always done by bad critics who have failed to be poets; this is a valuable weapon but a dangerously superficial maxim, because it obscures the main crux about poetry, that being an essentially suggestive act it can only take effect if the impulses (and to some extent the experiences) are already there to be called forth; that the process of getting to understand a poet is precisely that of constructing his [sic] poems in one's own mind. (Empson 1930: 61–2)

This is an important insight into Empson's own method, which relies on the meticulous unpacking with the aid of the *New (Oxford) English Dictionary* of the multiplicity of latent or competing meanings which press upon the reader. But it also serves here as a reminder that the author of one of the foundational documents of literary criticism was well aware that criticism was itself a supplement to the 'words on the page', and that criticism in turn rested (at least implicitly) on a constructive theory of reading. The object of this chapter is to examine the relationship between the practice of criticism and creative writing. It centres on the heyday of 'literary criticism'. This is not a piece of wilful historicism: rather it proceeds from a belief that residual forms of literary criticism still provide a pedagogic basis for the study of literature in British universities. Literary criticism, we shall argue, is an articulation and elaboration of the reading process by which virtual or so to speak counterfactual texts are created. The very notion of ambiguity (at the core of all versions of the new criticism) implicates the reader in the mental activity of sifting, prioritizing and holding in suspension possible meanings. Reading is in any case a process of inference and gap filling, and we shall recur to the subject of 'reader response' and reception theories in the next chapter. As a professionalized form of reading, criticism – even in its most conventional forms – is a process of so articulating those inferences as to make them available for pedagogic dialogue. Critical writing thus erects constructions of what the text means (or might have meant, or could not say for itself) in other words than those it used itself.

In the last chapter, we argued that the conventional distinction between critical and creative practice was in fact unstable and ripe for deconstruction. In developing the theme of this book, our case about literary criticism develops three broad and interconnected areas. In this light we seek to spell out something already touched on in the previous chapter: the complex relationship of criticism as a genre of writing and pedagogy to other, 'creative', genres. In doing so we examine an explicit argument concerning the symbiotic relationship between criticism and writing: the Arnoldian thesis that a healthy state of criticism is the precondition for 'great' writing. Throughout we make a case that criticism is a form of supplement: a process of re-making that foregrounds its own interpretative performance (what Derek Attridge refers to as 'the creative act of comprehension' 2003: 91) as a form of production. This in turn connects to a more oblique argument. That is, that despite the association of literary criticism (especially in its US 'New Criticism' form) with condemnation of the 'heresy of paraphrase', the pedagogic practice of criticism has *always* been a form of alternative creation.

But if criticism is a supplement to the text, existing in a dialectical relationship of service or mastery with its source, it is also a supplement at another level again. Thus in filling out and making available to critical dialogue what the text does not (in so many words) actually say, literary critical practice also takes issue with the everyday process of reading. It is, as Information Technologists say, counter-intuitive. Ordinary reading, as I.A. Richards sought to demonstrate empirically in the famous protocols that underlay *Practical Criticism* (1929), is altogether too slipshod for the high calling of criticism. Ordinary reading founders on the twin hazards of utility and escapism, of goal-oriented practicality and self-indulgent sentimentalism. Where the effect of what Louise Rosenblatt was to call 'efferent reading' was to 'push the richly fused cognitive-affective matrix into the fringes of consciousness' (1978: 40), the task of criticism by contrast was to summon it back. From the work of Q.D. Leavis onwards, then, the foreseen mission of literary criticism was simultaneously to spell out what an 'ideal' reading of the text would achieve anyway, and to estrange and discipline the act of reading itself. This was the 'training of sensibility' which was central to the whole enterprise (e.g. F.R. Leavis 1932). To enable the student reader to become self-disciplined, it set about establishing model readings which were in themselves re-creations of the source text. This is a subject to which we shall return later in the chapter. But first we must outline a thesis about the relationship between creativity and criticism.

THE FUNCTION OF CRITICISM AT THE PRESENT TIME

Before returning to explore the idea of critical activity as genre, we must attend to an often overlooked aspect of the campaign for criticism. For an understanding that criticism and creative production were symbiotically linked goes right back into the 'culture and society' tradition, whose illumination was the starting place of Raymond Williams' work. The point of this brief excursion is to demonstrate that many prominent exponents of criticism saw their craft as existing in a kind of symbiosis with creative endeavour. It is well known that the Leavis circle adapted from the Arnoldian tradition the idea that forming and nourishing an 'armed and conscious minority' was all that stood in the way of commercially driven cultural disaster.[24] In the second issue of *Scrutiny* Leavis could treat it as a given that 'criticism undertakes its essential function of keeping an edu-cated body of taste and opinion alive to the age of testing, nourishing and refining the currency of contemporary culture' ('What's Wrong with Cri-ticism' 1 (2)). What is less often observed is that this heroic endeavour was not confined to the production of a caste of critics. From Matthew Arnold via T.S. Eliot through to *Scrutiny*, the cultural ecosystem was understood as comprising complementary critical and creative processes. The argument of this section is a simple one: that one of the givens of literary criticism in its formative years was (though lost to sight in more recent histories of the subject) that criticism was not an activity secondary upon the creation of literature, but was indeed a precondition for that creation. Criticism, in a tradition which the *Scrutiny* school took for granted, existed in a dialectical relationship with creative practice.

This is an argument to which Matthew Arnold returned again and again.

Paving the way for creation: Matthew Arnold on criticism

The critical power is of lower rank than the creative. True; [but] ... Another is, that the exercise of the creative power in the production of great works of literature or art, however high this exercise of it may rank, is not at all epochs and under all conditions possible; and that therefore labour may be vainly spent in attempting it, which might with more fruit be used in preparing for it, in rendering it possible. This creative power works with elements, with materials; what if it has not those materials, those elements, ready for its use? In that case it must surely wait till they are ready. Now, in literature – I will limit myself to literature, for it is about literature that the question arises – the elements with which the creative power works are ideas; the best ideas on every matter which literature touches, current at the time. At any rate we may lay it down as certain that in modern literature no manifestation of the creative power not working with these can be very important or fruitful. And I say *current* at the time, not merely accessible at the time; for creative literary genius does not principally show itself in discovering new ideas, that is rather the business of the philosopher: the grand work of literary genius is a work of synthesis and exposition, not of analysis and discovery; its gift lies in the faculty of being happily inspired by a certain intellectual and spiritual atmosphere, by a certain order of ideas, when it finds itself in them; of dealing divinely with these ideas, presenting them in the most effective and attractive combinations – making beautiful works with them, in short. But it must have the atmosphere, it must find itself amidst the order of ideas, in order to work freely; and these it is not so easy to command. This is why great creative epochs in literature are so rare. This is why there is so much that is unsatisfactory in the productions of many men of real genius. Because, for the creation of a master work of literature two powers must concur, the power of the man and the power of the moment, and the man is not enough without the moment; the creative power has, for its happy exercise, appointed elements, and those elements are not in its own control.

Nay, they are more within the control of the critical power ... Thus it tends, at last, to make an intellectual situation of which the creative power can profitably avail itself. It tends to establish an order of ideas,

> if not absolutely true, yet true by comparison with that which it displaces; to make the best ideas prevail. Presently these new ideas reach society, the touch of truth is the touch of life, and there is a stir and growth everywhere; out of this stir and growth come the creative epochs of literature. (Arnold 1864)

The Newbolt Report of 1921 was by *Scrutiny* standards much more lackadaisical about the function of criticism.

> We have a traditional culture, which comes down to us from the time of the Renaissance, and our literature ... draws its lifeblood therefrom. But the enormous changes in the social life and industrial occupations of the vast majority of our people ... have created a gulf between the world of poetry and the world of everyday life ... Here, we believe, lies the root cause of the indifference and hostility towards literature which is the disturbing feature of the situation, as we have explored it. Here too lies our hope; since the time cannot be far distant when the poet, who 'follows wheresoever he can find an atmosphere of sensation in which to move his wings', will invade this vast new territory, and so once more bring sanctification and joy into the sphere of common life. It is not in man to hasten this consummation. The wind bloweth where it listeth. All we can do is to draw attention to the existing divorce, and to suggest measures that may lead to reunion.

> The interim, we feel, belongs to the professors of English literature. The rise of modern Universities has accredited an ambassador of poetry to every important capital of industrialism in the country, and upon his shoulders rests a responsibility greater we think than is yet generally recognized. The Professor of Literature in a University should be ... a missionary in a more real and active sense that any of his colleagues. *The Teaching of English in England*, Section 237–8

'The wind bloweth where it listeth': self-evidently, the Committee subscribed to a naive romanticist version of creativity. Nevertheless, in addressing 'Literature and the Nation' they too advanced an argument that the work of the professors of English literature was necessary in the transitional period before the next great poet should arise. To that extent their vision of 'the teaching of English in England' was underpinned by a successional history of culture which saw critical and pedagogic activity as preparing the way for the writer who would finally be able creatively to assimilate the new conditions of life. The idea, in short, was widespread in the milieu from which literary criticism arose. With the example of T.S. Eliot, *The Criterion* and *The Calendar of Modern Letters* constantly before them, the New Critics did not start off, at least, prioritizing

criticism over creation. But, again like the Eliot of 'The Function of
Criticism', they saw the critical and creative processes as symbiotic with
each other.

One last example, before we return to the examination of criticism as
genre. In 1929 a young Cambridge postgraduate wrote an essay on
'Future Developments of Literary Criticism' for an English essay prize.
The essay (which won him the prize, the then munificent sum of £30)
also, and in the long run more significantly, won him the friendship of
Queenie and Frank Leavis. In summarizing his survey of the state and
possibilities of criticism in the moment of Eliot's *Criterion* and Richards'
Principles and *Practical Criticism*, L.C. Knights concluded:

> An atmosphere of healthy criticism is essential for art. Not only were
> the great creative ages of the past critical ages; that which is weak in
> our literature is due in large measure to bad criticism, or lack of
> criticism. The conventional acceptance of a certain mode led to the
> production of much bad 18th century verse. Wordsworth's inability to
> take up an objective critical attitude caused him to combine the
> greatest poetry with an occasional line almost grotesque. The weakness
> of later 19th century Romanticism, is that its emotion is not tempered
> by intellectual criticism. This deficiency is already being made good.
> The classical criticism of the future will be cool, analytic, and logical;
> but in this keen atmosphere creation is possible, and literature may
> once more renew its strength. (1929: 68)[25]

In the context of our own argument, this confluence of Arnold and Eliot
constitutes an important reminder that in its formative moment literary
criticism saw itself as having a role symbiotic with the emergence of new
creative literature.

A KIND OF CONSTRUCTION

> There is then creative reading as well as creative writing. When the
> mind is braced by labor and invention, the page of whatever book we
> read becomes luminous with manifold allusion. Every sentence is
> doubly significant, and the sense of our author is as broad as the world.
> (Emerson 1971: 58).

> [He] was meant, if people ever are meant for special lines of activity, for
> the best sort of criticism, the imaginative criticism; that criticism
> which is itself a kind of construction, or creation, as it penetrates,
> through the given literary or artistic product, into the mental and inner
> constitution of the producer, shaping his work. (Pater 1905: 28–9).

As literary criticism moved to develop a pedagogic base, it sought to demonstrate to students and the 'educated public' what fully engaged readings might look like. And in making new readings, the advance guard of literary criticism were able to take for granted what we have labelled a constructivist tradition. Criticism was thus embedded in a more-or-less overt theory of reading. But in turn reading was seen as an active process, a process of energetic but disciplined mental production. Indeed, the intellectual energy summoned out for that production forms a key criterion in the work of both Richards and the Leavises for the worthwhile poem. Thus F.R. Leavis, writing about Gerard Manley Hopkins, enunciates what became a commonplace:

Hopkins is really difficult, and the difficulty is essential ... If (as Mr I.A. Richards pointed out ...) we were allowed to slip easily over the page, the extremely complex process called for would not be allowed to develop. The final, adequate reading will not be a matter of arduous struggle (though a sense of tension and resistance is usually an essential part of the effect), but it will have been made possible by previous intellectual effort, the condition of various subtle and complex organizations. (1963: 134–35)

While no single tradition holds together figures as various as Coleridge, Emerson, Pater, Vernon Lee and Percy Lubbock (not to mention Richards himself), they all in some degree subscribe to a theory of literary process grounded in psychologies of reading. The relevance to this book and this project is that – contrary in many ways to its subsequent reputation – literary criticism rested from the beginning on something akin to a constructivist theory of active reading.

It is possible here only to gesture towards a chapter of intellectual history which would be well worth fuller exploration. Brief reference to two figures in the pre-history of literary criticism must suffice, both with their roots in the *fin-de-siècle*, both in the circle of Henry James. Vernon Lee (Violet Paget 1856–1935) – woman of letters, aesthetician, and novelist – was widely known in the 1920s for her collection of essays, *The Handling of Words and Other Studies in Literary Psychology*, which, published in 1923, antedated by a year Richards' *Principles of Literary Criticism*. Much of what David Lodge referred to as this 'rather neglected pioneering book' (Lodge 1966: xi) 'formulates a reception theory *avant la lettre* ...' (Mieszkowski 2005: 102) and is given over to close linguistic analysis of passages from authors who include Carlyle, Stevenson, Hardy (a discussion of *Tess of the d'Urbervilles* to which Lodge returned some 40 years later), and James himself.

The Co-operation of the Reader with the Writer: Vernon Lee

For the things which we write in our books, the Reader has to read into them.
Of course all art depends as much upon memory ... (1927: 72–3)

For if, as the new science of Aesthetics is beginning to teach, the preference for a picture, a building or a song – indeed the feeling and realizing of its presence – depends upon stored up and organized experience of our own activities, how far more exclusively does the phantom-reality called literature exist only in the realm of our recollections! It is not composed of objective, separately perceptible lines, masses, colours, note-sequences and note-consonances; it has no existence, no real equivalent outside the mind; and this spoken sound, the written characters, have no power unless translated into images and feelings which are already within us. *What's Hecuba to me?* ... The Writer makes his book not merely out of his own mind's contents, but out of ours; and in the similarity, the greater or lesser equivalence of these contents, lies all the possible efficacy of literature ... (74–5)

We have seen ... that literature requires the co-operation of the Reader with the Writer: the Reader must bring all his experience to the business, all his imagination and sympathy; he must enter deeply into the Writer's work, help to make it live, and thus receive a strengthened and purified life in exchange ... (94)

Here I was back at my old belief that literature takes effect solely by the co-operation, the interaction of him who reads with him who writes. As regards [the art] of Literature, I had ... long recognized that the Writer has always to draw upon the Reader's stored-up experience, and can tell him something he does not yet know only by evoking and rearranging what he already knew. (189–90)

So it is that the idea that reading literature is a work of co-operation would not have come as a surprise to the New Critics. Our other exhibit here is Percy Lubbock (1879–1965), novelist, critic, friend of Edith Wharton, friend and editor of Henry James. Two years before *The Handling of Words* he published *The Craft of Fiction*, another synthesis of a kind of close reading with a speculative reader psychology.

But how is one to construct a novel out of the impressions that Tolstoy pours forth from his prodigious hands? This is a kind of 'creative reading' (the phrase is Emerson's) ... The reader of a novel – by which

I mean the critical reader – is himself a novelist; he is the maker of a book which may or may not please his taste when it is finished, but of a book for which he must take his own share of responsibility. The author does his part, but he cannot transfer his book like a bubble into the brain of the critic ... The reader must therefore become, for his part, a novelist, never permitting himself to suppose that the creation of the book is solely the affair of the author. The difference between them is immense of course, and so much so that a critic is always inclined to extend and intensify it. The opposition that he conceives between the creative and the critical task is a very real one; but in modestly belittling his own side of the business he is apt to forget an essential portion of it. The writer of the novel works in a manner that would be utterly impossible to the critic, no doubt and with a liberty and with a range that would disconcert him entirely. But in one quarter their work coincides; both of them make the novel.[26] (Travellers Library Edition 16–17)

The work of reading (and by implication the work of the teacher critic) was a work of collaboration and reproduction.

CRITICISM AS SYMBOLIC CREATION

We now return finally to an argument sketched at the beginning of this chapter. That is, that even at its most severe, the genre we know as literary criticism, in seeking to know and make known what the text did not overtly say, found itself having to articulate alternative para-texts of its own. Notwithstanding literary criticism's deep ambivalence about the materiality of performance (often expressed, for example, in distaste for the dramatization of Shakespeare or impatience with textual scholarship), we might argue that the practice of criticism in writing and in pedagogy was itself a type of performance, a symbolic reconstruction of the source text. Let us also note how many university critics in Britain and the US have also been practising writers, thus issuing an existential reproof to the theoretical division of critical/creative labour. A tally of better-known names might include William Empson, Allen Tate, Lionel Trilling, Richard Eberhart, Robert Penn Warren, Yvor Winters, Anthony Hecht, David Lodge, John Hollander, Raymond Williams, Antonia Byatt, John Holloway, Joyce Carol Oates, Malcolm Bradbury, Alison Lurie, Tom Paulin and Susan Sontag. Indeed, as Dawson points out, the US New Criticism grew up, as it were, in the hands of modernist poets, from whom it gained much of its intellectual authority (Dawson 2005: 72–9). If the critical genre, as it engages with specific texts, is itself a form of

reconstruction, then it has more in common with 'creative' forms of
'writing back' than is usually acknowledged.

In the final stage of this chapter we will seek to make a more specific
case through the brief analysis of three sample passages. Our first example
comes from *The Pelican Guide to English Literature* (Volume 2, ed. Boris
Ford, *The Age of Shakespeare*, 1955) – itself one of the monuments of the
literary critical movement. The passage we have chosen comes from
Derek Traversi's discussion of Shakespeare's late plays, and concerns Act
Four, Scene Four of *The Winter's Tale*. Traversi begins by quoting Perdita's famous speech:

> O Proserpina,
> For the flowers now, that, frighted, thou let'st fall
> From Dis's wagon!

In the oral tradition of pedagogy from which the text derives, quoting is
itself of course a kind of performance, the demonstrative work of the
teacher-critic being achieved through reading aloud in lecture or class as
much as through the overt analysis that followed. Having quoted the
speech, Traversi goes on to locate it within the metaphorical architecture
of the play. This requires not only picking out how the passage alludes to
and recapitulates the imagery of the play, but in doing so creating a para-
text, a story about *The Winter's Tale* that overtly reconstructs the play's
own implicit meanings. Its story of the play only obliquely concerns the
narrative data. To borrow an analogy from structural linguistics, the
critical story reads off connotation in such a way as to detect and lay bear
the symbolic 'deep structure' that underlies all the surface phenomena of
the text. This account of what, so to speak, is *really* happening in the play
– an exploration of the nature and progress of psychic maturation –
effectively erects a further narrative upon the existing narrative structure
of Shakespeare's text. Plot turns into theme. The implication that this
primary narrative is one which any intelligent and suitably trained reader
could have found unaided does not detract from this being an act of
critical *poiesis*.

Over-wintering: Derek Traversi

Beautiful as the speech is and for all its conclusiveness as a sign that
the spring of reconciliation has dawned, the love it expresses still lacks
the necessary maturity which only experience can provide. The
emphasis laid, in the imagery, upon spring, that is, upon birth,
inexperience, virginity, is subtly balanced by an implicit sense of
death, which the vitality indicated by the reference to the royal flowers

– 'bold oxlips' and the 'crown imperial' – can only partly counter. The flowers to which Perdita refers are 'pale' and 'dim'; they 'die unmarried', in unfulfilled promise, having failed to 'behold Phoebus in his strength'. Like the friendship of Polixenes and Leontes, this is an emotion which, insofar as it is unprepared to meet the challenge implied in the passage of time, is destined to die.

Florizel's reply in turn expresses, with at least equal beauty, a similar desire to live outside time, to hold up the course of mutability in a way that is ultimately impossible. When he says to Perdita:

> . . . when you do dance, I wish you
> A wave o' the' sea that you might ever do
> Nothing but that,

his emotion, though expressed in language and rhythm where the effect of simplicity represents the final perfection of art, is still nostalgic, still an attempt to evade the pressure of mutability, to escape from the problems presented by maturity into a permanent dream of first love. The conclusion is, inevitably, the same as that implied in Perdita's speech. The meeting of the lovers is a sign that Spring has been born, indeed, out of Winter tragedy; but Spring needs still to pass over into the Summer which is its fulfilment, otherwise it must, in the very nature of things, wither. In terms of the dramatic action which concerns us, the spring-like beauty of this love is not yet mature; in order to become so, to take up its place, not rejected but completed, in the full balance of the play's conception, it needs to be reinforced by the responsibility, the human concern implied in the deeply spiritual penitence of Leontes. That is why, at this moment of idyllic celebration, Polixenes enters to cast across it the shadow of aged, impotent anger, taking away his son, threatening Perdita with torture, and falling himself into something very like Leontes' sin. A final meeting at the court of Sicilia must precede the final reconciliation. (270–1)

We cannot of course treat Traversi as representative on all points. But it is fair to assert that in its search for the underlying metaphorical structure (the 'full balance of the play's conception') the holistic practice of literary criticism creates a parallel text in the guise of spelling out something already there. The drawback of this invitation to inventive response is that it turns easily into a technique for extracting essence, the critical text in turn coming to be mined by students and followers for a master code. Thus the pedagogic process of which literary criticism is the exemplar and guardian rests upon a formalized process of re-writing the text.

Two more, shorter examples will round off this phase of the argument.

Both concern *Macbeth*, a play which Caroline Spurgeon, Wilson Knight
and the *Scrutiny* school concurred in finding metaphorically dense. Our
first example comes from Wilbur Sanders' discussion of the play in his
unjustly neglected *The Dramatist and the Received Idea* (1968). It is a
commentary on Macbeth's debate with his wife (Act One, Scene Five), a
fraught dialogue which leads to – or perhaps reinforces – Macbeth's
decision to murder Duncan:

> His capitulation, however, uncovers a central failure in Macbeth's
> nature – a failure of self-knowledge. His wife's misinterpretation of his
> genuine scruple as a mere cat's timorousness leaves him powerless
> because he has no better knowledge of his own real motivation. In a
> similar way he is paralysed by the shadow of his own potential evil
> when it rises like a ghost across his path, because he cannot
> acknowledge it as his own. Its power to tyrannize over his better
> nature is dependent on his inability to recognize it. If he could say,
> with Prospero, 'this thing of darkness I/Acknowledge mine', its power
> to appal and master him would be partially broken. Not being able to
> say this, yet seeing the evil rising demonstrably from his own 'horrible
> Imaginings', he is torn asunder, divided against himself, thrown into
> despair. Because he never acknowledges his potential evil, it perpe-
> tually terrifies him in shapes of external coercion. (1968: 287)

Literary criticism had its own theatre, and that theatre could perhaps
be described as a *psychomachia*, a struggle within the self. This *agon* might
be variously located within the simulated character in the text, within the
dramatist, or indeed within the reader critic. Criticism in this vein is
itself a drama, but a drama whose location has moved inwards, away from
the materialities of stage and theatre. The very power of criticism to
irradiate the symbolic structure of the text could, paradoxically, lead to
an intolerance for mediations, production, technology. Where, we might
ask of this school of thought, is this play? The answer in the tradition
discussed here seems to be that in its paradigmatic form it is a drama of
the mind. A. P. Rossiter, the great spokesman of 'ambivalence', uses *Lear*
('humanity perforce must prey upon itself/Like monsters of the deep') and
Troilus as lenses through which to identify what Macbeth has become. He
continues:

> [At] this level, *Macbeth* is the tragedy of success. Macbeth becomes the
> embodiment of everything antagonistic and self-directed; and yet he is
> made the symbol of the utter emptiness of mere antagonism and self-
> assertion. The two contrary experiences – determination to force one's
> way on everything ... and the despair at the impossibility *and* the
> futility of doing so – are brought to co-existence in the mind. It is *in*

us that Macbeth, his Lady and Banquo happen. They are not three persons, but one event in a poem. Murderers and Porter apart, all the rest of the *human* cast are antitheses to the two protagonists: often they have different names, but one essence or being. (Rossiter 1961: 218–19)

This commitment to *psychomachia* reminds us of the literary critics' affinities with the contemporary current of psychoanalytic ideas, and its Coleridgean antecedents. But it also had profound pedagogic implications. The narrative of maturity, of the emergence of the mature, the integrated personality through a struggle with self-indulgence and self-ignorance, became the paradigmatic critical *Bildungsroman*. It is a central part of what its theory critics refer to as the essentialism of liberal humanist criticism. Of course, the technique of teasing out verbal detail to lay bare the text's symbolic deep structure has always generated telling insights. But in pedagogic practice it also led to a discourse which progressively withdrew cultural activity and exchange from the public material world of making, publishing or staging culture. Even authorial biography came to be seen (as so often in discussions of Shakespeare) as an inner, psychic biography, an embattled journey to maturity. What Eliot called the 'intolerable wrestle with words and meanings' came to be seen as an inward strife. This observation restates from a pedagogic angle Francis Mulhern's argument about *Scrutiny* and the repression of politics, the evacuation of the public world (Mulhern 1978). Such an inward turn meant in turn that engagement with the text was an inner rehearsal. We return thus to the point of the present book. As publishing, staging and embodiment became increasingly invisible, so too did pedagogy. A theatre of mind interacting with mind (or mind in dialogue with itself) had little space for mediations. Our object in our project as in this book is not to reject out of hand the instruments of literary criticism, but to press for a rematerialization of pedagogic practice.

4 A Certain Effort of Transformation: Student Writing in Theory

What is singular about any artwork is its redeployment of the resources of the culture, understood as sets of relations rather than concrete objects; and this redeployment, because it introduces new perspectives and relationships which can be understood as the implementation of new codes and norms, always offers the opportunity of imitation, translation, parody and forgery. The singular work is therefore not merely *available* for translation but is constituted in what may be thought of as an unending set of translations ... (Attridge 2003: 73)

[E]ither literary criticism is ... completely determined by the pre-existence of a domain, the literary works, and finally reunited with them in the discovery of their truth, and as such it has no autonomous exis-tence; or it is a certain form of knowledge, and has an object which is not a given but a product of literary criticism. To this object literary criticism applies a certain effort of transformation. Literary criticism is neither the imitation nor the facsimile of its objects ... (Macherey [1966] 1978: 7)

As John Searle puts it, it is the illocutionary force and not the locution that signifies the speaker's intent. And if the teacher wishes to close down the process of wondering by flat declaration of fixed factuality, he or she can do so. The teacher can also open wide a topic of locution to speculation and negotiation. To the extent that the materials of education are chosen for their amenableness to imaginative transfor-mation and are presented in a light to invite negotiation and spec-ulation, to that extent education becomes a part of what I earlier called 'culture making'. The pupil, in effect, becomes a party to the nego-tiatory process by which facts are created and interpreted. He [sic] becomes at once an agent of knowledge making as well as a recipient of knowledge transmission. (Bruner 1986: 127)

In the last chapter we argued that literary criticism – the hegemonic practice of English Literary Studies between around 1950 and 1985 – could in some ways be retrospectively understood as a specialized practice of re-writing. In this chapter we go on to explore the reciprocal implications for this book's subject matter of the new 'theory' paradigm as it progressively re-shaped the English Studies landscape from the mid-1970s. The object is not a summary overview of intellectual history. It is rather an attempt to read the theory reformation pedagogically: as an educational intervention, and one with deeply contradictory implications for the student experience of English Studies. We then seek to connect this analysis to the themes of a book whose concern is with the practice as much as the content of university learning. We shall need briefly to examine aspects of theory in terms of our account of re-making. Transformative writing can have a heuristic value in side-stepping the forms of competitive intellectual aggrandizement too often associated with the transmission of theory as educational knowledge. Conversely, 'theory' may itself be understood as a praxis of re-writing. Writing, as we have argued throughout, enables deeper engagement, students coming to understand theory as process – in terms of metacognitive choices rather than as blocks of facts or truths that can be translated literally and without remainder from one context (the lecture, textbook or Internet) to another (the essay or exam).

What began in the 1970s as a polymorphous attempt to prioritize and fundamentally to reframe the study of culture had enormous, if generally unexamined, consequences in the domain of learning and teaching. Many paradoxes unfolded from the implementation first of structuralism and then almost at once of poststructuralist 'theory' as an educational programme. (For examples, see Evans 1993: 129–158; and critique of 'reading for mastery' in Armstrong 2000.) Unrolled in British higher education, a mix of anti-authoritarian, heteroglossic and dialogic movements was widely experienced as authoritarian, magisterial and monologic, in effect an incitement to surface-level compliance. Lacking either philosophical training or wider reading, too many of its students found themselves ill-equipped to cope with inequalities of intellectual and cultural power. Even what had started out as conceptual and   linguistic playfulness could be experienced empirically as a set of   propositions to be learned in order to satisfy the unaccountable whims of lecturers. Propositions that were in their nature metaphorical, exploratory – ludic even – could thus come to be experienced as authoritative truth statements. Let us think for a moment about the propensity to neologism: to get the point of neologism, students have to have some awareness of the language from which neologism is derived, and against which it reacts – or why indeed an existing term would not suffice. Otherwise they find themselves dutifully learning up terms invented, by, say, Barthes or Cixous – out of a kind of anti-authoritarian *jeu d'esprit* – as dogma. This is not of course to imply that teachers of theory were unanimously devoted to aggrandizing the symbolic power of their caste at the expense of their students. But it is to suggest that the incorporation of difficult and generally heuristic thought styles into the traditional educational genres of lecture, seminar and assessment by essay (whether coursework or timed examination) widely had the effect of generating a form of pedagogic relationship which disempowered all but the most articulate, confident or culturally well-equipped students. Being asked to subscribe to apparently counter-intuitive propositions could and did excite a minority of students to sign up joyously for the campaign to scatter fallacies to left and right. It could also (and in our experience more frequently) lead to grudging compliance or sulky alienation.

Though obviously there have over the years been many exceptions, the apostles of theory were generally in too much of a hurry to recognize the implications of the gulf between their own intellectual formation and learning styles and those of their students. In the circumstances of the later 1970s and 1980s the urgency of the situation was widely felt to require the rhetorical enlistment of students. While there were exceptions, in most cases the need for coadjutators trumped reflection upon pedagogic ironies. Many leading figures in the propagation of theory were of course concerned with how the new domains were to be learned. But they tended to work at the level of curriculum and substance, rather than pedagogy. Thus the movement gave rise to introductory books (e.g. Eagleton, Methuen New Accents series), 'readers'/anthologies (e.g. Lodge, Rice and Waugh, Easthope and McGowan, Rivkin and Ryan) or guides (e.g. Selden, Barry, Green and LeBihan, Bennett and Royle). But, and despite the short-lived series of Learning/Teaching/Politics Conferences (LTP) during the mid-1980s, the radicals of theory on the whole left the reform of teaching alone.

In what follows, we argue that a re-assessment of forms of learning and assessment is necessary if the majority of students are to be able to avail themselves of the cultural power of theory as process rather than simply to learn to gesture towards theory as product. Implicit in the forms of writing this book advocates is that they enable students *as writers* to theorize texts at the same time as recognizing their own location as educational and expressive subjects. We are no more arguing that the study of what has become known as theory is a waste of time than – in the rest of the book – we are arguing that unconstrained free expression should replace the meticulous study of texts. But we are proposing that the forms of engagement with the infinite riches of culture typically offered to students require supplementation if they are to kindle contemporary intellects and imaginations. We are experimenting, in short, with a perlocutionary practice of theory.

Let us take a specific example from the early days of the 'Writing for Reading' module. As a Level 2 option this was being studied alongside compulsory modules in Critical and Cultural Theory. The approach taken to the module represented an attempt to assimilate to British conditions what we had learned from David Bleich (including, obliquely, his earlier book *Subjective Criticism*, 1978), from Robert Scholes (especially *Textual Power* (1985) and *The Crafty Reader* (2001)), from feminist literary practice, and from the 'academic development' thread within DUET. In identifying the need to supplement conventional modes of instruction and assessment, we acted on a belief that 'theory' as educational practice made too many assumptions about the conceptual and rhetorical equipment of students. It had, in short, failed to theorize its own pedagogy. In particular, and because of not altogether ill-founded suspicions about the naiveties of expressivism (see Chapter 2), it stuck with a puritanically narrow repertoire of writing – principally the analytical essay.

The Fall of the House of Usher

A focused group activity. Group members have read the story and preferably sampled some other Poe in their own time, perhaps making use of e-texts such as those available through Project Gutenberg. The tutor could start by talking about the close affinities (from Pierre Macherey on Ann Radcliffe) between theory and Gothic, suggesting that the pedagogic domain can itself be read as a site of transformations, initiation, ghosts, transferences, hauntings, cryptography. (The ivy-clad tower and gothic lancets have a trace existence on the websites, and could invite visual collage.) Literally or metaphorically, a hypertext of writing activities (graffiti on, around and over the text – writing on the castle walls) simultaneously invigorates working with story and with theory.

Take the opening and invite re-writing in different genres (cf. Pope 1995) – actual examples have included: Western; naturalism; children's fiction; journalism; film scenario (we trialled this in the days of *The Blair Witch Project*). Group then focuses on what aspects of the existing opening come into prominence as a result. At the very least this preliminary activity enables collaborative tackling of ideas about genre, lexical field, codes, the orientation of reader expectations, openings as acts of demonstration, etc. They could alternatively pick out key signifiers for their own poems.

Simple beginning – the house: collect fiction/film titles involving 'house' and as a group collect metaphorical implications.

House ... 'eyeless windows' ... re-write interior spaces. As so often, we can take cue from text itself:

It was possible, I reflected, that a mere different arrangement of the particulars of the scene, of the details of the picture, would be sufficient to modify, or perhaps to annihilate its capacity for sorrowful impression ...

*... narrator looking into the tarn to reframe what he is seeing and avoid being
overwhelmed ... Re-arrange it: rewriter tries a different projection. Alternatively, how and using what signifiers could we domesticate this scene and
make it safe? (Explore the counter image of the homely through homebuilders'
websites or brochures.)*

More specifically in the context of this chapter:

Examples of theory themes which can be opened up through writing activity

- Realism ... unrealism ... monstrous ... taboo ... repression.
  Recreate the back story.
- Try out Barthes' five codes (students have dwelt in particular on
  the semiotic and to some extent cultural code ... what for
  example are the signifiers of 'Gothic'?). Break up a selection of the
  story into *lexias* and write commentary in the style of *S/Z*.
- Cultural code: an updated version ⇒ where are the equivalent
  spaces for writers today? Where would you set a twenty-first
  century *House of Usher*? And why?
- Linearity, secrets, incest, mystery and narrative ... change
  narrative stance.
- Feminism (what if there were a female narrator? ... Invert gender
  structure of the story). How might we set about a comparison
  with 'female Gothic'?
- Absences that constitute presences.
- Masculinities – doubles and childhood friends. What is the text
  saying about the masculine subject?

In the manner of my friend I was at once struck with an incoherence –
an inconsistency; and I soon found this to arise from a series of feeble
and futile struggles to overcome an habitual trepidancy – an excessive
nervous agitation. For something of this nature I had indeed been
prepared, no less by his letter, than by reminiscences of certain boyish
traits ...

- Metafiction: construction of the artist and the aesthetic. Artist as
  dabbler in the forbidden? (Talk to them about *Faust*?)
- Freud: dream, condensation and displacement (try inserting as
  dream into realist text); the uncanny.
- Binaries: as a group draw up table and debate positioning of
  elements.
- Parallel texts: use *House of Usher* as a lens through which to look at
  another narrative of haunted interiority. Invite students to explore
  how we might use one text as a theory of reading in relation to
  another. Might need suggestions from the tutor: for example
  Lawrence's 'The Blind Man'.

- Horizons of reference: intertext and cod intertexts. Role of titles, counterfeit medieval learning (anyone remember Coleridge's marginal annotations to 1816 *Ancient Mariner?*) and the 'Haunted Palace' ballad.
- Gothic checklist: create taxonomy of key features for identifying Gothic text, and apply to other examples or partial examples (e.g. Angela Carter's *The Magic Toyshop* or stories in *The Bloody Chamber*).
- Reader response: start from occasions on which reading prefigured (e.g. narrator reading to Roderick during the storm), and explore inferential gaps left in the text.

Our case is that writing activities enable more various engagement than simply learning up 'schools' or theorists. They involve students in the root questions that 'theory' seeks to address. So our approach links textual phenomena to everyday language: to link – shall we say – Gothic animism and the animism of day to day metaphor (the fog will be reluctant to lift, the car refused to start, the transponder chip says 'Oi' . . .)

Interruption and re-framing have the effect of estrangement. Structured writing, even when it appears to take an almost mechanical form, is itself a mode of enquiry. Practical experience of the weight of cultural codes takes students back to the root questions that 'theory' seeks to address. Nor can these questions be seen as static. Re-writing is, we propose, in itself a practice of theorization, a re-enactment for the student as apprentice writer of the dialogue inherent in the discovery and re-invention of frames for perception. The learner can thus explore the simultaneously liberating and constraining operation of what Kenneth Burke called 'terministic screens' (Burke 1966). In choreographing a rhythmic movement between estrangement and identification, structured writing out of and back into theory enables students to discover for themselves what many years ago, and in the context of his own concern with 'the impact of theory on teaching' Robert Scholes dubbed 'textual power' (Scholes 1985: ix). On the basis of the Sheffield writing modules, Robert Miles came to a very similar conclusion:

In particular I want to argue not only that the tendency of contemporary theory to question boundaries and demarcations undoes the unhelpful categorization of practice versus analysis, vocational versus academic, creative writing versus English, but that creative writing can helpfully, and rigorously, question contemporary theory. To put it another way, 'contemporary' theory helps bring out what is uncompromisingly 'hard' in so-called 'soft' creative writing, while creative writing in turn helps bring out the disconcertingly soft in hard theory.

('Creative Writing, Contemporary Theory and the English Curriculum' in Monteith and Miles 1992: 35)

MAKING SENSE

This book envisages the re-instatement of the student as a writing
subject: as someone whose equipment for learning rests not on the
memorization of dogma, but springs from an awakened desire to make
sense through the practical performance of a repertoire of ideas. In the
context of theory, as throughout, we argue for a dialectical process (one,
incidentally, through which it is simultaneously possible to demonstrate
a deconstructionist case for side-stepping the privileging of one term over
another). This variety of educational praxis involves a dialogic movement
between generating items of specimen text and engagement with the
intellectual dynamics of the already written. Throughout, we seek to
promote a dual focus on the student as apprentice maker; and on theory,
as prompt. We suggest that the teasing, allusive, invigorating resources
of theory may themselves prefigure the practice of re-making in which we
wish to involve our students.

The next stage of this chapter suggests what we as teachers might do
next. We shall refer (as a framing device) to the structure we evolved for
'Making Sense', a Level 1 module on theory and critical practice, one of
whose objects was to prepare students for the Critical and Cultural
Theory module at Level 2. Here, once again, Robert Scholes provided a
nodal thought:

> The first step towards any kind of critical independence is the study of
> constraint. This is one reason why the submission involved in reading
> is important. A student needs to feel the power of a text, to experience
> the pleasures obtainable only through submission, before he or she can
> begin to question both that pleasure and the requisite submission.
> Criticism begins with the recognition of textual power and ends in the
> attempt to exercise it. This attempt may take the form of an essay, but
> it may just as easily be textualized as a parody or countertext in the
> same mode as its critical object. As teachers, we should encourage the
> full range of critical practice in our students. (Scholes 1985: 41)

There is a world of difference for students between learning up
declarative statements about the constraints imposed by language and
culture ('we did Marxism last week; we're doing Feminism now') and
experiencing the emergence of unbidden codes and memories as they try
to write their own countertexts. The course whose outline we borrow here
was underpinned by our belief in the need – on however small a scale – to

attempt textual production as a precondition for conceptual under-standing and analysis. The module comprised six interlinked units:

1. Representation
2. Self, subject, author
3. The aesthetic
4. Text and structure
5. Readers and reading
6. Culture, history and society

In what follows we concentrate on just two of these: *self, subject, author* and *Readers and reading*. Other elements will shadow the main discussion as allusion and cross reference. Whatever reservations we may entertain about the theory of 'learning outcomes', we find it useful to describe this process in terms of what we would like students to be able to do. Threaded through the rest of the chapter are two interlinked proposals: that literary production is a powerful key to a grasp of theory, and that, through writing, students can acquire the tools to theorize their own experience of educational institutions and of themselves as learning subjects. In turn, these are supported by a third proposal, another voice in this polyphony. That is, that many aspects of 'theory' as mediated within English Studies *themselves* prefigure the process of writing as re-making. For example, the search for fissures, absences, inconsistencies that char-acterized so much of 'theory' after Macherey can be seen as itself a process of re-writing. After all, what Macherey draws out of Althusser and the tradition of praxis is precisely a Marxian version of knowledge as activity: 'not the discovery or reconstruction of a latent meaning, forgotten or concealed. It is something newly raised up, an addition to the reality from which it begins ...' (1978: 6). So it is that such interventions paradoxically present parallels with the account of criticism as re-writing sketched in the previous chapter. After all the 'absence that constitutes a presence', apart from becoming a mantra in some theory circles in the 1980s, was also the basis for powerful if disputed critical interventions like Edward Said's reading of *Mansfield Park*. Leaving aside the many problems attaching to the critical privileging of the not-said, the invo-cation of what the text could not say for itself is effectively as much an act of re-writing as is the new critic's teasing out of the master metaphor. Both endeavours implicitly model for the student an entitlement or even obligation for productive critical labour: revealing through re-writing that which was concealed, or which existed in what Iser once referred to as the 'penumbra of excluded possibilities' (1978: 72).

SELF/SUBJECT/AUTHOR

Self, Subject, Author: A Level 1 engagement with theory

This 'I' which approaches the text is already itself a plurality of other texts, of codes which are infinite ... or whose origin is lost. (Barthes 1975: 10)

We start with names and naming, moving on to characterizations and the stories people tell about themselves. The collection of examples from the field of everyday life leads on to the exploration of selfhood as polyglossic.

Look up some examples of places where people describe themselves or tell their story (e.g. magazine advice columns) ... What are the current vogue words for describing personal experience or the nature of human trouble?

The names we are known by call us into different roles (Sally, Sal, Sarah, Mrs or Ms S. Bowles, Mrs William Bowles, Mum may all be the same person, but each name implies a different form of relation and a different aspect of the self.) List your own names, and the contexts in which they are used, then think about the different versions of you that go with them.

As subjects we are to some extent shaped by the discourse of institutions (e.g. schools, hospitals, mother and toddler groups, universities). Collect examples of the language of the university: how does it shape your role as a student?

Look up dating columns in a magazine or newspaper. How would you describe yourself in these terms? What have you had to leave out? What aspects of yourself come into prominence?

Do writers tell the truth about themselves? Choose an incident from your own past. Write a short (two paragraph) description of what happened ...

Look through a family photograph album, or the holiday pictures saved on a laptop. What messages do the photos encode?

Find some examples of autobiographical writing. How does the speaker of the story present him or herself?

The aim is to create small scale theory scripts as a basis for further engagement with theoretical argumentation.[27]

As Lucy Newlyn notes of her creative/critical workshops, looking back on the whole process it is possible to see each of its separate stages as an exploration of questions fundamental to literary theory. (2003 I: 67)

In attempting to write out theoretical insights, students are here effectively trying out ideas about the interpellation of the subject, the self as palimpsest of quotations, about authorship, and the heteroglossic nature of utterance. In a culture where much of the dominant discourse of self is derived from forms of counselling and proposes the authenticity of the inner you, this procedure may well be experienced as counter-intuitive. In that case, the teacher's role is – as so often – to contain the anxiety of learning (Salzberger-Wittenberg 1983; Knights 1992, Ch. 2). The pedagogic sleight of hand is to invite engagement in the writing activity *before* offering a theoretical gloss on what has been achieved. Thus, students are for example empowered to swim with the current of dialogism that goes back to Vygotsky as well as Bakhtin. John Shotter usefully summarizes:

The 'movement' of my inner life is motivated and structured through and through by my continual crossing of boundaries; by what happens in those zones of uncertainty where 'I' (speaking in one of my 'voices' from a 'position' in a speech genre) am in communication with another 'self' in another position within that genre ... (Shotter 1993: 124)

Lectures or other declarative statements on the teacher's part play a complementary role. As teachers, we are of course responsible for using our own knowledge to speak back to the evolving experience. (Though we must strive not to overwhelm with the 'final' or 'correct' version, coming back, like the realist narrator, with the authoritative summary.) But unless students have the experience of writing small-scale theory scripts, teacher-dominated elucidation will mean little to most of them (other than as a threatening and unaccountable language of domination).

There is a reciprocal thread: that 'theory' speaks to the pedagogic situation. In this discussion of the student as emergingly self-conscious educational subject, the neo-Freudian tradition is very much to the point. Shoshana Felman classically explored the resonances for the pedagogic situation of Freud's theory of transference. 'This new mode of investigation and learning', she argued,

has a very different temporality than the conventional linear – cumulative and progressive – temporality of learning as it has traditionally been conceived by pedagogical theory and practice. Proceeding not through linear progression, but through breakthroughs, leaps, discontinuities, regressions and deferred actions, the analytic learning process puts in question the traditional pedagogic belief in intellectual perfectibility, the progressistic view of learning as a one-way road from ignorance to knowledge. (1982: 27)

The temporality she describes speaks strongly to our sense of the temporality of learning through writing. We might appropriate from Bakhtin an idea of the chronotope of the classroom. The portfolio of attempts, fresh starts, re-draftings, cuttings, comments and post-it notes is not simply a linear progress record, but the prosthesis of mind in process. Into it leak unsuspected codes, eruptions of the individual and cultural unconscious. The Freudian traditions (grounded as they are in the analytical here and now) make up one example in support of our contention both that 'theory' prefigures acts of re-writing, and that 'theory' can be repositioned as insight into the situatedness of learning. The different temporality which Felman identifies speaks to our sense of the different temporality of the 'active reading' experiment. In a consumer culture promising instant gratification, the role of pedagogy may actually be to delay the straightforward move from problem to solution, so protecting the time of reading. There is a direct parallel with the 'third space' of Donald Winnicott's *Playing and Reality* (1971, and see Chapter 8). The understanding of meaning as sequence of events which reader-response theory (see below) takes from Stanley Fish enables us to theorize an important perception: so much of teaching is protecting the right and obligation to do strange things (writing variations on a sentence, arguing about non-existent events) from the imputation – overt or implicit – of wasting precious time. If nothing else, the process of writing is a valuable weapon in the struggle (whether with students or with university managements) over what constitutes valid use of time.

Fictions of pedagogy

One way of getting at the meanings of the pedagogic setting and of the relationships of the classroom is to invite attention to texts that have themselves foregrounded those relations. From finding and reading samples or extracts, students could be invited to create their own intertexts, or to create collages drawing on their own fragments of memory. Coleridge's 'Frost at Midnight' would be no bad starting place:

And so I brooded all the following morn,
Awed by the stern preceptor's face, mine eye
Fixed with mock study on my swimming book...

Campus novels – from Malcolm Bradbury and David Lodge to Zadie Smith's *On Beauty* – are another obvious source, as are Muriel Spark's *The Prime of Miss Jean Brodie*, or Alan Bennett's *History Boys*. Ursula in the classroom could be lifted from *Women in Love*, while another and different source would be U.A. Fanthorpe's campus poems, e.g. 'Felicity and Mr Frost' (which has the advantage of itself being an intertextual re-writing as well). Students could go on foraging expeditions for examples from classic texts (*Portrait of the Artist as a Young Man*), remembering too both the sub-genre of governess scenes (*Villette*) and the school and classroom in children's fiction from *Harry Potter* backwards. Throughout, the object is to foreground, make explicit, and then re-work the genres and codes through which learning and teaching are represented. Experimental writing can then take the form of drawing out the propensity of schooling fiction to move either in utopian or dystopian directions. To make the point again: such an activity does not simply license the indulgence of memory. It can also, if appropriate, lead back into what anyone would accept as 'rigorous' critical scholarship: for example a dissertation on the affinity between schooling fiction and forms of Gothic.

Once again, we are talking about the 'study of constraint'. In interleaving memory, craft and text, students can be supported in thinking through the precise and local meanings of gender, class, age and power. Or indeed the force of unconscious meanings within the group.

It is in writing that students can experience the impurity of messages at the same time as the pressure of the medium upon the message, of the forms of language and culture upon what they are trying to say. Intentionality ('but can she have meant all this?') is not the least topic illuminated by the act of writing. No amount of telling will substitute for being in the presence of what Denys Harding called the 'hinterland of thought' (1974, Chapter 10). For, as he elsewhere puts it, if we ask a poet 'what his [sic] poem is communicating we imply that he first had some idea of the meaning and then translated it into the words of the poem. In fact what he had to say was not there until he said it.' (1974: 171) We seek to open up to students the lived experience of finding something not there until you said it. We have repeatedly found individuals and classes energized by the excitement of finding before them verbal objects that were simply not there 25 minutes earlier. And the dialectic between reading and writing, vitalized by even the smallest verbal sketch, is finely poised. Harding is quoted by Wolfgang Iser in support of his own phenomenological theory of reading.

What is sometimes called wish-fulfilment in novels and plays can . . . more plausibly be described as wish formulation or the definition of desires. The cultural levels at which it works may vary; the process is the same . . . It seems nearer the truth . . . to say that fictions contribute to defining the reader's or spectator's values, and perhaps stimulating his desires, rather than to suppose that they gratify desire by some mechanism of vicarious experience. (Iser 1978: 158)

This intereaction between self and text, the textuality of self, points forward towards livable theories of reading.

One more point before we move on from 'self and subject'. Because writing is so often associated with a psychologized or individual notion of expression it is important to assert that writing of the kind advocated here is not simply a vehicle of 'self-discovery' or 'finding your own voice'. A spiral of reading ⇒ writing ⇒ further reading can also, within conditions of adequate security, be used to open up questions about the cultural situatedness of the self as at once addressee and agent. Again, the educational environment may provide our text – students being invited individually or in small groups to collect evidence and write about the patterns of exclusion or empowerment they encounter in the here and now of the university environment. The rituals and conventions of the educational genre provide powerful sources for the 'study of constraint'.

Reflexiveness in a Level 3 special topic

. . . the social situation in which students work – the regular gathering, the steady physical formation of a collective body – is deliberately bypassed in favour of a more private, authority-heavy dyadic relationship in which the student is encouraged more to adapt to the teacher's perspective than to proceed in an authentic negotiation – since the teacher's final binding judgment is always anticipated. If the class were treated as a 'thought collective' on the other hand, there could be no a priori sense of either the group's perspective or its judgment, and a genuine negotiation of meanings could proceed. (Bleich 1988: 195)

Students are invited to foray out in small groups as ethnographers to collect and read signs – notices, noticeboards, fliers on walls, the labelling of pigeonholes, the prohibitions or welcomes displayed on doors, the semiotics of university space. (The digital camera and the photo mobile have made this activity easier than it used to be.) The material so collected becomes material for class analysis, group presentation, collage, or the ground for found poems – or the opening of their own campus novel.

Insights so generated can be worked up, depending on the precise inflection of the session or module, towards semiotics; agency and power; the 'political unconscious' of the university; the vocabulary and discourse of education; autobiographical vignettes about their own experience of schooling or of arriving in a new institution; the academic sociology of gender, age, or class; material for the investigation of Kafka, or the realist (or Gothic) novel.

INTERTEXTUALITY

From the heteroglossia of self to the polyphony of text, Barthes' affirmation of the 'writerly' has spoken throughout to our own pedagogic endeavour (see epigraph to Chapter 2). His demonstration that even the most 'readerly' text can in some sense be re-read as writerly moves beyond text as object to text as site of activity, a perpetual bestowing of names and definitions:

> To read, in fact, is a labor of language. To read is to find meanings, and to find meanings is to name them; but these named meanings are swept towards other names; names call to each other, reassemble, and their grouping calls for further naming: I name, I unname, I rename: so the text passes: it is a nomination in the course of becoming, a tireless approximation, a metonymic labor ... (Barthes 1975: 11)

In pedagogic terms, the loosening up of the bonds of naming, the articulation of the codes through which names are naturalized is a primary act of estrangement. Implicitly or actually we put to students the questions: under what name does this group know you? Who do you wish to be known as in this class? (Though we are then able to demonstrate that those choices are themselves drawn from the available *langues*.) Our module deals first with representation because the ambiguities of representation, the figurative nature of language, and the impossibility of simple positivist re-assurance run through the units that follow. As is also the case in the Althusser–Macherey tradition, the very imperfections and obscurities of the text are the starting place for reading as creative re-fashioning. Later in *S/Z*, Barthes seizes hold of the communication theory contrast of message and noise:

> In relation to an ideally pure message (as in mathematics), the division of reception constitutes a 'noise', it makes communication obscure, fallacious ... uncertain. Yet this noise, this uncertainty ... are given to the reader so that he may feed on them: what the reader reads is a

counter-communication; and if we grant that the *double understanding*
far exceeds the limited case of the play on words ... and permeates ...
all classic writing ... we see that literatures are in fact arts of
'noise': what the reader consumes is this defect in communication,
this deficient message; what the whole structuration erects for him
[sic] and offers him as the most precious nourishment is a
counter-communication; the reader is an accomplice ... of the discourse itself insofar as it plays on the division of reception ... (145)

The noise (of figurative language, of apparently redundant detail, of
narrative diversion and *cul-de-sac*) *is* the signal. A pedagogy of re-creative
writing seeks to foster patience and a willingness to wait: the student
(and perhaps the teacher too) must learn tolerance for the noise both of
the text and of the classroom.

For the reader student, the process of writing puts into play motions of
mind and feeling that can themselves be renamed within the genre of
theory: power, intertextuality, *langue*, code. We might even take heart
from the fact that poststructuralist theory has itself on occasion given rise
to poetic texts, or to hybrid forms such as those practised by Hélène
Cixous in *Sorties* or *The Smile of the Medusa*.[28] In the early years of the
importation of Parisian theory into England, *S/Z* itself metamorphosed
intertextually in Veronica Forrest-Thomson's hands into a poem of that
name which begins by quoting Barthes on *Sarrasine* and turns into a
meditation on writing.[29] A pedagogic endeavour such as we are trying to
describe is inevitably fascinated by all that we have come to know as
'intertextuality': culture and the individual text envisioned as palimpsest
of quotations. To Freud's processes of condensation and displacement,
Julia Kristeva adds a third: the 'passage from one sign system to another',
a transfer which sets up a new positionality.

> The term intertextuality denotes this transposition of one (or several)
> sign-system(s) into another; but since this term has often been
> understood in the banal sense of the 'study of sources', we prefer the
> term transposition because it specifies that the passage from one sign
> system to another demands a new articulation of the thetic – of
> enunciative and denotative positionality. (*Revolution in Poetic Language*,
> in Moi 1986: 111)[30]

Theories of intertextuality from Barthes to Kristeva and Genette
constitute luminous examples of theory pre-figuring the act of re-
writing. Simultaneously, and as another example of the 'double
perspective', the emergence of fragments, memories, allusions, veiled
quotations in students' own writing, enriches their understanding of
cultural transmission and re-enactment. For very much the same reasons

we as teachers are apt to make use of or draw attention to salient examples of fiction or poetry as re-writing (see Appendix 2.) All such hypertexts and appropriations challenge the simple division between critical readings and creative re-writing.

Throughout this chapter we have been simultaneously concerned with writing as the performance of theory and theory as pre-figuring re-creative writing. Forms of dialogism are implicit in these attempts to grasp accounts of self and of intertextuality. Todorov quotes Bakhtin:

> I achieve self-consciousness, I become myself only by revealing myself to another, through another and with another's help. The most important acts, constitutive of self-consciousness, are determined by their relation to another consciousness (a 'thou') ... It turns out that every internal experience occurs on the border ... The very being of man (both internal and external) is a *profound communication. To be* means to *communicate* ... (1984: 96)

Literary and constructivist educational theory here share a common rootstock. Our route back to the textual classroom leads through L.S. Vygotsky:

> [An] interpersonal process is transformed into an intrapersonal one. Every function in the child's cultural development occurs twice: first on the social level, and later, on the individual level; first between people ... and then inside the child ... This applies equally to voluntary attention, to logical memory, and to the formation of concepts. All the higher functions originate as actual relations between human individuals. (1978: 56–7)

In the Vygotskian tradition the acquisition of language and of consciousness is itself a form of intertextuality. Through adding to their linguistic repertoire, the 'subjects' of the textual classroom are creating their own mapping tools for the exploration of their boundaries and affinities with their peers, their teachers and their texts. In literary terms, the constructive effort to make sense is affirmed and articulated through theories of reader response. Literary texts 'initiate "performances" of meaning rather than actually formulating meaning' (Iser 1978: 27). Once again, theory (the sort that can be summed up and lectured about) clears a trail for re-writing practice. All we are suggesting is that the phenomenology of reading which Iser blended from ingredients of Gestalt and Freudian psychology requires extension outside the internal drama of the contemplative mind. The pen, the pencil, the computer keyboard – so far from being simply the invisible media of assessment – provide the material basis for dialogues between readers and between readers and texts. And to the tutor falls the task of creating and safeguarding what (in the unwieldy phrase of Vygotsky's translators) is known as the 'zone of proximal development'.

Readers and Reading

The iconic signs of literature constitute an organization of signifiers which do not serve to designate a signified object, but instead serve to designate instructions for the production of the signified. (Iser 1978: 65)

We have both found this area of 'theory' work one which most engages student groups, and has, over the years, been well supported by reader anthologies, most recently Andrew Bennett's Longman Critical Reader (1995).

Ceci n'est pas une pipe ... Start by reading aloud a passage that involves a range of kinetic response. Ask the group to shut their eyes and read to them ... e.g. the tree-climbing episode from Ian McEwan's *The Child in Time* (1987). Play inferencing games on an overhead projector or whiteboard.

Provide a contrasted set of novel openings on a sheet and set up a prediction exercise. Dwell on clues that might orient the narrative. From a palimpsest of notes to re-writings – e.g. simple (first to third person), more complex: fantasy as realism, etc. The object is to invite awareness of meaning as event, of the role of the reader as collaborator in building a symbolic architecture.

It remains to gather the threads of this chapter, and point towards the more practice-oriented chapters that follow. Theory (like literature or any other cultural text) represents equipment for enquiry. So, too, and reciprocally, does writing. Neither promises a direct or uncomplicated narrative of learning, a straightforward progress from ignorance to knowledge. We have sought to articulate a theory and practice of social learning, inserting the materiality of the pedagogic situation (its risks, false starts, dead ends and sudden new beginnings) into the materialism of theory. Our underlying theme has been that a binary mindset which poses theory over (re)creativity is inherently unstable. Further, that a pedagogy of writing does not have to lose its potential for critique – that, on the contrary, it may actually enable the student to undertake critique from a position of heightened confidence in her own critical stance. Nevertheless, collaboration – the mutuality of workshop practice – could profitably replace competitive *agon*. We advocate a process which *interrupts* the drive of both pedagogy and of theory towards a triumphant metalanguage.

Finally (and with Barthes, among others, still in mind), we want to spell out something about pleasure. Earlier, we noted that one component of the 'Making Sense' module was a unit on 'the aesthetic'. The ground base of that unit was a demonstration that humans are rarely satisfied with the merely necessary. Students were sent out to do their own fieldwork on the proposition that even in the smallest and most local examples humans strive for excess: to transform necessity into visual, auditory, tactile, sensory pleasure. Further, that they develop meta-languages for commenting upon, comparing and sharing that pleasure. Students themselves captured examples of the latter from sources as various as conversations about music, fashion magazines and football commentary. At a further level, that module, like the Active Reading project and this book itself, seeks to re-affirm the role of pleasure in the literary pedagogic process. So much in the instrumental rationality of contemporary learning and teaching orthodoxy reinforces what Louise Rosenblatt called 'efferent reading' (Rosenblatt 1978) – harvesting the written medium for useful material directed to an extrinsic end. If our project is about anything, it is about restoring and licensing sensuous pleasure in engagement with text.

Part II

Teaching, Learning and Assessment:
Writing for Reading

5 *Making a Start*

THE BEGINNING OF MODULE OR CLASS AS LIMINAL MOMENT – INTELLECTUAL, SOCIAL, AFFECTIVE

In May 2002, at the Sheffield 'Next in Text' Conference, the Jamaican writer, poet and performer, Jean 'Binta' Breeze, delivered a keynote lecture[31] in which she gave the following advice to prospective teachers and English practitioners:

- Be honest in the classroom – don't deny the power structure that exists
- Be comfortable – in your shoes, your dress, your attitude
- Improvisation – encourage this in your own and your students' work
- Become a participant – use drama games in class
- Entry – think about how you 'face' the class – it sets the tone/mood for the day
- Use personal storytelling – this will encourage tutees to share their experiences

Although these ideas have been paraphrased and bulleted, they all remain points worthy of discussion, and the single one which stays with me over time is the focus on 'entry', thinking about how you 'face' the learners for the first few minutes of the workshop or seminar. At first the idea of setting a tone or 'mood for the day' seems an antiquated one, something perhaps out of place in today's outcome-driven modules and this in itself speaks of a gap, something missing perhaps from the increasing pro-fessionalization of the discipline known as English Studies. Like it or not, however, the first few minutes of a new module do exist and we do have to work out a practical way of dealing with them. In the context of the active reading module, the first few minutes are perhaps even more significant given the anticipated differences in perception that such a module inevitably creates. Not only are there the usual 'What have I signed up for here?', 'What do I have to do to pass the module?' and 'What's the new tutor going to be like?' anxieties to be experienced on any new course, but these are likely to be joined by potentially more serious worries such as 'How much of myself do I have to give away here?', 'Where will I have to read out my stuff?' and 'Will everyone think my bits of writing are rubbish?' We can add to this list more module-specific – I'm tempted to say 'educated' – anxieties about whether this is a creative writing module or not, whether assessment by portfolio will be harder than an exam, and how and why it relates to the practice of reading anyway.

On the other side of the desk (as we have questionably become accustomed to labelling the experience) are other worries – intellectual, social, affective – not so very far from those of the participants themselves. Again I'm tempted by a cathartic list, but these issues are going to vary so widely according to such variables as level of experience, time of day, teaching resources, attendance numbers, handouts, room size and so on that I merely point them up at this stage. Returning to Binta Breeze's stress on the performance aspects of teaching (and trying hard to keep Samuel Beckett at bay here), how should we make our entrance – fast, slow, loud, quiet, worried, shuffling papers, carrying equipment or nothing at all? These issues are, alas, not negligible and cannot be allowed to 'just happen'. Once the boundary between corridor and classroom has been crossed, we are, inescapably, in the position of the professional modelling their discipline before others. Specifically we are modelling what seems to be a particularly narrow learning experience, one that is part writer's workshop, part academic seminar, part creative performance and part critical debate. It is this hybrid background that marks it off from conventional expectations that might be held about the usual higher education encounter with the teaching staff. Not only is there more 'up for grabs', but also at this stage nobody really knows what they're grabbing for. All of a sudden this seems a very high-risk environment and you begin to wonder (a) what on earth you're doing and (b) if it is all worthwhile anyway. If only I'd written a normal module. This feeling of uncertainty and high risk, however, is not one that goes away, given the nature of the active reading experience. In fact, it is the only honest, genuine and even pedagogically adequate feeling to have. The only real question is how to model the uncertainties of the active reading experience in such a way as to increase participants' confidence and trust, while not undermining the progress they have made in other modules on their degree. Increasingly, I see that the biggest strengths of transformative writing are making people at home with multiple readings, and then enabling them to locate themselves in that home. A greater recognition of the conflicting uncertainties and semantic possibilities of a text can only be achieved by focusing on the very processes and procedures through which we come to understand the world around us and our position in it. The first few moments of the seminar have to be meta-cognitive ones – because modelling meta-cognition will become the norm for the metaphorical and symbolic exchanges of the weeks that follow, through draft work to assignment submission and thereafter. For this reason there is something enduring to be gained from Thomas Hilgers *et al.*:

> What more might it take to help students achieve proficiency as writers, thinkers, and problem solvers? It might take little more than providing experiences that encourage awareness of what they are doing as they write, and, furthermore, awareness that how what they are doing, even in apparently disparate situations, is ultimately working to solve potentially related sets of epistemological or rhetorical problems. (1999, 348)

GROUND RULES IN THE FORMATION OF A WORKSHOP

There is no shortage of literature on the formation of conditions for a writing workshop.[32] Creative writing in particular has been a focus for attention in this area. What is less clear, though, is whether the same conditions should prevail in the setting up of the active reading seminar. The latter, let's remember, is still very much an academic enterprise within the confines of an institutional setting, part of a staged module with specific learning outcomes. Moreover, it sits within the overall context of a level of study within the larger undergraduate degree. Naturally, certain features may be recognized by participants of creative workshops, but it is important to flag up differences at the outset to learners who may mistakenly be entertaining purely creative writing expectations.

A key component in week one of our own active reading module, 'Writing for Reading' (a Level 2 option), is the writing contract. The idea of having a contract in which students come up with their own set of rules is hardly revolutionary but it remains, in our view, essential. It has several key functions in the overall structure of the module: it hands a level of responsibility over to the participants from the outset; it helps in the maintenance of a boundary between the workshop and the world; it begins to build up trust and group identity within the seminar; and not least, of course, it provides a yardstick for acceptable behavioural attitudes which should be followed in the weeks to come. More often than not, those who have signed up for 'Writing for Reading' have no experience whatsoever of formulating a contract within an educational setting. The room goes silent and clearly we need to provide examples of the kind of thing that might be useful. Like any teaching situation, this calls for real judgement on the part of the practitioner. Too many examples of ground rules and you've done the job yourself; too few and you've provided no guidance at all. For this reason I bring along a few

examples of contracts to draw on. There's an example in the box below
from our 2004 cohort.

Working Contract for Class Group Work
('Writing for Reading' module, 2004)

1. Constructive criticism only please
2. Take the work seriously – no laughing out of turn
3. No malicious attacks (personal)
4. Writers need to give a pre-warning if they intend to introduce
    material that might cause offence (contentious ideas/language,
    etc.)
5. We don't have to share our work out loud if we don't want to
6. Where the writer's permission has been given, the other Writing
    for Reading group can read our work
7. Everyone to start the seminars each week at 9.15 am prompt

---

It is worth spending a moment with each of the criteria that this
cohort of active readers have set themselves. (1) is a very common one
that reappears in a number of guises; it is also one I take as a positive sign
that the group are engaging seriously with the task of contract formulation. They know from the handbook that over the next 15 weeks
they will be sharing their output, both formally and informally, and they
need to construct certain workable defences. This is a good idea, apart
from which they have already identified for themselves two fundamental
concepts behind the module – constructive building or making, and
criticism itself, critical activity that is likely to move beyond the page.
(2) is a rarer example: it is a recognition of what we said earlier about
behavioral attitudes – the participants clearly want to be able to control,
even to outlaw, certain modes of expression. Quite what 'laughing out of
turn' would involve and when it could be identified is somewhat vague –
but this is no cause for concern. I like the way this group seem to
recognize the emotional and affective possibilities that may lie before
them. (3) has a clear relationship with both the previous entries but now
I'm beginning to think that they've said this already – they are emerging
as really quite a worried small group. How am I going to handle this? (4)
is another common rule that is good to see. Matters of censorship were
not given as examples but the group have independently seen the need for
some rudimentary code of practice when it comes to 'material that might
cause offence'. The idea of a 'pre-warning' is excellent and has been used
to very good effect in real situations by several active reading workshops.
(5) is a rule I make, even if the students don't and it's one that sometimes
surprises other English practitioners – surely the whole point of writing

with a group is to share your work and benefit from others' ideas and support? To an extent this is right, but the safeguard provided by not having to share your writing accomplishes even more essential tasks: it provides space for real creative and personal freedom in a participant's output and it also encourages experimentation and informal jottings that might otherwise be self-censored. The real reason it is included in all our active reading groups is not hard to fathom: it protects those two or three writers every year who engage in writing for reading as a therapeutic and autobiographical activity – more of which in a moment. (6) is about sharing and about permission. The 'walls' or boundaries of the group need to be set, and if, as in this case, other 'Writing for Reading' workshops are running in the same year, will groups be allowed to share material across the whole level? In this case, yes – but this is not often the case; generally groups wish to preserve their own identity and security within the confines of their own group space. There are certainly advantages to be gained by sharing work across different active reading workshops, however, if participants are willing to do so. Since issues surrounding 'permission' in general run to the core of the whole trans-formative writing agenda, these are considered more fully in Chapter 6. (7) is an entirely different criterion and a reminder that simple, practical rules regarding times, places and activities can usefully be included in the contract.

It usually takes 20 minutes or so for group members to come up with their ground rules, either in pairs or threes. I write them on the whiteboard using the exact words and phrases employed by participants and adjust them as we go along. They are typed up for the following class in exactly the wording agreed upon, and we all sign our own copies for filing, with the proviso that we can return to the contracts at any time in the future if we find we need to change a certain rule. Active reading tutors make a point of returning to the contracts as a matter of course in the middle weeks of the module just to check that the criteria are still in place, but so far I personally have never had to make an amendment. By that time writers have internalized the ground rules and have settled into a way of working within the group to such an extent that they are surprised to actually see the contracts again. This generally means that the ground rules have served their function, but from time to time as draft work builds up and more material is shared in class, the occasional rule is genuinely invoked by members. It is certainly no bad thing to remind everyone that they did actually sign the document at the outset, and that they should include it in their final portfolio of submitted work at the end. Lastly, it should be said that a variety of punitive measures can be taken against rule-breakers and an equal variety of warning systems involving yellow cards, red cards and three strikes rules can be used. Ultimately of course the tutor may have to have words in private with persistent offenders, but these cases are rare and at least nine times out of ten the group adopts unconscious or semi-conscious self-censoring actions. Tempting as it is to explore such paralinguistic coughs, whispers, blasphemies and ironic gestures, we move on now to consideration of the specific qualities of the verbal arts workshop as a pedagogic form.

THE VERBAL ARTS WORKSHOP AS A VALUABLE ADDITION TO THE REPERTOIRE OF PEDAGOGIC FORMS

Increasingly, as practitioners developing active reading modules, we have come to experience the verbal arts workshop as a valuable and specifically different space. Attempting to account for its value and difference is no easy matter since the texture and grain of our activities give rise to a learning environment that is ephemeral and hard to capture on the page. Perhaps one way of approaching this exposition is to consider certain activities that we might ask learners to undertake in the verbal arts workshop that would rarely be asked of them in a standard university module. Four topics seem to me to be worthy of inclusion under this heading: time out of the seminar space; movement within the seminar space; active tutor involvement; and performance elements in the workshop.

When peer observers are invited to witness an active reading workshop, they can be bemused by what they perceive to be an absence. One such colleague a few years ago remarked, 'there seemed to be nothing going on'. Far from being concerned with this reaction, I was delighted as it marked very clearly for me the valuable differences in pedagogic approach that we employ. One such reason for this is that the writers are often quite simply not 'where they should be' – in their designated room for the time slot allotted for them by centralized timetabling. They are, quite literally, out and about. Setting exercises that require the participants to move beyond the boundaries of the classroom is a higher risk scenario for the tutor. Things can certainly go awry, the commonest issues being that students fail to return at the agreed time, or they simply do not take the task set as seriously as they would in the tutor's presence, or certain individuals simply leave altogether and do not come back at all. And then there's the weather, the dynamic of the group, and a host of daily variables to consider. So why persist in asking learners to go off and do things outside the workshop? One reason is positive feedback from the students themselves. Not only do they seem to enjoy going off and doing things in pairs or by themselves, but they seem to remember the experience. It marks off their active reading module from other classes in which they sit unmoving from start to finish without any freedom of movement at all. Another reason is simply variety: it breaks up the workshop time in different segments and revivifies the minds of the group. With realistic attention spans for most of us being around 20 minutes, I find this is about enough time at the start of the workshop to explain the day's task, the reasoning and theory behind it, and what my clear expectations are for its completion.

A further advantage is one which we active reading tutors hold close to our hearts, and this is pacing. The entire active reading experience is deliberately formulated to decelerate the interpretive and semantic processes. Writing itself of course slows your thoughts down as you commit words to the paper or screen in front of you. This reduction in pace that is necessitated as much by the physical activity of writing itself as by the thinking behind your intervention in a source text is a valuable one, and working outside the seminar room further slows participants, giving them time simply to take in what they are seeing, how they are seeing it and why it is taking place. In the box below, we have reproduced three quotations used by Christian McEwen during a London NAWE Conference in 2004 and mated them to a slowing-down exercise devised by Colin Evans for the Sheffield DUET Workshop in 1999:[33]

Fair-Weather Writing Exercise: 'The Time of My Life'

First, read the following quotations and discuss them in small groups (20 minutes):

1 But one day I stopped in front of a Cezanne still life – green apples, a white plate and a cloth. Being tired, restless and distracted by a stream of bored Sunday-afternoon sightseers drifting through the galleries, I simply sat and looked, too inert to remember whether I ought to like it or not. Slowly then I became aware that something was pulling me out of my vacant stare and the colors were coming alive, gripping my gaze till I was soaking myself in their vitality. Gradually a great delight filled me, dispelling all boredom and doubts about what I ought to like ... Yet it had all happened just by sitting still and waiting. If I had merely given a cursory glance, said 'Isn't that a nice Cezanne?' and drifted on with the crowd, always urgent to the next thing, I would have missed it all.

Marion Milner: *A Life of One's Own*

2 A mild morning, the windows open at breakfast, the redbreasts singing in the garden. Walked with Coleridge over the hills. The sea at first obscured by vapour; that vapour afterwards slid in one mighty mass along the sea-shore; the islands and one point of land clear beyond it. The distant country (which was purple in the clear

dull air) overhung by straggling clouds that sailed over it, appeared like the darker clouds, which are often seen at a great distance apparently motionless, while the nearer ones pass quickly over them, driven by the lower winds. I never saw such a union of earth, sky, and sea. The clouds beneath our feet spread themselves to the water, and the clouds of the sky almost joined them. Gathered sticks in the wood; a perfect stillness.

Dorothy Wordsworth, *The Alfoxden Journal*, 3 February 1798

3   I have learned that what I have not drawn I have never truly seen, and that when I start drawing an ordinary thing I realise how extraordinary it is, sheer miracle.

Frederick Franck

Next you need to take your writer's journal and find a specific place *by yourself* outside the building. Stay in exactly the same location for half an hour and write a description of exactly what you see before you. Limit yourself to a specific set of objects and a single viewpoint and simply set down on paper what you observe. (40 minutes)

Return to the workshop room and to your small groups to share your writing results. Relate them to the experiences of Milner, Wordsworth and Franck, above. (30 minutes)

Plenary reflection on process and thoughts arising. (15 minutes)

The above task shows how transformative writing can be triggered by a structured process of re-reading carefully selected passages. It also shows the heteroglossic nature of the task itself and suggests how intertextual resonances might arise when texts speak across one another paratactically. Perhaps the majority of teaching activities come about in this way as a third tutor picks and mixes the ideas of tutors one and two. Indeed we can see that this is how pedagogic cultures emerge within a discipline, as interested parties rightly engage in a process of academic cross-fertilization. As in the above case, such an admixture does not necessarily occur immediately: the DUET task had to wait five years for reinvigoration by the NAWE talk, or, put another way, it took five years to answer the searching question posed by Colin Evans about writer pacing.

But back to the seminar room: as it happens, the helpful assertion by my peer-observing colleague that nothing seemed to be happening was not on a day when the active readers were out of the room itself. They were all very much present and engaged in quiet group tasks. I suppose it must have seemed more like a library to an observer who walked in. The students were actually drawing a poem I had given them, more specifically drawing their own interpretation of key images that related to the narratives and sub-narratives of the text. Some were doing storyboards, some were using a collage technique and others were just doing their own thing by using the array of coloured pens I had brought with me for the exercise. From time to time one member would drift across the room to chat to another person about their interpretation. A couple of people went out for a mini-break. One pair finished early and stuck their A3 paper to the wall. Someone else was doodling images on the whiteboard and a few were drinking from cans or having a snack. Such freedom of movement within the actual workshop space is a key element of the active reading experience and one, naturally, with which certain groups are more at ease than others. Some groups, as we know, prefer to be far more settled and formal than others. What I am suggesting is valuable and different in the verbal arts workshop is an attitude to freedom of movement that is not the norm for traditionally delivered learning experiences. It is an approach which seeks to give participants almost, if not quite as much freedom of bodily movement as the tutor herself enjoys. Undisruptive freedom of movement is encouraging and empowering for active readers, unless of course it has been vetoed by the group itself in the initial group contract.

Active tutor involvement is the third topic that makes an impact on the value of the verbal arts workshop as a pedagogic form. In simple terms, we strongly recommend that the tutor performs most of the tasks set for the students in the same time-frame as the students themselves. Why do this? Shouldn't the facilitator be doing other things like monitoring the small groups or preparing cogent responses to questions that might arise or thinking about summarizing the session outcomes? Certainly, yes – but the tutor can access all these activities by actually participating in the writing task itself. Active involvement by the tutor throws up in the most direct way possible the very questions, outcomes and affective issues likely to be raised by the group members themselves. There is also the related advantage of greater authenticity. It is simply more honest if the tutor has had a go at the activity as well as the group itself: it breaks down the boundary between practitioner and learner, as well as highlighting the subtle difficulties of the task which the tutor has either forgotten or never actually experienced first hand. It also means that you have something yourself to share (or to choose not to share) with the rest of the workshop. Bluntly put, you are in the same boat. There are an array of issues and interesting things to discuss here, especially when it comes to the reactions of the students when they hear you read your own response to the task. I'm going to put these on hold for the moment, though, and return to them later. Suffice it to say that the mistakes that are made by active tutors in active task participation very rarely turn out to be detrimental to the group's learning experience, even if they feel embarrassing or tragic at the time. If, on occasion, the tutor's performance of the task is not as good as the student's, so much the better. Again, it's a higher risk environment but we are at all times purposely modelling the uncertainties of the drafting process, of meta-cognitive activities and of openness to interpretation here.

That the verbal arts workshop should include performance elements that mark it off from other pedagogic forms is not a shocking discovery. Or, put another way, it's not the surprise to English professionals that it often is to the participants themselves. In the box below are some of the commoner activities that might take place.

- Tableau
- Role-play games
- Performance poetry
- Mini-dramas
- Mime activities
- Creative visualization
- Condensing and expanding tasks
- Boundary games
- Listening tasks
- Object construction
- Monologue and dialogue performance
- Enactment activities
- Narrative and historical re-creations

There are a host of cautionary tales here as might be expected. Knowing exactly when and with which groups to engage in some of the above is a fine art and one which, in my view, can only be gauged on the hoof. This is not to say that some can't be timetabled and built in from the outset, but, like anything, overdoing it or doing them at the wrong moment can prove intellectually fatal to both tutee and tutor alike. At the right time, however, and when conditions allow, and by giving the participants due warning as appropriate, these are the very activities which give rise to the value and difference of the creative verbal arts workshop. Nor do tutors have to be stereotypes of the theatrical, over-emotional persuasion beloved of celebrity television shows. Charismatic pedagogy has, as we know, been almost universally derided and rightly cast aside. Yes, every tutor is performing in the sense of modelling certain discipline-specific methods and approaches; no, the tutor is not a per-forming seal or someone seeking to be the emotional focus of the group.

CRITERIA FOR WRITING ACTIVITIES – PRIVATE VERSUS SHARED MATERIAL

Of course the reluctance of 18-year-olds to voice openly matters relating to emotion and ethics should not be surprising. It is fully documented in the literature of adult development. (Haswell *et al.* 1999: 18)

We have already said that in the group contracts we insert a clause such that writers are not ever required to share their output unless they feel happy to do so. The boundary between what remains private and what is shared with the group is already a particularly important area for any student, but in the context of modules that employ a creative writing element, it is further highlighted. We are, after all, expecting active readers not only to be able to improve upon their own communication skills, but also to become better readers of others' work as critics and editors. How can this be done if a certain workshop is quiet week after week with participants who, for whatever reason, are not willing to share their textual responses with each other?

One such exercise (which we adapted from Barry Palmer) is called 'Theme and Variations'. With no requirement to complete every single part, it might easily take a number of adapted forms and is printed in the box below.

Theme and Variations Activity

A. Theme
   Think of an incident you can recall vividly, either from childhood or more recently. Write two or three sentences, in the first person and the past tense, summarizing this incident. This is the theme for your variations.
B. Variations (you may omit variations you don't like after number 4)
   1 Rewrite it in the present tense   ('is' not 'was')
   2 Rewrite it in the second person   ('you' not 'I')
   3 Rewrite it in the third person   ('s/he' not 'I')
   4 Rewrite (3) reversing the gender of all characters (change names if you have to)
   5 Describe the incident as another person in the story might have seen it
   6 Choose one of the variations and rewrite it adding a simile
   7 Select a noun from the theme and write down as many adjectives as you can to describe it

---

8 Select a significant word or phrase and write down all the words and phrases that come into your head as you think about it

9 Retell the incident without nouns or pronouns (don't worry about the grammar!)

10 Write a few sentences reflecting on the incident from the perspective of today

11 Write a short dialogue with a person you trust including their comments on the incident

12 Imagine someone who might be critical of your part in the incident and write down their comments

13 Expand your account of the incident into a longer narrative, using language which is as concrete and sensuously vivid as possible

14 Rewrite as the first paragraph of a short story

15 Rewrite in the form of a script for a short scene in a play or film

16 Rewrite as a draft for a poem (or part of a poem) including reflections on it

17 Rewrite it in the form of a parody of a particular writer or genre you find interesting.

You will be given the opportunity to read to the group bits of what you've written that you find interesting.

The exercise asks students to begin with a few sentences from their own past, even returning to their childhood, written in the first person and past tense. After setting up these two or three sentences as their 'source text' the exercise then asks them to put these sentences through a number of technical and substantive variations. This is a task which we tend to set as 'homework' rather than live class work, as it tends to elicit higher quality responses in terms of personal reflection and topic choice. People tend to feel more content writing about their personal history in the security of their own space, at least to begin with. Also, they know that they are simply not going to be required to share their material in class unless they want to. And in addition, the physical and visual prompts for personal reflection are more likely to be at hand at home (photos, letters, home videos, pictures, mementos). Certainly, this exercise can be returned to in workshop time if the group dynamics allow, and there is without doubt constructive reaffirmation to be gained by returning to it if they do.

We start with some of the advantages of this exercise and some examples we have permission to re-use. To begin with, the task places a focus on the production of a little personal writing, which participants are usually pleased about because it gets them off to a start on the module. Then, by gradually changing point of view via pronouns, tense and grammatical activities, it starts a process of critical self-awareness as the material becomes more and more objectified, more and more like a passage from a novel or biography that someone else has written. The participant is forced, by the very nature of the subject in language, to recognize that the 'I' they first produced is merely a construction, a position to be negotiated and renegotiated in a number of possible narratives and text-worlds. They begin to see their own life as part of a social story that goes beyond their own personal memory of it. Perhaps they even begin to experience their own life events within a wider geographical and historical framework. Indeed, there is applied evidence from the late 1980s onwards that literature students benefit explicitly from the actual familiarity of the material they are working with because it tends to encourage a more rhetorical mode of interpretation:

> Our findings suggest that there may be occasional instructional gain in having students read and write with familiar topics – however difficult – because that seems to elicit rhetorical strategies in students and keep them from falling back on the 'knowledge-getting' and 'knowledge-telling' modes that trouble Haas and Flower when used exclusively. (Haswell *et al.* 1999: 24)

Returning to the 'Theme and Variations' exercise, there follows an example of the initial theme Kay wrote last year. Note that the content is familiar to her, if not a familiar event *per se*:

Theme

Anthony invited me over at 7 pm prompt. I thought this was rather strange considering the fact that he usually tells me to come round 'whenever I want'. When I arrived he covered my eyes with his hands and lead me to the dining table. It was covered with flowers, candles and Chinese food. I knew at that exact moment what that evening entailed. He asked me to be his wife!

She has followed all the instructions except one, producing a passage of six sentences rather than 'two or three'. It is in the right tense and person and is indeed a vivid incident from her own life. Asking students to become active readers begins, as it must, with a close focus on language – which, of course, also provides the tutor with the opportunity to do some remedial grammar work with the group as necessary (back to relative clauses and noun types ...). After performing the required technical exercises, Kay opted for variation 17, a rewrite in the form of a parody of a particular genre. Genre parody is not a popular choice, especially in the early weeks of the module; still less is it typical to go for a parody of Byron's *Don Juan*. This was her first draft:

First Draft

She arrived at his house at 7:04
His attire was grand; he'd made an effort
His wandring hands now covered my eyes
For he'd prepared a glorious surprise
She never loved anyone more
The thought of losing him, it made her cry
But she need not worry, for her he adored

Like any first draft, it's a bit of a rough effort: is it parody or pastiche? Is it set in the twentieth or twelfth century? Why is it a line short for a Byron stanza? But it gains marks for providing evidence of drafting, for being experimental and for working closely with her own initial theme sentences. I don't want to spend too much time on this example, so here is Kay's final draft:

Final Draft

She arrived at his castle in 704
His attire was grand; he'd really tried,
She knew she'd never love anyone more,
The thought of losing him, woe betide!
She need not worry. For her he adored.
With gentle touch and trembling care, a sigh,
His wandring hands now covered her eyes,
For her, he'd prepared a glorious surprise!

Now everything becomes clear. She has been working on Byron in her Romantic Literature module and found a stanza from *Don Juan* itself which she liked. Closer than that, in fact: she found a line of Byron's that she wanted actually to include in her own variation. Thus from stanza 113 where Byron wrote 'Its gentle touch and trembling care, a sigh', Kay changes the possessive to a preposition and writes, 'With gentle touch and trembling care, a sigh' as the sixth line of her verse. Since students are required to provide a supplemental critical commentary on every piece they write for their portfolio, we now have a record of Kay's thinking and the whole process:

Commentary

I wrote this octave in parody of Lord Byron, as I was currently writing an essay on *Don Juan*, Cantos II–IV. This sequence of Cantos consists of eight-line octaves, with a rhyme scheme ABABABCC. For example:

Both were so young and one so innocent,
That bathing passed for nothing: Juan seemed
To her (as 'twere) the kind of being sent,
Of whom these two years she had nightly dreamed,
A something to be loved, a creature meant
To be her happiness, and whom she deemed
To render happy. All who joy would win,
Must share it – happiness was born a twin!

I turned my Theme into an octave. Although I did not stick entirely to the rhyme scheme (ABABABBB), I did try to achieve Byron's tone and use of humour in the couplet. Byron uses the rhyming couplet at the end of certain stanzas for a punch line. For example in 36 [. . .]
  To try and make it sound like Byron, I incorporated a line from stanza 113 into my octave:

Its gentle touch and trembling care, a sigh

Therefore, I have written an alternative version of both my theme and of Byron's work by incorporating his words into my stanza.

It is clear that this student wanted to include the piece because it evidenced other significant changes relating to metrical concerns (octave) and the rhyme scheme (end couplet), as well as affective considerations (humour). By combining her own life story incident with a second source text from the Romantic canon, Kay has moved into more ambitious territory. Additionally, she has shown an ability to move between modules, making links at various levels between her understanding of one set of generic values (autobiography) and another (lyric poetry). This movement in the participant between private and public worlds in the text can sometimes facilitate a move from silence to enunciation and verbal participation with other writers in the group. A good way of doing this is simply to ask individual writers to share their work aloud in pairs, making full use of the room space available. Failing that, just asking them to have a chat about the processes they went through in completing the task, inviting a straightforward explanation of what they were doing, is often a practical answer early in the module.

But what are the disadvantages and dangers of starting 'Writing for Reading' with such an exercise, and what happens when it goes wrong? Any and all of the following have occurred: students fail to complete the technical language aspects and get them wrong, raising the usual anxieties that they 'really should know this by now'; students have no experience of writing about themselves in the third person, as an object rather than a subject in the world; students make inexperienced or over-ambitious choices of which variations to perform on their own particular theme/life incident and end up with little of value; students get into deep water too soon by selecting a childhood trauma which then leads to a therapeutic/cathartic type of writing which over-exposes material that they thought would never surface in public. This last area has very significant educational literature attached to it, and its relevance for active reading modules is not to be underestimated. I have marked active reading work on three memorable occasions that clearly came directly from criminal incidents: substance abuse, child abuse and theft. Like many writing tutors, I have also seen work which is clearly helping the author to get over bereavement, failing family relationships and hospitalization.[34] Applying the Level 2 learning outcomes to such writing can often seem frivolous and irrelevant. It is certainly problematic when it comes to giving feedback. All told, however, it is probably wrong to label such responses to 'Theme and Variations' as disadvantages. More that it underscores the absolute necessity of the ground rules the group sets up in its contract.

UNDERLYING PURPOSES WHEN WORKING WITH DIFFERENT CULTURAL EXPECTATIONS

Deborah Tannen has written persuasively on the importance of recognizing 'structures of expectation' that operate between perception and narration:

> I have thus far shown that structures of expectation are constantly mediating between a person and her/his perceptions, and between those perceptions and the telling about them. These expectations operate on all levels, from the broad level of context and activity (interview, subject of experiment) to ideas about episodes and actions, to objects and people. (1993: 41)

Tannen raises some points here that are central to students of Literary Studies and it is our contention that a recognition of the complex ways in which we frame and transform our expectations as individuals can provide a meaningful focus of attention in the active reading seminar. This sounds ambitious for the opening few workshops, yet it can be achieved by introducing participants to a range of different types of text from the outset. The sooner people begin to recognize the constructed and mediated nature of alternative types of writing, the sooner thay can try out those differing modes of expression in their own interventions. While Tannen observes the rather obvious point that 'structures of expectation are constantly mediating between a person and her/his perceptions', she also makes the essential second point that structures of expectation come between our perceptions and our 'telling about them'. How often, for example, do we reframe, re-emphasize and re-adjust certain details of a story to a slightly different audience? How often do we alter our register in language according to the social situation, the perceived expectations of our hearer or our guessed-at effects upon our listener? The discourses we consciously enter and leave as our day progresses are multi-layered, polyphonic and unstable. Writing our words down in the form of jottings, scribblings and notes slows the processes in which such changes are encoded and come about. Apparently, informal writing thus holds the key to refreshed ways in which we might begin to think about identifying rhetorical expectations in different varieties of text.

Changing tack here, we are constantly struck by the similarities that our students exhibit with those learning another language, in particular with the post-beginner, pre-intermediate level of language learners. So it was no coincidence when we came across the following passage from the introduction to an EFL (English as a Foreign Language) resource book by Anthony Bruton and Angeles Broca:

> So, the idea in *Active Reading* is to give these learners exposure to a variety of different types of informative text, so that they become familiar not only with the language, but also with different types of texts. (1993: v)

Although there doesn't seem to be much to this, there's plenty to unpack. Quite apart from falling on the same 'active reading' phrase, EFL learners are given 'exposure' to a variety of text types. This is a powerful metaphor for English professionals and educationists alike as it concerns the most fundamental question faced by any tutor: *what* texts should I teach? Indeed the care with which certain texts and passages are chosen for inclusion on the syllabus is hardly a new one, and we are so used to relating this topic to theorization of the literary canon that we hardly notice it any more. It has, in effect, been defused by its status as an essay question up and down the country. So the 'what' question, the exposure metaphor and the emphasis on variety and familiarity – there's that word again – are obviously bridges between the language acquisition of the EFL school and the kind of active reading that we have in mind for our literature students. It seems that with active reading in both contexts we are inducting group members into another language as well as into another set of texts. We are, in fact, introducing them to an entirely new set of cultural and educational expectations and expecting them both to cope in private while playing the game in public.

While on the topic of language acquisition, a second American book with 'active reading' in the title can be mentioned here, one that began to place the idea of meta-cognitive reading practices within two separate developing contexts of the time: the new transferable skills agenda in higher education which we have already addressed, and also the closely related discipline of critical thinking or 'Active Critical Thinking' (ACT). Central to both these approaches in the late 1980s was the idea that people read different texts for different purposes so that an awareness of why we are reading a particular text *as we read it* is significant. Ediger, Alexander and Srutwa put it as follows:

> Reading for Meaning is based on the assumption that people have different purposes in reading. Some read for enjoyment, or to obtain general knowledge or specific information. Some read to decide whether to continue reading the material. The good reader uses reading strategies appropriate for the specific type of reading and purpose. This book encourages students to be aware of *why* they are reading and to use appropriate strategies. (1989: iv)

Here is another reason to use a wide variety of text types in the active reading workshop, texts that come from real life as well as from academic genres. Bus timetables, shopping lists, data tables, posters, health and safety notices, temporary signs and so on have all found their way into our seminars as examples of different writing and reading strategies: reading for information, for pleasure, for escape, for memory, skim reading, speed reading, re-reading, for summary, for review and so on. The greater the variety of writing types introduced, the greater the likelihood that these types will become part of the full imaginative repertoire of the participants' own interventional writing when they come to experiment with their draft work. It gives them more options when responding to more literary or conventionally high-status texts, as well as asking them to see writing production on a continuum between the daily and disposable and the lasting and irredeemable. Of course, the link to literary genres is an important part of the active reading process and a full development of genre work is certainly a key objective of the workshops.

This is not the place to launch an exposition on genre theory, but we shall seize the moment to underline our belief that failures to recognize the features of established genres can signal wider misapprehensions about the workings of society at large. This is because many under-graduates who may well have read the high priests of cultural studies on the topic of genre still comprehend the issue back to front. The idea that critics have somehow created genre categories in order to make sense of the writings with which they are faced is forever pervasive and tempting to students because they, like us before them, want to sort into 'the right box' the stylistic attributes of varying texts. This view, alas, is entirely upside down. Moreover, disabusing participants of this notion can become a module-long challenge in itself, but in this task we have been constantly helped by importing the words of Margaret Himley:

> Genres emerge, then, in a culture as conventional responses to parti-cular and recurrent situations – situations where discourse can mediate or accomplish some social action. Inaugural speeches, eulogies, letters of recommendation, ransom notes, users' manuals, and sermons, for example, have taken on conventional forms *because* they arise in recur-rent situations with similar structures and elements. Genres, in sum, are defined here as 'typified rhetorical actions based on recurrent situations'. (1986: 139)

If anyone has put this better, it remains to be found. The solution to the wayward thinking that critics have somehow invented generic categories for their own dubious gain is put to flight by Himley's cogent, exem-plified, socio-cultural explanation. It is easy enough to bring this text along and for everyone after 15 minutes to agree that her argument is correct (there has, on occasion, been stout resistance); what is less easy is to prevent learners from falling back into the easier and more 'common-sense' view in the weeks to follow. It is, however, yet another reason for working with a wide variety of writing from the widest possible pool of 'recurrent situations'. Once students begin to recognize the powers society invests in generic expectations, new avenues toward personal and professional development open up before them.

Having established that one of the aims of our workshops is to help participants become more aware of their own 'structures of expectation' as well as those of society at large, and having suggested that they, like foreign language learners, benefit from critical thinking skills and 'exposure' to a variety of text types, we can now move to simple launch-pad activities which begin to promote such awareness and progress.

SIMPLE LAUNCH-PAD ACTIVITIES FOR INITIAL WORKSHOPS

In this section we are going to look at three introductory activities which we frequently use to get modules going. They are 'maximum access' writing tasks in that they seek to include and encourage all levels of participants in creative thinking from the very start of the module. They are also indicative examples only, drawn from across a number of workshops, mainly DUET-inspired, and are certainly not expected to be taken as mandatory. Because these are start-up tasks, designed to last about 10–15 minutes each, instructions can be given in one line. I try not to fall into the trap of over-explaining them but you sometimes get the 'can I do this' permission anxiety that was flagged earlier. The important thing is to remind the new participants to let themselves go, to let their subconscious ideas surface if they can. Also, they need to be made aware that there will be an opportunity to share what they've written. Once one person has taken the risk to share the result of these mini-tasks, usually enough follow to make the activity worthwhile. There's not usually too much invested in them to give individuals pause.

Launch-pad activities for early group workshops

- Describe a thing, a person or a place ... Then something happens ...
- These are pieces I have written in my time ... List the kind of things you've set down on paper ...
- What's in my drawer? List the items in your drawer or handbag ...
- Write a letter to a friend or colleague about your experience here so far ...
- Write a short dialogue between two people of different social status ...
- I would like to write ... I wouldn't like to write ...
- Write an 80-word biography of yourself in the third person ...
- Give an object you can see a voice. What has it seen? Use the first person ...
- The stuff in my head ... List all the things on your mind at the moment ...
- You're talking to someone but they can't remember who you are ... write it out!

A number of these informal launching activities involve the compilation of lists. Listing, scribbling and jottings are the early stages of drafting, and provide possible building blocks for development at a later stage. The list is itself a literary device and I sometimes take in examples of flora and fauna lists from antiquity to prove this (*The Odyssey* specializes in these,[35] and of course Chaucer and also many eighteenth-century texts). More importantly, we are modelling the beginning of the process of externalization that writing involves. It is recognition that the first jettison of thoughts, snippets and fragments is a significant part of the creative reading methodology. It also helps people relax and get into the groove, removing themselves from the pre-occupations, problems and worries of the world outside the workshop itself. 'Ice breaker' is not a word I use for such mini-tasks as it seems to assume the existence of frosty relations in the first place. Since I have never been struck by such a scenario, the metaphor remains somewhat lost, not to mention negative, for me. Something like 'boundary activity' or 'check-in/check-out' seems a better way of phrasing such exercises, which can equally be used at the end of the seminar as a way of easing participants away from the main theme of the day. With Level 1 participants I do still use adhesive name badges for the first session as I like the clumsiness and physical commotion it causes – especially since a few forget to take them off after the class and wander nonchalantly off with them still attached. That aside, the ten examples above are not randomly chosen and do function well for setting both the mood of the seminar and some of the underlying expectations discussed earlier.

It is obvious that people complete such exercises at different rates, so managing the pacing and choosing the time at which the tutor should gather up the writers to share their output is an important consideration. Following the Tavistock tradition of maintaining strong boundaries when such tasks are actually in operation,[36] intervention during the writing phase is avoided, with a preference to spend a little longer in the explanation of the task at the start if necessary. Since the active reading tutor will also be engaged in the process, it is important not to get too immersed in it yourself and to keep an eye on the small signs of how the participants are getting along. Resisting the temptation to gather things up too quickly and ensuring learners are given the time to complete what they're doing takes some getting used to – but this is no different to any English Studies seminar where people are engaged in timed constructivist learning activities. When one or two people only are still writing it's generally a good idea to send out a signal that you are aware of this so that the group learns that it will give consideration to the slower pacing of others. Sending signals that require the group to learn certain attitudes and behaviours, and to ascertain the boundaries of acceptable workshop conduct is not an under-recognized area of pedagogical research. It is an area, however, that is rarely brought to the participants' attention themselves as they are actually in the workshop or class. There is, in our view, much to be gained by pointing out certain group behaviours, signs and gestures as the dynamic develops from week to week. Meta-critical and meta-cognitive breaks in the proceedings can be built into the work of the group at relevant intervals. Whether this takes the form of a five-minute review of why we were doing what we were doing, a ten-minute diary entry of how we felt about the last task we did, or a full one-hour reflective plenary at the end of the module, gathering up both academic and affective reactions to what has been achieved does not really matter. The main thing is that every week meta-cognitive reflection becomes an accepted and normal undertaking within the active reading group. We understand from peer and student feedback that such a reflexive attitude to group work both enables the individual to achieve deeper involvement with the text and also goes some way to creating the kind of dynamic of trust and emotional strength that allows communal access to purposeful acts of the creative imagination. If all goes well, it can be easier and more productive for people to write in the silence of a large group than it is for them to write by themselves. This, alas, is not all good news as it brings into the equation another set of problems for those who exhibit markedly passive learning traits, but we'll return to this topic in the next chapter.

6 Developing the Group

DEVELOPMENT OF MUTUAL SUPPORT AND MODES OF SHARING

I mean in my own case I came in early in June just to see what was up, you know to buy the books and on the door there was you know that and the other book so I went and bought it, well I bought them all – and every day at about 11 o'clock I used to make myself a cup of coffee and I'd read one story, you know, and then put the book down but it was in the mind, it was thinking of it, what can I do with this, where can I go and if I was writing that story what would I have done and later on I'd go and sit in front of the screen and I'd put everything, pour my mind into it and then go back and that's where some of the stories have come from ... (Jeanne)

I say that because with writing about texts I think I have understood them better, I've got more out of them – erm, I don't know it's difficult to put into words, I think erm, [*pause*] I suppose when you read a text you do sort of, it's like the exercise we did on Monday where we had to pick out keywords from the short story. I suppose when you read you subconsciously pick out the bits that are most important to you, so erm so, and I think in writing you dwell on whatever's more important for you, if that makes any sense. (Fiona)

I suppose to understand your own writing it's good to read around what other people are doing and vice versa, in order to read you've got to write and understand like in 'Introduction to Writing' really, maybe parodying people to understand what they say it's best to really write in the same style like in 'Learning Skills' I wrote a, wrote a poem on your poet and you really really understood what the poem was about then, and look I did Larkin and I really understood that he wasn't necessarily all negative (*and are you doing that on this module as well?*) Yes, yes especially like with the Gertrude Stein and when you realise that it wasn't just you know ... (Jenna)

In this chapter each section opens with the voices of active reading participants who have something to say about the module they are doing. The quotations, which are reproduced just as the words came out, are taken from mid-semester (week 6) tutorials which we hold in order to monitor student progress with this different type of approach to learning.[37] In seeing what the learners have to say mid-module, I (CTD) am going to use this chapter to address the developmental or mid-stage aspects of active reading, examining in this first instance ways of developing mutual support and sharing.

Jeanne, above, has clearly adopted a good working routine, using the same time every day to read one of the set text short stories. She has a coffee, finishes reading the source text and asks herself 'what can I do with this, where can I go?' This is a very honest and clear expression of the first stages of the process we are describing. She is thinking of the short story as a mineral resource – she is going to do something with it, make something out of it, change it into something else of her own devising. In doing so she is thinking spatially, 'where can I go?' The story will be taken somewhere else, transported in other directions, to another location perhaps. In a real sense she is going to transform her raw material into a written product that she herself has created. I think it's fair to say that some of the time writers have a fairly conscious idea of where it might go, but much of the time they certainly do not. Often it is only in the actual process of writing out their responses to a text that a line of narrative or argument or interpretation emerges. It can be as if the act of writing itself makes manifest latent, hidden or concealed ideas that were waiting to be brought to the surface. Again, there is no shortage of evidence and testimony for this, not least from the world of counselling and psychotherapy.[38] The important thing here is that Jeanne, already a good independent writer, could bring her questions about where to go and what to do with the story to the workshop each week. There she was not always met with the same enthusiasm about her own project that she herself displayed, but the group feedback certainly nudged her in certain directions from time to time.

Whereas Jeanne was using the group for specific support with her narratives, Fiona found the workshop activities and exercises more useful in triggering ideas and responses. The keyword task she is referring to is summarized in the box below and is a powerful tool for increasing the self-awareness of participants who assume that there is only one possible (or main) interpretation of a text, or even that theirs is the only right (or 'correct') answer to a piece.

Keywords: 'Revealing the Reader'

Read the following passage from a short story by Edgar Allan Poe. Use a highlighter to mark up the ten most interesting keywords (words or phrases that seem to stick out from the rest of the passage for you):

I had swooned; but still will not say that all of consciousness was lost. What of it there remained I will not attempt to define, or even to describe; yet all was not lost. In the deepest slumber – no! In delirium – no! In a swoon – no! In death – no! even in the grave all *is not* lost. Else there is no immortality for man. Arousing from the most profound of slumbers, we break the gossamer web of *some* dream. Yet in a second afterward (so frail may that web have been), we remember not that we have dreamed. In the return to life from the swoon there are two stages: first, that of the sense of mental or spiritual; secondly, that of the sense of physical, existence. It seems probable that if, upon reaching the second stage, we could recall the impressions of the first, we should find these impressions eloquent in memories of the gulf beyond. And that gulf is – what? How at least shall we distinguish its shadows from those of the tomb? But if the impressions of what I have termed the first stage, are not, at will, recalled, yet, after long interval, do they not come unbidden, while we marvel whence they come? He who has never swooned, is not he who finds strange palaces and wildly familiar faces in coals that glow; is not he who beholds floating in mid-air the sad visions that the many may not view; is not he who ponders over the perfume of some novel flower; is not he whose brain grows bewildered with the meaning of some musical cadence which has never before arrested his attention.

Amid frequent and thoughtful endeavors to remember, amid earnest struggles to regather some token of the state of seeming nothingness into which my soul had lapsed, there have been moments when I have dreamed of success; there have been brief, very brief periods when I have conjured up remembrances which the lucid reason of a later epoch assures me could have had reference only to that condition of seeming unconsciousness. These shadows of memory tell, indistinctly, of tall figures that lifted and bore me in silence down – down – still down – till a hideous dizziness oppressed me at the mere idea of the interminableness of the descent. They tell also of a vague horror at my heart, on account of that heart's unnatural stillness. Then comes a sense of sudden motionlessness throughout all things; as if those who bore me (a ghastly train!) had outrun, in their descent, the limits of the limitless, and paused from the wearisomeness of their toil. After this I call to

mind flatness and dampness; and then all is *madness* – the madness
of a memory which busies itself among forbidden things. (From
'The Pit and the Pendulum', Poe 1994)

Do the words you've chosen form a pattern or share anything in
common? Write the ten words and phrases down and build them first,
into a short imagist poem of your own, and second, into a short
fictional paragraph. (40 mins)
   Share the results with your neighbour – did s/he pick out the same
words? Psychologists tell us that our choices are never accidental and
that unconscious processes guide our selection; what does your own list
of words tell you about the kind of reader you are? Does a text read you
in the same way that you read a text?

In her recognition that 'I suppose when you read you subconsciously pick
out the bits that are most important to you', Fiona moves towards the
conclusion that, 'I think in writing you dwell on whatever's more
important for you'. By asking learners to share their chosen keywords in
the workshop, if they feel able to, an opportunity is given to work with
this significant idea in some detail. Participants are either delighted to
find that their neighbour has independently chosen the same keywords, or
interested to hear reasons for different choices. It is true that you can back
up this exercise by the gentle introduction of some reader response theory
– I tend to use Norman Holland in this case[39] – but the real lesson perhaps
lies in the suggestive opening up of themes and topics which students had
either not recognized as being important to themselves or had, for
whatever reason, previously undervalued. They suddenly become 'strangers to themselves' as Kristeva puts it, and begin to comprehend the value
of such defamiliarizing techniques. This is another task which elicits
results that are somewhat personal, always subjective and frequently
enlightening. It is also a kind of listing, the benefits of which have been
indicated in the previous chapter, and again it requires a close attention to
the actual lexis and lexicography of the source. Word selection is such a
useful focus for writers that group work which focuses on such a taken-for-
granted aspect of communication is restorative and empowering. It links
very naturally with historical studies regarding the care and craft of
writing, an alternative or lost experience for many in today's instrumental
society. Unbeknown to Fiona, her use of the word 'dwell' was a loaded
one. It goes back to discussions of pacing and the way in which the act of
writing forces the writer to slow down and dwell on the reading undertaken, but it also connects to significant theorization by Heidegger,
Derksen and others that dwelling is a more fundamentally appropriate
signifier for our relations with the world than simply living or being.[40]
Again, the relevant quotations can be brought to the seminar for perusal.

While Jeanne and Fiona were using their groups in directed ways for advice and the shared exercises, Jenna seemed to see a wider use for the more reciprocal and holistic benefits of the active reading seminar. We know this because she is relating the work she is doing on our module to two other modules on her degree, 'Introduction to Writing' and 'Learning Skills for English'. In time-honoured fashion she is displaying classic learning strategies of building on what she already knows while extending her repertoire into the unknown – in this case Gertrude Stein. This raises another of the key messages of transformative writing: the importance of using highly experimental texts to promote equally experimental attitudes and freedoms in the members of the group. Apart from imagist poetry, which I'll return to in a moment, a short story by someone like Stein or Jean Rhys can really open up discussion, especially when you ask the group to perform their own parody of the writing style. In one memorable seminar we found it very difficult to gather things up for the day because a kind of hysteria was setting in with each Stein-inspired contribution. It was a breakthrough for everyone in the room and suddenly we all understood anew what the *avant-garde* could mean.

LIVING WITH THE RISKS AND RESPONSIBILITIES OF PRODUCING TEXT

Erm – creative criticism – I'm very passive I must admit when I do read I would say I was quite a passive reader actually – erm (*but what do you mean by that?*) I just read what I think on the page and I think well that's your interpretation, you're a very good writer and I'm very sort of, er, I should criticise more. Erm, I think more open group forum would help me with that – be a bit more forthcoming. I mean I'm guilty for it too I always put my work down and think maybe I won't read this so more open group forum. (Lauren)

No. I don't think there is. I think that writing and reading's two, two separate things you can write about what you've read and like make a different context and stuff like that but I think reading and writing about it, no, two different processes altogether. I don't see – you can write about what you've read. There's a slight link, you can write about, say, all the stories changing like the tenses and stuff, person, like that, but – but I don't see a direct link between writing and reading – but no, not in that respect. (Graham)

By saying 'I always put my work down and think maybe I won't read this so more open group forum' might help, Lauren is voicing something that is both the biggest risk and the biggest responsibility of the transformative writing group. Indeed, if a group is quiet or has individuals who are not confident enough to share their work, how can any transformation be expected to take place? After all, it's not just that we are hoping to effect a positive change from one text to another via our writing practices, but also that we're hoping to achieve a positive change in the participants themselves, one that enables them to improve their range of literary understanding and communication at the same time as developing their cognitive skills and social identities. It is not necessarily the help a bystander might think it would be for students to admit to this lack of confidence and passivity toward text and class in private. In fact, the members of one small group went on week after week complaining about the lack of their own interaction in class and that of their peers, but this did not in itself prevent another silent class the following Thursday. We tried the full panoply of recommended pedagogic tools to break this unsupportive atmosphere (guest speakers, change of seating, revisit contract) but to no avail. At times like these the active reading tutor has to admit that there can be insurmountable obstacles to the dynamic of a particular group – in the case concerned I held on to the old hope that poor oral contribution might be an indicator of higher reflective and writing capabilities, but no, the portfolios were neither better nor worse than those of other cohorts. Lauren, who was not a member of this group and overcame her crisis in confidence very well, reminds us usefully that the anxieties faced by students are not fabricated but very real and challenging. Not only may a writing group contain those who are alarmingly resistant to writing, it may include those for whom the very processes of writing production are an issue.

With the risks involved in producing and sharing text of your own in a group also comes the responsibility of so doing. If others are sharing their material openly and encouragingly, it's surely the case that I'm expected to do the same. The society of the group mirrors and mimics the behaviours of society at large, sometimes even exaggerating the behaviours (both good and bad) of the outside world. Embedding strategies of participation which introduce and enhance a sense of group responsibility is therefore to some degree a prerequisite for the level of success that follows. I say 'to some degree' because normally we encounter students who certainly are willing to play the game of the HE English seminar. They are aware of the rules of engagement, of the normal procedures for joining and leaving, and of the generic expectations that are likely to fall upon them from time to time. It's an animal they recognize. The student who isn't willing to play the game, or who takes on the role of group joker, group outcast or group rebel risks not simply failing the assignments but also the censure of other group members. While the former can take a long time to manifest itself, the latter can be devastatingly quick. And while certain things can be done by the tutor to minimize the effect of a group which is poor at self-censoring, very little can be done to alter the adoption of a self-harming role within that group. Graham, above, was one such individual. Silent one week and overbearing the next, the temptation to play up to his mates was often too strong to resist. Sometimes it actually helped the progress of a set exercise; more often it hindered others from expressing more appropriate ways forward. As seen above, Graham knew that one of the outcomes of the module was to recognize the links between writing and reading practices, and was therefore determined not to give me any evidence of this on tape. Since I could use only meta-linguistic markers in support of this contention (the tone of his voice, the way he was sitting, the facial expression and body language), the words transcribed show only half the story. Graham's opening sally, 'No. I don't think there is. I think that writing and reading's two, two separate things' indicates a not uncommon form of resistance to risk-taking and responsibility. When faced by potentially harmful or truthful information, the ego defends itself in complex and effective ways. Breaking through such defences is not my business as a HE facilitator, but I am content to let them play out longer than almost all my colleagues. Unless behaviours become dangerously disruptive, the message can be safely given to writers that they will have the responsibility not only of producing their own material, but also of producing the kind of working atmosphere that operates best for them. Failure to intervene on the tutor's part is often mis-read by participants as a weakness in her or his professional judgement, yet it is often inexperienced or ineffective practitioners who fail to allow such resisting participants to model their anxieties in front of others. Gradually, risk-taking builds confidence in the group; together, group members discover responsible strategies for moving forward.

WORKING ON AND THROUGH THE SOURCE TEXT

Yes because I think when you're reading it does help you obviously with your own writing because you get erm other authors' points of view, other styles of writing, the way they do things, it does, it does influence your own work and without that I mean like you could just be sitting there writing a load of nonsense, load of nonsense really, they do help you – a starting point to develop your own work. (*Is that because they're experienced writers?*) Yeah, yeah definitely. I don't think there's a right and wrong way of doing, doing that but it does help you set an example of different ways of writing after you've read other authors' texts. (Kathryn)

Yes, definitely – I think by us trying to write and copy these styles and everything I think it shows you how much, you know, what it – just what it says – writing *for* reading, coz you really do have to redraft it all the time and I haven't really, I've been trying to redraft and stuff and I've done it more now than I have done essays and things which is quite strange, but yeah, definitely [*pause*]. (*Do you think they're linked in any other ways?*) I think, you probably have to actively think about it, the way you're writing like how it can be interpreted, you know what kind of audience you're aiming for – if you're going to really write creatively you've gotta have in mind what kind of audience you want it to go out to (Rachel)

Kathryn talks about developing her own work in response to source texts which 'set an example' for her. By stating 'I don't think there's a right and wrong way of doing that', she has realized that the meanings and styles she is creating are in a constant flux and process of negotiation. Working with the concept that writers negotiate their communications via careful and reciprocal relations with other writers and audiences is perhaps the central tenet behind a pedagogy which asks people to work with and through selected source texts. It is not just a simple case of acknowledging 'the way they do things' but a case of asking 'is the way they do things any use for me?' This is an effective learning trigger, one akin to problem-solving activities in other disciplines. Just because Flannery O'Connor and Anita Desai work with unacceptable assumptions made by minor characters, does this mean I should have minor characters who act like this? If Jackie Kay and Bill Herbert write using street slang and dialect, does that mean I can use regional variations in my own poems? The insistence upon a source text is the essential difference between creative writing and transformative writing: the former requires the writer to use the imagination for the greater part of the scripting process – to make things up; the latter is always responding to another text with the goal of changing it into something else. For the creative writer the finished product is motivated by the creation of an autonomous and self-sustaining artistic product. For the active reader, the motive is not to produce such a text as an end product (although s/he may achieve this) but to produce a transformation in their understanding of the text with which they started. The text the active reader drafts and writes to its final point is only the middle part of the whole process. By far, the most important sector is to come: the return to the source text and the explanation of how and why the interpretation of it has now changed as a result of having written about it. This is an entirely alien and counter-intuitive process for almost every participant in our modules. Satisfactory reasons for this are long overdue serious research, but it seems that this final stage holds the key to progression beyond dutiful and compliant responses to text and world. Possible answers are listed below:

- Learners expend energy in responding to the source text, and more energy in transforming it into their own creative response text. Perhaps the third stage of returning to the source is too much of an emotional or intellectual drain.
- Learners see no benefit or point in returning to the source text after having written about it in an interventionist manner. Perhaps they have not been taught the value of this final reading stage.
- Learners are not used to understanding re-reading as a different activity from reading. Perhaps they have not studied or considered the cognitive differences between the two processes.
- Learners are tepid critical thinkers. They have not recognized that critical persistence is the mainstay of objective academic discourse; they are missing intellectual stamina or rigour to finish the job.
- Learners are so pleased with their own creative response to the text that they cannot see any point in returning to the original. They perceive that they have mined this mineral resource to the full.
- Learners are unhappy that their response text has not measured up to the perceived quality of the text by the first author; returning to it would only exacerbate or prove this fear to be so.
- Learners have shorter attention spans and want to move onto something new; they have become bored with redrafting and rewriting the source text. Why prolong the agony?
- Learners have enjoyed producing their own transformative writing and have enjoyed sharing it with the tutor. Going back to the source text would spoil the dynamic because once again the tutor would be returning to her old role as theorist and teacher.
- Learners enjoy disclosing their creative writing; they do not enjoy disclosing creative reading.
- Learners are pragmatists or theorists; they find it hard to be reflective practitioners and to close Kolb's reflective learning cycle.
- Learners find that if their creative output is only an intermediary tool in the pursuit of something else and not an end in itself, it is somehow devalued or sullied.
- Learners do make the return but find it hard to express any changes in their interpretation of the source text; it is not an easy thing to accomplish.

It would not be hard to carry on with this list and we have little hard evidence to discriminate between the above categories beyond the informal feedback which inevitably comes the module leader's way. Certainly it is not always the case. Some groups take very well to the idea of going back to the original short story and putting their own resulting texts back alongside it to see how their initial understanding has altered via the process of recasting it into something else. Participants who are able to do this, and who enjoy doing it, tend to be those who write convincing commentaries and supplementary explanations on the pieces they themselves have submitted in their portfolios. Many times when fellow practitioners from other universities have asked me about the methodology behind active reading modules, they seem to hear the first two steps (read source text; re-write it) and jump to the conclusion that it's all over and they have now 'got it'. It is, they say, very similar to a class they run on their own creative writing module where they ask their writers to rewrite other texts for practice in making them better writers themselves. This works quite well, they agree, before moving off around the room. But this is wholly to misunderstand the radical and most empowering aspect of our approach which is, I begin to think, a very narrow and highly specific rhetorical venture: the return to the source text once you have written about it is a return to an earlier self. The active reader meets herself on the other side of the creative/critical divide and sees that if she herself has produced at least two readings of the first writer, then the intended message of the source text was always in some sense a lie. Such an enactment of Wimsatt and Beardsley's famous argument not only removes the security net of authorial intention, but also replaces it with the spectre that the rewritten text she herself has produced is also estranged and illegitimate. In fact, it forces a Lacanian *méconnaissance*.

If Kathryn reminded us of the importance of returning to the source text, Rachel emphasizes the necessity of drafting, 'coz you really do have to redraft it all the time and I haven't really, I've been trying to redraft and stuff and I've done it more now than I have done essays and things which is quite strange.' Rachel is starting from a perfectly reasonable position: she can see the point in redrafting critical essays in order to improve the mark on her assignments, but she has never really thought about the creation processes of the very texts that her essays are about. It therefore seems 'quite strange' to her to be engaged in an operation which (a) she has never really thought about and (b) shows creative writing to be as intellectually tough a proposition as theoretical interpretation. The activity of drafting has lent her a new respect for the different types of text that creative writers produce.

There are a number of ways of building in recognition of the importance of draft work. You can assign it marks, of course, in the final summative assessment and you can simply tell people to try again, to make a second attempt at their contribution. One of the more successful ways, however, is to allot actual editing time after the completion of a task. For example, I personally favour strict word-limit exercises where the writer has to produce an exact number of words in response to a task. If I give the workshop 20 minutes to write a 100-word seascape which reflects a person's emotions, I'll stop the exercise exactly at 20 minutes (don't forget that the students have watches too and will monitor your rule observance) and then, since the group believe the task to be over, I'll give them a full 10 minutes to make their 100 words even better, asking them to delete weak phrases and expressions, alter unclear devices, re-punctuate the grammar or find more convincing synonyms, while reducing the original 100 words to 80. By now they're getting fidgety and want to move on. Stage three is to give them (and yourself, because you're also doing the task) another 5 minutes to really make final adjustments and tuning, while aiming for exactly 70 words. Then comes the meta-cognitive move. We don't share our work yet – it's all in the delay here, but instead we spend another full 10 minutes reflecting on how our texts changed through the editing and tightening processes. I remind participants that this meta-cognitive writing is the most important writing they'll do in the day, that for my purposes, the actual content of their final 70 words is neither here nor there. There are a number of writers who you can use to back up such condensation exercises, from Ezra Pound's *ABC of Reading* (1951) to Charles Olson or Stevie Smith.[41] It helps to have them to hand in advance. We often build such thinking around work on haikai, rengas and tankas, attempting to turn whole chapters into three lines of verse or 31 syllables. That certainly focuses the mind.

Of course, demonstrating the existence of draft work is not as easy as it sounds. Does the tutor expect manuscript scribbles, illegible first jottings or more considered presentation of deletions and accretions? How many drafts should be included as evidence? And the common 'well I don't really draft it at all, it just comes out as it is so I'd have to go backwards and invent drafts' (this is quite fun, incidentally, as a proper writing exercise in case you haven't tried it). Fortunately we've built up a veritable bank of previous participants' material to show how they all solved the same problem in a multitude of ways. Some students use word or text-manipulation software to create hypertext-type documents showing how their original drafts developed. Others employ different colours, text boxes, lines and arrows. Some of the best do in fact move from hand-writing a messy first attempt to word-processed perfection, while others are little more than a pile of marginalia that seem to show little connection to the eventual submitted top copy. Tracing paper has been used to physically layer one stanza on top of the next, with corrections showing through, diaphanously. And then there are the usual mind maps, note columns, parallel texts and graphic images to help things along. Perhaps these variform approaches begin to account for our insistence on a supplemental commentary for every piece submitted, joining the dots for casual reader and external examiner alike. We do not accept any work that fails to show the processes by which it came into being. Even if only minimal changes have been made (and yes, we do

require our writers to discriminate between the quality of their drafts),
the expectation is that a lengthy justification will appear by way of
accompanying review or exegesis. Re-reading this, it sounds as if we are a
bit carried away with process, which isn't the case. We do take time to
share and celebrate the transformed writing itself, often with renewed
respect for what has been achieved, and simply to enjoy the results.

EVALUATING EXAMPLES OF TRANSFORMATIVE ACTIVITY

> If say you read something so you're writing something about it, you
> get a different idea about it, and then coz you're re-reading it you've
> got a different thought in your mind about it, I think, one of your
> ideas, because you interpret into it, so you get a different ... you think
> it's better or more interesting, or worse. (Kerry)

> Well someone's writing might not be great but it'll just be a different
> twist on what someone else has done to a certain extent (*So in that sense
> culture all the time is rewriting itself?*) Yeah, but it'll keep going for ever,
> it won't just stop, d'ya know what I mean? Someone will come up
> with something really, sort of abstract-looking that somebody else
> has done (*Well I think that's a good thing really – it means we have some
> kind of communication going on*) One big melting pot? (*It is a melting pot,
> yeah*) – just recycling that's all it is and that's always good (*Intellectual
> recycling ...*) – rather than just having loads of, er, crap. (Johnny)

Often the strongest and most meaningful feedback takes on a very
informal, ungrammatical or half-formed appearance. Only when the tutor
reflects and transcribes what the participant has said is the full force of
the content grasped. Two things strike me when looking back at what
Kerry said: her interest in evaluating whether the first text was 'better or
more interesting, or worse'; and her creation of a new phrasal verb
because we simply don't have a word for active inference-making in the
English language, 'to interpret into' (a hybrid of 'look into' and 'interpret', I suppose). Both of Kerry's ideas bear directly on the topic of this
section: evaluation of transformative writing. At a basic level Kerry is
absolutely right. The transformation of a piece of writing into your own
re-written text will alter it so that it seems better or worse, or perhaps, in
Johnny's phraseology, a bit 'er, crap'. It is worth mentioning that this can
indeed happen: sometimes work is produced in a workshop that is in
many ways more impressive or convincing than the ur-text. Given the
time and feedback available, this is perhaps not so surprising, and of
course it's quite common for professional writers to hammer out a dud
sentence or clause or metaphor here and there. Since we perform a lot of

reading aloud in class, a valuable addition in itself, poor rhythms and less than sonorous prose stand little chance, in all fairness. But it works the other way too, and three or four times I've had classes fall silent, struck by the reading of simply unimprovable passages. At such times someone usually breaks the silence with 'Well, I'm just going to give up!' or 'Ugh, that's good!' or some such expletive. If you suspect that such a passage is coming up, it's nice to end the seminar on it and just leave the room without comment, but you have to be sure of the dynamic (plus you can't keep doing this one ...).

The main substance here, though, is not evaluation of the source text by going back to it, but evaluation of the transformative writing that the student has produced. We ask our groups to peer-assess two thirds of the way through the module (week 8 of 15). Below are the six criteria we request they use when commenting on each others' work. They are semi-structured criteria because if you're too specific not all writing submitted is necessarily relevant; if you're too broad you haven't given the participants enough guidance. In general, for bridging the gap between critical and creative work, semi-structured handouts and tasks are easily the most beneficial for learners. Plenty of white space for the peer-assessment feedback to the writer must also be left on the page. Inducting the participants into the potentially threatening arena of useful peer review is never easy. The vast majority of people (especially those with no teaching experience at all) find it difficult but not impossible to see their own shortcomings; the same people find it impossible *full stop* to voice weaknesses in others, as if it is some kind of crime against society. When it comes to writing down these weaknesses on paper and fixing their views of their friends' work in ink, you might think you'd asked them to hit the writer in person. Fortunately, Level 2 students do have some history of the positive benefits of feedback on their Level 1 modules, so they can at least recall the constructive aspects of what they are being asked to do. To close this section with something to ruminate on, then, these are the marking criteria questions we employ:

In the portfolio, has the writer ...

1 produced a body of *experimental* writing (creative/critical)?
2 considered a *variety* of styles and forms (language/voice)?
3 engaged in a process of critical *self-reflection* (via commentaries)?
4 provided evidence of attention to the processes of *drafting and editing*?
5 *presented and organized* material in a clear fashion (signposting)?
6 worked carefully to craft and construct *creative links* to the source texts?

APPROACHES TO GENRE, STYLE, LEXIS, NARRATIVE VOICE AND POETIC FORM

The workshops were designed to demonstrate that the activities of creative writing and critical analysis are mutually enhancing. They clearly succeeded. On the critical front we have observed in ourselves a greater awareness of form, and a greater ability to comment on it. This has come not just from increased practice in the use of technical terminology, but from the practical experience of writing to a particular specification. [. . .]

Furthermore this enhanced sense of form is spilling over into the way we see the activity of writing essays. Students are paying more attention to the construction of their arguments, to the length and shape of their sentences, and to how their prose sounds when read aloud. All this has come from seeing essays as *analogous* to poems. (Newlyn 2003 I: 87)

Lucy Newlyn, who runs a poetry workshop series at St Edmund Hall in Oxford (see earlier, p. 38), is also trying to help students bridge the gap between creative and critical writing. Her attention to form here shows that it is certainly one of the supporting arches under that bridge. It is also one of the hardest areas for English practitioners to communicate to students of any degree of experience. Working with students from non-traditional backgrounds, as we do at Teesside, places an even greater importance on developing writer confidence through linguistic play and formal experiment. Indeed, form is far more threatening than content for many Literature Studies students, because not only can you be just plain wrong about metre, tropes and technical elements of prosody, but also you can be shown never to have known even the basics. We have found that transformative writing practices to some extent defuse the anxieties surrounding such problems because they give hands-on, weekly experience of form to the group members. I would not personally endorse a pedagogy of 'monkey see, monkey do' but this is to misrepresent the benefits of what Newlyn calls 'writing to a particular specification'. These are not blind copycat exercises, because experiments with metaphor, hexameters and free indirect speech are never the same twice. They may spring from unreal, imagined scenarios but they are very real learning outcomes, embedding formal processes by grooving repeatable techniques. In most cases, students welcome the strict rules of, for example, poetic composition because it gives them clearly defined boundaries. The more obscure the form, the better it seems to go down, so that arcane and marginal metres and structures are suddenly reborn from the mists of antiquity. Quite why students prefer triolets[42] and tankas to limericks and sonnets is not obvious to me, but perhaps the call of the marginal speaks more volubly to the diverse cultural and social make-up of our student body; maybe non-traditional forms simply welcome non-traditional writers.

HOW STUDENTS TAKE CONTROL OF LEVELS OF DIFFICULTY

John Turner, a teacher of creative writing at Sheffield Hallam University, makes an important point about allowing students to express themselves freely. He suggests that tutors should be confident enough 'to go with what's coming from the people you're working with' so as to 'workshop their own language, culture, experience.'[43] By doing things like taking a portable keyboard along to increase the group's awareness of rhythm, his general approach is to unlock people's creative potential through verbal experimentation. If students are going to be at ease with each other and with the process of knocking language about for their own purposes, the freedom to utilize diverse material from their own experience is essential. I would add to this the idea that such measuring up to individual interests, enthusiasms and traumas is one of the primary ways in which students take control of levels of difficulty. Educational progress, as we know, does not climb in a perfectly steady gradient; it jumps, shifts sideways, leaks under doors, then finds itself back on track. It takes three steps forward and two steps down. It hits a moment of enlightenment, epiphany even, then goes dormant for a few weeks. All writers need to grow accustomed to treading what to all appearances is a very wavy path through these murky surroundings. Sentences come out wrong, set tasks do not give the expected results, a passage doesn't sound right, a low mark in another module throws the learner off balance, and so we go on. How does the English practitioner deal with this mess? Is she expected to take control of it on behalf of the students or to empower them with strategies which might facilitate their own taking control? How is it best to do this? John Turner, again, uses teaching practices which involve 'validation of life experience' and is not afraid of 'giving credibility to local voices.'[44] One way to go about this is to set writing exercises which borrow source texts from the local community. You could either have local writers come to the institution, as we do with our writers in residence and Royal Literary Fund Fellow at Teesside,[45] or you could simply send participants out into the field to collect samples of local voices via overheard conversations, free newspapers, eavesdropped mutterings, local radio or more structured interviews. These are all things we have done, but once again we stress the fact that this is not creative writing per se but creative reading via transformative writing. What makes it the latter is the production of a formal source text, for example, a transcript of the dialogue heard in the street, a top copy of the recorded interview, a structured textual record of the source material, wherever it came from. This then takes on the status of the source text like any other, and from it come the interventions that we have spoken of elsewhere. Finally, of course, the writer goes back to the source text and writes a commentary on how his or her transformation has affected their first reading or interpretation of it, even though the self-same person discovered the language and documented it in the first place. I'll sketch out an example for clarity:

Exercise: 'Café Racer'

1   Writer goes to a local café and overhears a conversation.
2   Writer returns and accurately documents this data (this is the source text).
3   Writer transforms the source text into a creative draft (e.g. a play, poem).
4   Writer redrafts and edits their response into a 'perfect' final form.
5   Writer returns to source text and comments on the processes undertaken, what was actually done, as well as on how it changed his/her initial interpretation of it before the transformation.

The level of ethical clearance required for such activities does need a little prior attention, and certainly students need to be realistic about what they can achieve 'in the field'. Whereas a pure creative writer might sit in one spot and simply observe the subject of her or his composition, slowing down the observation process in order to pick up minute details of sound, sense and sight, the active reader is always thinking in the first instance of gathering actual text, oral or written, from which to begin. The creative writer is gathering sensation, detail, scent, intention, but the creative reader is simply collecting transcribable text with a positively Arnoldian or Livesayan disinterest.[46]

Validating local voices and happenings is certainly one way of making experience count in the workshop, and of working with different levels of difficulty in the same physical space each week. Every person is engaged in their own text-world, selecting for themselves the difficulty rating of their next dive into the pool of active reading. They are, in effect, gradually building a body of experience as well as formulating the very criteria on which they will be judged in their assessment. In fact, as we shall see in Chapter 9, all the work that is submitted at Level 3 has specifically to be marked against its own bespoke aims and objectives; to do otherwise would be meaningless.

To close our current discussion, there is one aspect of active reading that is reassuring for us all in relation to levels of difficulty and setting the height of the bar to be vaulted. This is the fact that a final piece of writing that is in itself quite poor can still gain a first-class mark. Yes, an impressive, autonomous and well-written final piece is desirable and does push the grade up, but the quality of the writing *in itself* is not the make or break criterion that it is in traditional criticism. So long as the portfolio shows evidence of variety, self-reflection, drafting, links to the source, and experimental use of language, it is likely to do well. The odd missing syllable, rough phrase or poor ending is not going to impact disastrously on the percentage achieved. Like a puzzle in algebra, the success of active reading is couched very largely in the process itself, in the 'workings'. Similarly, it is about showing that you have developed a workable methodology for recognizing and creatively solving the stylistic peculiarities of another sign system. Some solutions are inevitably (to use an anachronism) more 'elegant' than others, and sometimes you have to say 'well that's not the way I would have done it' but there again, do we not say the same things when marking traditional essays?

7 Assessment and Feedback

INITIATIVE HANDOVER

As we have seen to this point, a transformative writing and active reading module makes use of concrete learning outcomes and the demonstrable acquisition of certain linguistic and communicative capabilities. These are predetermined and written into the module guides, handbooks and descriptors. They are reinforced as necessary in handouts, overheads and practical activities and tasks. In some cases they may be modified in learning contracts, negotiated statements of intent or bespoke commentary paragraphs which deal with a student's specific aims and objectives. So far, then, so good: let us assume that these necessities are in place and that the quality procedures of the institution are being evidenced and delivered. What next?

It would be reasonable to assume that at a mid-point in the module, some kind of natural or inevitable shift might occur in the participants' approach to their output. We might like to think of certain individuals either having a eureka moment where their work magically moves on to another level, or perhaps handing in a redraft that is appreciably better than anything that has gone before, or maybe just uncovering the secrets of active reading via a common-sensical and logical progression through hard-won cogitation and critical maturation. Well, funnily enough, yes, these things do happen, but they only happen in the context of peer support, tutor guidance and sensitive cooperation. Quite when they happen, along with how and why, is the subject of this next chapter, as indeed are the obstacles which prevent them from happening, the sites of resistance and anxiety in the production of real writing for real audiences. In making consideration of these topics we inevitably move towards assessment, revision and reflection, all three of which find their target firmly nailed to the return of the active reader.

Often the factors that prevent the handover of initiative to the workshop group stem not from the unwillingness of the students to experiment, or from an innate lack of confidence in sharing material, but rather from the facilitator's own fear that she or he has inadequately prepared the readers for their first solo flight. What results is a kind of delay, a deferral or procrastination in the realization that the processes of active engagement with the texts are already in place and have been for some time. The basic methodology for transformative writing is not in itself hard to comprehend and it is often the case that good initial work is being produced by week three or four of the module, certainly by those who are apparently in sympathy with the approach, or those whose learning styles map on to the tasks undertaken. This is not by any means to advocate an early wholesale handover of initiative to the group, but it is a call for practitioners to be more aware of the signs of student competency in their early stages. These signs might take the form of, for example:

- A desire by the writers to choose their own source texts
- A recognition in the students of how their drafts are changing their work
- A certain freedom developing in the variety of styles used
- A focus on the processes and theories of reading as topics in themselves
- A linking of their own life experience to textual situations and events
- A growing appreciation of the devices and skills employed by published writers
- A growing confidence in the quality of their own writerly responses
- A willingness to criticize and offer support to others in the room
- A critical and reflective attitude to the written work of peers
- A recognition that they are beginning to read differently now
- An increasing capacity for active listening via jottings and note-taking
- A rudimentary questioning of form, genre and punctuation
- A plausible positioning of self, text, group and tutor.

However, this is not intended as a set of tick-boxes and it is not as if, having witnessed, say, five of these in the classroom you can, like an astronaut, jettison formative boosters and proceed to initiative-handover stage. We might pause for a moment on the last bullet point, however, as it (more than the others) raises important issues relating to responsibility and social positioning. The word I have used is 'plausible' and the nexus we are exploring is quaternary and properly dialogic in Bakhtin's sense: the four voices of self, text, group and tutor as they intermingle and power-adjust both within and without the workspace.

The achievement of plausibility – intellectual, social, interpretive – is not the sole aim of active reading *per se*, but it is perhaps the principal means through which high-scoring project work comes into existence. The candidate who, by avoiding the pitfalls and dangers of the implausible, has succeeded in negotiating possible, likely and provable links between the four categories above, is in a strong position to express her results. Put another way, the individual writer is an agent who, in discovering where certain discursive boundaries lie – boundaries policed by convention, economy, socio-spatial norms and institutional practices – finds creative and imaginative solutions in written form to competing and often conflicting data sets. Having done so she then expresses her results in ways which not only meet the requirements of the code and context but which augment and initiate constructive pathways for future group exploration. Start as we may with sources from Swift, Spivak or Shakespeare, active readers end by reconstructing their own narratives of plausible selfhood.

EDITING, REVISION, REWRITING

Editing work by active readers is significantly unlike any other kind of editing. This is because in an etymological sense, the kind of 'putting forth' required by active readers is of a fundamentally different nature. The process of bringing out the work rests as we have said upon an understanding of self, text, group and tutor and the dialogic processes of negotiation and semantic construction that are played out within the local meaning-making environment.[47] Thus editing becomes not a supplementary activity for participants, but actually the central activity of seminars and private learning time. It also becomes not something that is done after the primary activity of first drafting, but something that takes place before and during the very production of that initial outpouring. Proficient active readers, in fact, are people who are permanently in the editing stage of creative production and who remain aware of this point at a meta-cognitive level whilst actually performing editing-related activities. Indeed, a better question might be 'when are active readers not in the editing phase?'

Part of the reason for this increased importance of editing lies in wider technological advances: we edit on screen, we cut and paste, we import data and visuals from the web, we reconfigure our text messages and emails towards brevity and slang. In many ways, paring down the language has become part and parcel of our everyday existence in the information age, where a fast response is often valued over a crafted one. But we do not respond to this in a sentimental or pessimistic mode, railing against the fall in student standards or the apparent lack of reading that goes on or the instrumental nature of skills acquisition; instead, we use it as a positive indicator that creative language use and media production is taking individuals and society itself into new areas of shared interlocution. Take, for example, the genre-blurring that has increased in almost all types of utterance since the onset of postmodernity, the second- and third-level quoting and adaptive, parodic voicing that takes place in everyday conversations, the repetitions and creative reiterations of widely known cultural expressions and television mantras that we overhear in the corridors. These are forceful indicators that 'it's more in the edit' today than it has ever been, and, as English professionals, one of our tasks is to make manifest imaginative language use that is already extant in everyday literary and linguistic situations. Precisely because our editing skills are put to use in greater volume than ever before, there is a requirement for us to trace with our students the routes and mediated pathways of potentially complex modes of 'putting forth'.

TRANSFORMATIVE ASSESSMENT – THE PORTFOLIO

'Writing for Reading' is assessed by portfolio, and ideally students work towards submission of this folder of work from the outset. In practice, however, and partly due to the nature of the active reading process itself, different writers tend to produce work that will end up in their portfolio in fits and starts. One obvious reason for this is, as we have seen, the fact that members of the group are in a constant process of drafting and editing which alters the pace of their output as they renegotiate boundaries and learning outcomes week by week. For example, knowing that they will be credited for variety, perhaps their folder is looking fiction-heavy halfway through the module, so they need to move to other genres and text-types. Perhaps they have used the same strategy too often – changing the point of view to that of a minor character – and they need to try alternative modes of writing. Their work might not be experimental enough – utilizing the full force of a creative proving of language – so they will need to include more radical or imaginative attempts. As candidates know that they are required to show evidence of drafting (their 'workings'), how can they do this within the word limit if drafts are long and involved? These are the kinds of questions and negotiations which take place particularly towards the end of the module, when both time and outcomes become real and pressing concerns. Inevitably, there are those who have missed certain weeks due to illness, family crises and the usual panoply of obstacles which life throws at us, and often these are not the people who seek further support and guidance from the tutor. It is now that the practitioner should identify such students and offer to meet with them on a one-to-one basis so that they are at least clear about what is expected of them in the assessment. Yes, this is extra work for the tutor, but the benefits in terms of completion rate, quality of work returned and personal satisfaction are all there for the taking. Our attitude to active reading modules has to be that of the strong finish because this is where maximum support is required. Obstacles that have been somewhat abstract and deferred until week 12 of 15 suddenly take on a new meaning: they have to be surmounted in such a way as to score highly in the assignment. More traditional academic modules do not, in fact, share this focus on the last three weeks in the same way.[48] Again, this is due to the particular needs and requirements of an active reading approach, an approach which builds constructively as the workshops progress via a structured process of imitation, experimentation and confidence building. Apart from seeing students on an individual basis in the final weeks before submission, and checking that they know the marking criteria and learning outcomes in the handbook, how can he or she ensure a result that does each individual justice? We have found the following 12 pointers useful to ensure that the apprentice writer is in a strong position. Check that the participant:

1. Has produced a body of work in different writing styles with evidence of drafting.
2. Has included a flexible balance between class work and individual output.
3. Is aware of the word limit and has used it to maximum effect.
4. Has signposted the portfolio clearly throughout and has included a contents page and bibliography.
5. Has provided a self-critical reflective commentary on every individual piece of writing.
6. Has quoted appropriate secondary material from authoritative sources to support and supplement this reflection (e.g. reader theory, journals, writing magazines, websites).
7. Has not forgotten to include more experimental jottings, listings and marginalia to demonstrate the creative and imaginative aspects of form and language use.
8. Has made significant and appropriate links in every piece of writing to the relevant source text on which the piece is based.
9. Has actively reflected upon the way in which writing each piece changed his or her understanding of the original text with which s/he started.
10. Has, at some point in the folder, made use of the work of other group members (peer review; comment on advice given; group work produced and so on).
11. Has reflected on the tutor's input and feedback, for example, on drafts or in mid-module meetings.
12. Has produced, in sum, a portfolio of active reading work which demonstrates both their engagement with the module and is in itself a creatively crafted object.

One of the immediate features with which second markers of this module are struck is the wide variety in nature of the portfolios submitted each year. Despite the assignments being based on exactly the same set texts, there are so many possibilities available to each group member that the differences in approach, style, length, presentation and ways in which the outcomes are demonstrated are simultaneously daunting and uplifting. This is a module in which it is almost impossible, for example, to plagiarize material, copy the ideas of others in an uncritical or unaware manner, or deliberately to fake or transpose the results. The transparency of the process, after all, accounts for a large part of the mark awarded, and the module already has considerable licence and real freedom of response built into it. It is true that the make-up of the student cohort at Teesside is one of the most diverse in the UK so we should not be surprised by the bandwidth of the response; there is also evidence to suggest that the students who take 'Writing for Reading' are those who benefit from non-traditional modes of assessment such as the essay or exam. Students who have an image of themselves as weaker or struggling individuals after the first year seem to benefit greatly from the multiple possibilities on offer here.

It would be wrong to suggest, however, that nothing ever goes wrong in the portfolios – quite the reverse – and with the best will in the world on both sides of the tutor/tutee relationship, certain aspects of the portfolio are apt to run aground. Listed below are the commonest weaknesses and failures which crop up year on year, and we have ordered them in our own perceived rank of observance where 1 indicates the most common error and 20 the least common:

1   relatively poor signposting of how the portfolio operates
2   lack of a significant return to the source text in the commentary to explain how their understanding of the original has changed as a result of rewriting it
3   lack of depth in real formal comprehension (grammar, tropes, lexis)
4   failure to experiment with detailed, nuanced and crafted links between the source text and their own version
5   portfolio leans too much towards pure creative writing
6   lack of variety in the portfolio as a whole
7   poor physical presentation (font, colours, layout, diagrams, photos, screenshots and so on)
8   unimaginative use of the commentary on each piece
9   lack of research into reader/writer theory
10   poor use of journals and internet to support reflection
11   under-development of potentially strong ideas and topics
12   poor evidence of drafting
13   under-use of links to other modules and texts beyond W4R

14 misidentification of own strengths and weaknesses
15 workshop exercises poorly executed (or just plain wrong)
16 lack of contextual underpinning in the commentaries
17 poor choice of source texts
18 lack of bibliography/references
19 unconvincing actual quality and resolution/coherence of the final rewritten pieces
20 rushed or hurried work which shows little evidence of development

As part of the learning process, we need to spend a moment thinking about the more common issues above, in particular, perhaps, the top five. Poor signposting (1) can be addressed in a number of ways and is the perennial bugbear of this mode of assessment as a whole. Apart from sharing previous years' portfolios with each cohort and asking them to mark these against the same criteria upon which their own work will be judged (a valuable task in itself), there are two other recommendations to be given. First, and this is by no means new, it is a good idea to ask participants to map the learning outcomes in the module guide to each part of the portfolio as it is fulfilled. This may be as simple as adding the outcomes in brackets under each sub-heading, or it may be built under parenthesis into the supporting commentaries. However writers choose to do it, though, it increases the self-awareness of the student and has benefits in keeping the work relevant and on-topic throughout. Second, simply requiring a numbered contents page with proper headings which separate the re-written pieces from the reflective commentaries is considered essential – especially since external examiners need to find their own way around a potentially confusing array of responses. There is something that runs deeper than saying 'remember to structure your assessment clearly' here. Active reading asks imaginative readers to engage positively in a process of making the internal external; such a process is held hostage by interference from sub-conscious cognitive processes that are not always identifiable. It seems that the same barriers and ego symptoms which prevent direct access to an easy transition from mind to page also play themselves out in a structural sense upon the portfolio. This is more than asserting that objectivity is bound to get lost when producing subjective responses to a favourite text – it is more likely to be related to the isomorphism, incrementalism and 'phenomena of analogical thinking' addressed by Hummel, Holyoak and others.[49] Suffice it to say that further research might usefully be completed in this area.

The second commonest problem above was 'lack of a significant return to the source text in the commentary to explain how their understanding of the original has changed as a result of re-writing it.' Again, this is a conundrum which for many participants remains practically insoluble. More than any other criterion it requires the person to be an active learner and usefully indicates for the examiner exactly who those capable learners in the workshop are. Almost all candidates who make a *bona fide* attempt at the portfolio find it easy to write back against a chosen text in the active reading mode: this is rarely a problem. Still, as argued in Chapter 6, what candidates do find challenging, having rewritten the original piece, is then to return to it in order to analyse how their experience of writing back has altered their own first interpretation. If we could solve this problem, we could add perhaps 15 per cent to almost every folder of work. Those who do embrace the concept invariably see grades in the first/high 2.1 bracket, because these are the candidates who have been able at one and the same time to link thinking about their own creative output with meta-cognitive reflection on the whole learning process. Finally, as our own aid to reflection on this (and we offer no analysis of what follows ourselves), we have gathered three real examples of students' commentaries in the box below. What rank order would you put them in?

A. Liz's commentary on her re-write of 'The Heavy-Petting Zoo' by Clare Pollard

I wanted to convert the poem into a letter from one teenager to another, and attempt a text message using only 160 characters including spaces, and using only lexis found in the original poem.

The text message is not as concise as I'd hoped; it proved more difficult than I anticipated, but did make me realize how, as a poet, Clare Pollard had needed every word to work for itself in order to convey very specific meaning. I attempted two drafts and chose B rather than A because I feel it encapsulates the essence of the poem and sets the scene with its reference to 'A heavy-petting party'. I wanted the reader to empathize with the writer, just as I did when I read the original. I became more aware of the references to animals in the original whilst writing these pieces and the reason for the poem's title.

I feel the letter is more successful than the text message because it filled the gaps that the poem suggested. There is more emotion in the letter, and it is written from a personal viewpoint. The theme of teenage angst is echoed in the use of vernacular language and also the choice of font. I decided against using names, and setting the scene, in favour of a vitriolic emotional outburst, which I felt elaborated on the obvious upset inherent in the original poem. (Liz)

B. Gemma's commentary on her rewrite of 'Coming, Aphrodite!'
by Willa Cather

'She wanted to walk across the roofs in the starlight, to sail over the sea and face at once a world of which she had never been afraid' (H. Lee ed. *Secret Self 1: Short Stories by Women*, 1985: 60).

I decided to use this short quotation as it stood out to me as soon as I read it. To me the sentence portrays a woman who is now wanting her own independence and she decides this whilst looking at the scenery. Due to recent events in my life, I felt empathy whilst reading it and I felt as though I could relate to this very short piece of writing and I wanted to respond to it. I developed my poem around a recent visit to a beach on a windy December day and the poem portrays the feelings I felt at this specific time of my life. I wanted to achieve a sense of freedom and independence in my poem, which I feel the quotation is also trying to achieve. I am not entirely happy with the last stanza as I struggled with trying to convey my own exact emotions. I hope that readers can see the theme of freedom and a yearning for independence in my poem. I think I may have achieved this with my imagery of the wind, sea, rhythm and dancing and the idea of struggling. I also wanted to focus on the beauty of the landscape with the aim of creating an atmosphere for the reader. I tried to create the same one which I witnessed, but I know that this is not fully possible. Each reader will have their own mental picture and interpretation of it. Like the quotation, I do not address the question of independence openly or directly, rather with the use of images and metaphors. I present the poem to the reader as a personal experience with the use of first-person narrative, which may distance the reader as they may just see it as a personal poem. I prefer the final draft as I focus more on the role of independence in the final stanza by giving the wind a more central role. If I had more time I would have tried to involve more images or changed the poem to third-person narrative hoping that the reader could become more involved.

From doing this I found that even a short quotation could evoke certain emotions in a reader as this one did with me. Readers can also relate to certain issues and make their own interpretations of it like I have here. I have taken the quotation and taken it out of its context completely and represented it in my own way and included my own experiences to give it a new style: 'But really the word "poem" implies a space: what you would put into it might be just a piece of the world discovered – or – rediscovered from the flood of obscurity and forgetfulness that engulfs almost everything that happens to us. (Mills 1996: 72.) This exercise highlights how an individual reader can change the writing to suit themselves and develop their own ideas from it. (Gemma)

C. *David's commentary on his rewrite of 'Warhol at Wheatlands'* *by John Kinsella*

John Kinsella's poem 'Warhol at Wheatlands' was fascinating in that, for me as a reader, it projected a sense of difficulty in communication between two individuals who see the world in different ways. There is, I believe an empathy to be felt with the narrator of the poem as he seems to struggle to find some common ground. I thought it might be interesting, however, to persuade the reader to view the difficulty from the point of view of Warhol.

When one considers how few people would understand such an individual's perception of the world, it would also be worth noting how isolated that person could feel.

Draft one of my response didn't give the reader time to experience that possible loneliness. It was too short and to the point. The second draft however does allow the reader to respond to the emptiness felt by the two individuals who search the crowds of faces for a soul mate while still pursuing 'normal' lives.

In his poem Kinsella has Warhol as an uncomfortable guest. He is almost being viewed by the reader through the eyes of the narrator. It was my intention to move the reader much closer to the subjects of the poem, even if they could not empathise with the concept of not being understood by others. (David)

Moving on: apart from poor signposting and failing to return to the source text, our third commonest error in the portfolio is 'lack of depth in real formal comprehension'. Even after 13 or 14 weeks of studying different forms of text, a good number of candidates are still unable to appreciate the fundamental nature of the relationship between form and content. This is partly caused by the oft-cited, late-twentieth-century pedagogical shift which moved English away from detailed studies of grammar, punctuation and lexis, and partly a result of understandable undergraduate inexperience in the sensitive handling of language in its most sensible and vulnerable states. We certainly have no wish to join those bemoaning the current levels of syntactical knowledge (such complaints were probably on Socrates' lips in the *agora*), but neither can we endorse or reward work which ignores the richness of the linguistic variety available, or fails to identify formal shifts at the level of clause and phrase. For this reason we help participants from the start with, for example, the tangible effects of word order, ellipsis and modality in a text, and are disappointed when such topics do not feature in the assessment. Lack of confidence in advanced linguistic terminology can and does hamper demonstration of creative reading outcomes, and while it is certainly our responsibility to provide tasks and activities which teach and encourage pleasure in the formal analysis of literary expression, it unfortunately remains a weak point in many portfolios we see.

A 'failure to experiment with detailed, nuanced and crafted links between the source text and their own version' is our fourth commonest problem in portfolio assessment. Marks are available for experimentation and the best folders are always extremely competent here and remain open to experiment in many areas. Innovation, and the crafting of that innovation into something sustainable and rewarding, is a highly prized process and, while it is more typical of the work produced at Level 3, it can and does exist in the second year as well. To illustrate this point we have provided two anonymous examples, below, from previous years. The first shows use of extensive, crafted links between source and finished product; the second has some connections, but they are fluffed, rough-edged and under-explored. A marker's commentary is given for each example to highlight the imbalance.

'Places We Love' by Ivan V. Lalic (*Source text for both examples*)[50]

Places we love exist only through us,
Space destroyed is only illusion in the constancy of time,
Places we love we can never leave,
Places we love together, together, together,

And is this room really a room, or an embrace,
And what is beneath the window: a street or years?
And the window is only the imprint left by
The first rain we understood, returning endlessly,

And this wall does not define the room, but perhaps the night
In which your son began to move in your sleeping blood,
A son like a butterfly of flame in your hall of mirrors,
The night you were frightened by your own light,

And this door leads into any afternoon
Which outlives it, forever peopled
With your casual movements, as you stepped,
Like fire into copper, into my only memory;

When you go, space closes over like water behind you,
Do not look back: there is nothing outside you,
Space is only time visible in a different way,
Places we love we can never leave.

Part One: Pat's active reading, via transformative writing:

The places we share together just don't seem the same. You have shut me out. From our son's first butterfly movements in the womb, which filled us both with wonder, right up until his birth, we were one.

Now there is no room for me.

He fills your every waking moment.

It isn't that I don't love him – I do; but must your love for him be so exclusive?

Is it not possible to have space in your life for me too?

I miss so much, those times we shared which are now, sadly, just a memory.

I close my eyes and picture your casual movements; feel your touch in passing; smell your fragrance; but when I open them you're gone.

Too busy to see that the child in me needs you too.

Let me into your space.

It's so lonely having nothing only memories.

Marker's comments

This is an exceptional piece of 'writing for reading' which has many crafted links to the source text. You work in detail with specific words and phrases that clearly have meaning for you and yet you manage to add something further of your own to enrich the reading experience. The strength of your piece derives from your sensitive handling of stanzas three and four and your translation of the phrases 'Your son began to move' and 'casual movements'. You also work well with the major theme (shared place) and by re-using and re-casting specific signifiers (room, memory, love, place, nothing) your own piece takes on an emotional validity and finds a coherence and resolution that it might otherwise have lost. The spareness of your language, combined with its carefully achieved colloquialism, is the product of careful editing and drafting and you have achieved a rare simplicity in prose that can indeed match that of Lalic's poem. Your resulting text is successful because of a number of informed stylistic choices you have made along the way, including those relating to layout, punctuation, voice, register, tense and person. Plenty more to discuss here when we meet, Pat – very well done.

Part Two: Andrea's active reading, via transformative writing:

– Do you remember our first house, the magical time we had there together?
– I've never really left that place. I don't think I ever will.
– Do you remember our bedroom; so small we had to snuggle up close together?
– It wasn't the place for rows.
– Do you remember the street below our window, where we would watch the years roll by with the changes they brought?
– The many summers and winters we watched, changing the landscape in their definable ways. I feel now that I could open that door and see everything as it used to be. The good times and the bad rolled into one. I've still never left that place. I don't think I ever will.

Marker's comments

While I like the idea of your second draft turning the poem into a dialogue, I think it runs the risk of losing sight of key themes and lexis in the Lalic text. You've done well to pick up on the general handling of place and memory, but at times your piece verges on hackneyed sayings ('the good times and the bad', 'the years roll by') without real explanation for this in your commentary. I'm not sure 'definable' is the right word here (final speaker) – how does it link to the source text? You've done well in capturing the nostalgic atmosphere in your piece, but I wonder if this isn't being done ironically in the source text – did you make a deliberate decision to take it straight? Also, you seem to have missed the opportunity to develop/transform the highly effective imagery and language of stanza three (and elsewhere) – maybe you just chopped out too much of the poem? Nevertheless, you do get credit for experimentation and for your other draft response, and although the final piece perhaps isn't that strong, you have clearly demonstrated the processes involved in such an exercise. Keep going!

What do we mean by saying that a portfolio leans too much towards pure creative writing (error number 5)? A number of features can lead the marker to this conclusion. The commonest is an overuse of workshop warm-up exercises which have not derived from a literary (or other) source text. While it is right and proper to include one or two of these exercises for variety and idea development, they do not in themselves make a whole folder of work. Such portfolios exhibit a methodological weakness in that the writer has not realized that such imaginative tasks are a part of the process, a means to an end, rather than the end in itself. For this reason tutors do need to take care when using such short ice-breakers and intermediary exercises so that participants are fully aware of their function in the active reading cycle. After all, such exercises may be exactly the same as those we might expect to find in a pure creative writing module: work with characterization; with the senses, with the visual imagination, with question and answer scene-setting, and so forth. However, it is easy to identify summative portfolios which have simply worked these up a bit and have not found literary or cultural source texts of their own from which to work. In one case, a student became so comfy and proficient at these short check-in tasks that she was unable to see past them and produce proper active reading work of her own outside class time. She had become habituated into the mechanics of the short writing task to such an extent that the group's presence, upon which she became dependent, veiled her weaknesses elsewhere. Again, it is important for the tutor to identify such cases, if at all possible, during the course of the workshops. Just because a person is vocal every week, shares their work on a regular basis and seems to be enjoying the module is no actual guarantee that the assessed portfolio will yield an impressive mark. This is why the transition from workshop to submitted folder is the crucial step and why we maintain that the 'Writing for Reading' module is end-loaded. Guidance by the tutor in the final three weeks is imperative if the group members are to convert their energies and enthusiasms from the workshop arena into written material which fully does justice to their transformative abilities.

FEEDBACK

Students taking our modules make a greater personal investment in their assessment because it derives extensively from continued negotiation between the personal and the public, their inner and outer landscapes. Although there is some crossover, this is simply not the case with a standard critical essay on *Henry V* or *Jane Eyre*. It is certainly not the case in examinations where a disinterested critical objectivity continues to act as the gold standard for both register and theoretical practice. We have seen that the affective and emotional processes of reading are reflected upon at a meta-textual level for active readers and such an approach necessarily runs the risk of having to analyse and deal with material arising from unconscious or repressed long-term memory. Desire, volition, frustration and trauma are present in a number of drafts for any active reading year group, even if the specific writers themselves are indeed following the class rules and contract. Feedback, then, in its usual educational sense for higher education assessment tasks, is both an appropriate and an inappropriate term. On the one hand the tutor has nothing to gain by collapsing the formality of the normal systems of modular feedback in operation across the institution: indeed it is of no help to the participants to do so since they need reassurance regarding the status, validity and parity of the staged modules they have elected to study. On the other, to deny aspiring writers the opportunity for detailed comments on their output as transformative *writers*, as people who have personally risked far more than normal in their assessment tasks, is not a defensible position for most tutors either. To call the latter feedback, however, is something of a stretch, especially when therapeutic writing is often submitted in response to what we have elsewhere called 'healing texts'.

With these factors in mind, the feedback we provide on 'Writing for Reading' takes four forms: tutor feedback on draft work in week six; structured peer feedback by participants in week eight; informal formative feedback as required through the module; and written summative feedback on the final portfolio. The exact mixture of these received by each student will inevitably differ based on the type of reading/writing being undertaken. If we suspect a certain learner is struggling or is disappearing over the horizon in an unfruitful direction, we do intervene and spend more time with that person. If, however, a writer needs time to develop a piece of work on his or her own over a period of weeks, this is not regarded as a problem and we can keep an eye open from a longer distance. The net result is that, like drafting and editing, the feedback cycle becomes part and parcel of the actual process and progress of the module, not something disembedded or disaggregated from it. Again, this is true of several English modules in the English Studies section, but once more the personal investment outlined above magnifies its importance for our particular students.

Mention has already been made of the peer assessment and interim tutorial meetings in other chapters, but we have not yet provided examples of the type of written feedback that we use when grading the summative folder itself. I have given two examples in the box below. As previously, the chosen examples vary in quality. Both first marker's and second marker's comments are included for each, which, although somewhat laborious, does give an idea of the type of discussions that are likely to take place.

Pre-discussion Markers' Notes on Portfolio A (Blind Marking)

First Marker

Gets stronger as it goes and by the end you feel that this IS a decent selection of work after all. Source text for second piece (questions?) is a weak point but perhaps the strength of the graphic presentation of this folder compensates? I do think the parallel text format in A3 is rather suggestive and energetic throughout (not naff at all). Response to Jackie Kay is genuinely interesting and the commentaries do include secondary material with idiomatic terms (defamiliarization, determinism, etc). Another themed portfolio (autobiography) that works well. Only real drawback is the real shortness of all four source texts hard to say if this is a problem *per se*, but it does limit variety (which IS a criterion). Tanka is two syllables short and is unconventional anyway. Mmmm ...

Second Marker

You'd certainly given attention to the matter of presentation, and how to represent the process of drafting. There are a few mistakes (Peugot, qouatation, though 'smoother' may have been deliberate?), and the occasional oral slippage in commentary ('I would have went into more description'). The dialogue with Paul Mills was a recurrent organizing element throughout, and the investigation of how the dance narrative emerged demonstrated and heralded the mutual interplay of drafts and commentary. Dance as occasion and metaphor turned into a cohesive device as the portfolio went on. There is enough focused observation (and absorbed conceptual apparatus) in the commentaries to support the generalizations. There's an interesting set of decisions here to develop autobiographical themes throughout, and to use source texts where you do in an indirect, associative way. But this relative inattention to the verbal being of your originals is counterposed by the strong use you make of Mills and beyond Mills of the ideas and procedures explored in the module. It's a very personal take on the module, but closely enough anchored to warrant the mark which in any case the portfolio deserves.

Pre-discussion Markers' Notes on Portfolio B (Blind Marking)

First Marker

1   This is a very strong Hemingway commentary that includes mini-
    drafts within it. A clever way of meeting learning outcomes, yet
    remaining fluid and analytical. The actual creative response is the
    most impressive I've seen to this story (e.g. voice, register, structure).
2   Variety of respective poetic responses to Hemingway are by and
    large good (even the jokes) and this covers the experimental tag
    nicely.
3   The paperback plot summaries are a technical exercise in genre-
    switching and this is what they accomplish. I do like the com-
    mentaries from this student, however, that are relaxed without
    being sloppy.
4   At 2000 words or so, this is the dominant part of the folder and it
    is well executed and cleverly structured. The narrative has Carter's
    own original beginning followed by a number of possible middles
    and endings, arranged as a hypertext or multi-role-player game.
    The idea comes from Atwood's 'Happy Endings' in *The Secret Self*.
    This is first-class work: well written, drafted and experimental.
    Careful attention to structure and close details appearing from the
    Carter source. Excellent, if a bit risky.

Summary
The folder is backed up with his own research (Eaglestone/Barry *et al.*)
rather than with classwork – which is refreshing. It's also a bit long,
and you could quibble with a slight lack of variety (no drama) and
presentation (bit dull), but (1) and (4) are surely highly original first-
class material? We have a proper active reader here.

Second Marker

Thoughtful and reflective, capable of taking an overview of development of own work, reflecting on decisions and their implications.
Writing exercises suggest sustained and extensive attention and
development. Version of Carter's story with multiple plot options is
quite a complex and sophisticated task – not merely structural but
thematic. Introduction to portfolio was appreciated; conclusion evaluating 'success' (suggested in intro) would have been welcome. Variety
of genres, tones and voices is impressive – as is capture of quite specific
period and location of Hemingway.

Here is not the place to compare marking styles in detail (there are several tutors represented here) and it has to be said that final marks are achieved more in the dialogue between markers than in their initial guidance notes above. Assessment, as we know, is an inexact science in the Humanities, much as we would like, at times, to convince ourselves otherwise, but in general the marking criteria adopted (see previous chapter) are very effective at keeping discussions on track. External examiners are used in a moderating capacity for Levels 2 and 3: although we do not ask them to alter individual marks, they can rightly ask us to revisit a band or set of scripts.

To end our 'Writing for Reading' narrative on a positive note, though, it is fair to say that the four tutors who have marked this module for the past five years have without exception found the experience a particular joy in comparison with other marking duties. Having carefully read a cohort of transformative writing scripts, there is always a genuine and shared feeling that individuals are truly learning in the best sense of the word: learning to see and express their own social world with a renewed energy for others alongside a firmer grasp of self, expectation and language. Moreover, as a result of the evidence in the preceding chapters (support for which is growing across many higher education institutions at the current time), we firmly believe that the work produced in the critical/creative, active reading mode has freed many of our students up to perform better in the other components of their degrees. As we move in the remaining chapters, then, to address such topics as autonomy, professional development and negotiated writing projects, we continue to maintain that this last point tells a valuable story of its own.

Part III

Beyond the Classroom

8 Learning for Life: Transformative Writing in Professional Development

To be 'literate' means to be a social being. One is committed to 'read' the inner life of others, and to 'write' one's own life on the blank space of one's pregiven relatedness to others. In these terms, any literate act is a development of one's implication in the lives of others, and the cultivation of literacy always entails psychosocial, ethical, and political practice ... To cultivate literacy is to refine and enhance our mutual implication in one another's lives and to discover and exercise our mutual responsibilities. (Bleich 1988: 66–67)

The wood carver is delighted and not upset when the wood grain inside his block gradually reveals itself and by its obstinate twists compels him to modify his tentative ideas. (Ehrenzweig 1967: 72)

We typically conceive of concepts as packets of meaning ... But parable gives us a different view of meaning as arising from connections across more than one mental space. (Turner 1996: 57)

The primary focus of this book has been on teaching and learning within university English Studies programmes. In this final chapter we venture outside our immediate parish to explore the mutation of the subject matters and practices of 'English' outside and beyond the English degree programme. We take one area – therapeutic practice – as a major example and make brief suggestions about another. Curiously, it is in this domain that all our arguments converge. Thus, for one thing, as we pointed out in Chapter 1, 'English' (as a domain that overlaps with the practice of diverse communities of readers) has never been solely defined by university scholars. The study of English Literature has a long history in Adult Education going back as far as the University Extension movement of the 1870s. In the post-war period it became one of the most popular subjects in the extra-mural and Workers' Educational Association repertoire.[51] But further, implicit in the narrative of the undergraduate career which underlies this book is the idea that the kinds of learning with which English equips students are characterized by their implications for lifelong learning.[52]

In short, to address the undergraduate programme in a meaningful way requires us to think beyond its boundaries and beyond that particular, limited moment in the student lifecycle. English proposes itself as a subject which nourishes the learner as citizen and as fulfilled individual, and the modes of teaching and learning advocated in this book prepare the ground for the learning on which lifelong development is built. Study, we have implicitly argued, is itself a form of production, and enriched cultural and linguistic inventiveness a form of self-making (Greenblatt 1980 and compare Bruner 2002, Eakin 1999.) Since imaginative reading and writing are self-evidently not monopolized by English Studies, this insight applies as much to those readers who have not formally studied the subject. Language and letters are not so much a guide to what *is* as a collaborative invention of what *could be*. To move in and out of the wealth of the already written, re-writing, quoting and misquoting as you go, is a profoundly developmental activity. Many of the aspects of 'theory' on which we have drawn may be extrapolated into this realm, above all the idea – basic to this book – that reading at its fullest is not a passive process of consumption, but rather an active process of staging and enactment carried out on the basis of textual cues. This is not, we believe, a position antagonistic to theory. At its best, 'theory' has always been concerned, not so much with the substance of what we know, but how we know it. Our phrase 'active reading' is intended to foreground the idea that serious engagement with the text is after all a constructive and supplementary process even where it does not actually involve making alternative marks on paper. Active readers enter into a cultural ecology, taking sustenance from texts, and in return endowing texts with continuing life.[53] The preoccupations of this book with performance, with the discursive construction of identity, and with hospitality towards visitations of 'the other' can all apply to the more specialized domain of professional self-knowledge. Nowhere is that more true than in the border territories where professional development and therapeutic practice meet.

THERAPEUTIC PRACTICE

The tradition of mining literature for therapeutic ends goes back of course at least to Freud himself. As too does a distinctly Oedipal struggle over whether psychoanalysis or literature was in fact the master discourse.[54] More dialogically, over a number of years, a variety of professionals working in forms of psychotherapy, health and social care have been exploring ways in which imaginative writing and generative response to literary texts may have a significant role in setting free human powers of regeneration, whether in clients or in the professionals themselves (Bolton 1998, Knights 1995, Hunt 2000, Hunt and Sampson 2006).[55]

It is not appropriate here to do more than indicate the merest outline of the relation of literary to professional practice. (Interested readers are referred to the bibliography and notes.) Here – as an extension of the larger argument of the book – we seek to explore some of the principles involved in carrying our core proposals beyond the undergraduate classroom. In particular, we are interested in the insights to be derived from undertaking even small-scale, limited 'active reading' activities with those whose professional or personal identity is not that of an undergraduate student. We believe, in any case, that reviewing our principles in relation to this sphere is likely to feed back into priorities and perceptions in teaching for the BA: the undergraduate degree informed by its own prospective horizons.

Any such intervention into professional development carries the risks as well as the opportunities of dialogue between disciplinary tribes. The cultures of counselling and psychotherapy tend to have a very different orientation towards fictional text to that which by and large characterizes the English professions. When reading literary texts with such groups, we have repeatedly had to acknowledge that activities which 'English' takes for granted may seem trivial or even offensive to those who look to text to reveal psychological insight and substance. The depth model of mind (or of *mythos*) dominant in counselling and therapy does not sit comfortably with the propensity to cultural construction. To take what may be a core example, there are marked cultural differences in respect of the representation of pain or suffering. Working with counsellors on texts as different as Tillie Olsen's story 'Hey Sailor, What Ship' or Sylvia Plath's poem 'Nick and the Candlestick' I (Ben Knights) have sometimes needed to justify what was seen as the defended academicism of asking for verbal or formal analysis in the face of the emotional power of the subject matter. Thus the meeting between these disciplinary cultures in many ways re-activated an ancient debate over the cognitive meaning of tragedy. For many of those in such groups, the power of the material being represented trumped second-level discourse about how the representation was done. Intellectualization, for some counselling cultures, represents a form of betrayal. In short, we need to be sensitive to the implications of translation into other professional languages.

Speaking across the demarcation lines from English into other professions, what sort of things do we find ourselves wanting to say? We argue that we are talking about 'doing things with signs', on the basis of literary text as form of enquiry or investigation. Texts, we can say, are case studies whose value lies in the twin facts that their entailments to reality are cut (disaster will not follow from getting it wrong), and that they offer themselves for interpretative re-writing. We seek to draw on the common sources of constructivist psychology and dialogic theory to advance a textual practice that builds on narrative as dialogue (Morris 1994, Shotter and Gergen 1989, Shotter 1993, Holquist 1990).

We start such workshops by saying that we assume that participants will be very aware of issues to do with narrative, but that we intend to explore ways in which the literary discipline complements their own. This leads to an outline of what practitioners of our disciplines have in common: they are readers of signs and messages; they are aware of discursive framing and disclosure – and acknowledge the possibility of being lived by stories which are only partially understood. Listening readers have in common a curiosity about metaphor and analogical thinking, and about the often oblique ways in which different levels of self and identity may be represented. Where appropriate, we can draw attention to the long history of two-way converse between psychotherapy and literary criticism, from Freud himself through figures like Norman Holland to poststructuralist versions of psychoanalysis (Holland 1975, Ellmann 1994). We can point to insistent preoccupations with identity, with guilt, the unconscious, the family romance, with the uncanny, and with haunting – indeed to repetition as itself the underlying Freudian plot motif. We might at this stage suggest that making active searches for alternatives in the reading process is equivalent to being able to sidestep the compulsive narrative in the therapeutic encounter. From the literary side, we can draw on examples from a vast literary range, from Matthew Arnold's 'The Buried Life' to Anne Tyler's resonant opening 'Once upon a time there was a woman who discovered that she had turned into the wrong person' (*Back When We Were Grown-Ups*, 2001), to demonstrate the concern of both traditions with the appearance – or concealment – of identities under different conditions of narrative possibility. Both traditions resist generalization, or summing up human predicaments in reductive terms, and both are attracted by an ethical commitment to the idea of an encounter which leads to transformation. Further, we can share a view of narrative as a search for justice and the desire for justice: the child-like 'it's not fair' and the urgent need to get a fair hearing as the propellant for narrative and disclosure.

> Since then, at an uncertain hour,
> That agony returns:
> And till my ghastly tale is told,
> This heart within me burns.
>
> I pass, like night, from land to land;
> I have strange power of speech;

That moment that his face I see,
I know the man that must hear me:
To him my tale I teach.
(S.T. Coleridge, *The Rime of the Ancient Mariner*)

Furthermore, there is a continuum of narrative across the range from
face-to-face encounter to feature film, soap opera or novel. Self-evidently,
these forms require different levels of institutional embedding and turn
into tangible objects in diverse ways. But we should not make the
mistake of assuming that face-to-face varieties somehow occur in a space
outside culture. Language is itself an institution, and cultural conventions (counselling or psychotherapy are not exceptions) themselves produce discursive genres, so shaping not only the settings in which
narrative happens but also the forms it can take. At the least, literature is
a constant reminder of the management of reader appetite by genre.

What else? Language, we would want to say, is not only inescapably
rich in connotation, but also, crucially, it is performative and persuasive,
does not merely serve a representational function. The day's newspaper
headlines will yield a crop of examples.

IT'S OFFICIAL: IMMIGRATION IS TEARING BRITAIN APART

Even an imaginary or non-proximate reader is an addressee, and conventions of reciprocity and codes of relations govern what may be told. In
the workshops on which this section draws we explore story as an appeal
to the listener or reader: as a project of relation building. A telling self is
constructed in the presence of a listening self, and neither figure may
exactly map on to the actual persons present in the encounter (Young
1987). The story space may, for example, be dominated by the desire
to match or to dispute what we think our addressee thinks, to seek
recognition or approval – or for that matter to test the limits of the
interlocutor's tolerance. The teller may want to appeal for sympathy, to
impress, to compete, or to demonstrate the sort of person they would like
to be, and the possibility of narrative success or failure will impact on the
unfolding story. To put it schematically, the addressee is cast in an ideal
role which could (for example) be that of a parent, someone to shock or
from whom to seek comfort. Tsvetan Todorov summarizes the great
theorist of dialogue, Mikhail Bakhtin:

In their analyses Freud and his disciples always tend to play up
individual motivations ... but aren't the words of the patient, uttered
during the analytic session, determined as well, if not more, by the
interaction that comes into being in the microsociety formed by the
physician and the patient[?] ... What is reflected in these verbal

utterances is not the dynamics of the individual soul, but the social
dynamics of the interrelations of doctor and patient. (1984: 31–2)

So it is that to intervene in the storymaking process is to enquire into a
generative pattern of relationships. And for this purpose the fictional
story (or, of course, the poem) is akin to D. W. Winnicott's 'third area' of
human living, 'one neither inside the individual nor outside in the world
of shared reality', the 'potential space' of play. The 'place where cultural
experience is located', he says, 'is in the *potential space* between the
individual and the environment ... The same can be said of playing.
Cultural experience begins with creative living first manifested in play.'
(1971: 110, 100.) It is our case that in the space of the active reading
workshop we are licensing, in a similar sense, a form of play, though one
which is far from connotations of the frivolous. Parable, says Mark
Turner, 'serves as a laboratory where great things are condensed in a small
space. To understand parable is to understand root capacities of the
everyday mind, and conversely' (1996: 5). Our procedure has marked
affinities with what Richard Winter calls the multi-voiced 'patchwork
text' (Winter *et al.* 1999, and see below p. 147).

Reading for Clues

Here is the opening of a short story. Please read it and note down any
language or narrative clues that you pick up. What inferences can you
draw? Make a guess as to where the story is going next, then compare
notes with another person. When you have done that, see if you can
agree the outline of a plausible narrative following on from this passage.

Psychology

> When she opened the door and saw him standing there she was
> more pleased than ever before, and he, too, as he followed her into
> the studio, seemed very very happy to have come.
>   'Not busy?'
>   'No. Just going to have tea.'
>   'And you are not expecting anybody?'
>   'Nobody at all.'
>   'Ah! That's good.'
>   He laid aside his coat and hat gently, lingeringly, as though he
> had time and to spare for everything, or as though he were taking
> leave of them for ever, and came over to the fire and held out his
> hands to the quick, leaping flame.

In the next phase of the activity, we give out the following paragraphs of Katherine Mansfield's story 'Psychology' and delegate four groups to go through marking up, respectively: metaphors; reporting of thought processes; narrative turning points; and use of objects or 'props'. That group activity is itself the platform either for plenary discussion or an expansive writing activity working either forwards or backwards from the 'moment' of the short story.[56]

Engagement even with fragments of literary text will lead us on to a core argument, another instance of how the hybridization of habits and languages along the margins of disciplines may enable us to move beyond either. Thus part of our aim will be to persuade of the importance of going beyond simplistic notions about identification, mimesis or realism into questions about metaphor, narrative, style and gesture – engaging in those debates about how representation actually functions in social space. Personal and linguistic styles are never the direct expression of inner reality. At the heart of this case is an idea about indirection: about creative processes (and interpretation as itself a creative process), requiring us not to go at the subject matter head on, but through a mediating object. Symbolism, and the material obduracies of form, are as fundamental to the culture of therapy as that of 'English'. Enigma calls out interpretative energy. We draw here on the psychoanalytical tradition in the form of Anton Ehrenzweig's 1967 classic *The Hidden Order of Art*, above all his development of the idea that a 'new idea will inevitably be modified through its impact on the resisting medium ...' (1967: 72). His dialogic argument spills light on the convergence of therapy and literary practice as mediated activities of re-making:

Something like a true conversation takes place between the artist and his own work. The medium, by frustrating the artist's purely conscious intentions, allows him to contact more submerged parts of his own personality and draw them up for conscious contemplation ...

One has to explain to the student that a purely conscious control of the working process is neither desirable nor possible ...

True craftsmanship does not impose its will on the medium, but explores its varying responses in [a] kind of conversation between equals ... (1967: 72–3)

And he goes on to speak of a 'passive but acute watchfulness for subtle variations in the medium's response'. What is the relevance of this case about teaching art to our theme? Precisely this: we are not here offering up literature as a gigantic lexicon of psychological, sociological or ethical illustrations. Rather (and in the spirit of Louise Rosenblatt's distinction between 'efferent' and 'aesthetic' reading), we are arguing that repertoires of understanding can be powerfully expanded by conscious involvement in the *processes* of narrative and metaphorization. The learning is in the process, not in what the reader excavates from the text in any unmediated sense (see Knights 1995: 2–3).

Literary process engages participants in the material and social practices by which maps of significance are drawn and re-drawn; practices by which that which is oblique or indirectly glimpsed is articulated through the resonant image. So Ehrenzweig's argument about the artist's struggle with difficulty can in fact be applied to the reader as well. For the very resistances and difficulties in the text may actually stimulate all the more affective and cognitive activity. The text's management of difficult material is an incitement to symbolic engagement. Thus Margaret Atwood's 1988 novel *Cat's Eye* does not *tell us* about childhood bullying: instead it draws the reader into how a narrator makes sense of the experience of being bullied.

> Cordelia says, to me, 'Were you laughing?' I think she means was I laughing at her because she fell down.
> 'No,' I say.
> 'She was,' says Grace neutrally. Carol shifts to the side of the path, away from me.
> 'I'm going to give you one more chance,' says Cordelia. 'Were you laughing?'
> 'Yes,' I say, 'but ...'
> 'Just yes or no,' says Cordelia.
> I say nothing. Cordelia glances over at Grace, as if looking for approval. She sighs, an exaggerated sigh, like a grownup's. 'Lying again,' she says. 'What are we going to do with you?'
> We seem to have been standing there a long time. It's colder now. Cordelia reaches over and pulls off my knitted hat. She marches the rest of the way down the hill and onto the bridge and hesitates for a moment. Then she walks over the railing and throws my hat down into the ravine. Then the white oval of her face turns up towards me. 'Come here,' she says ... (*Cat's Eye*, 186)

What might an active reading approach to this passage reveal? An attempt to re-write in the past tense ('Cordelia said, to me') might well provoke reflection on how the act of telling deals with the threatening rawness of experience. There is an often overlooked continuity between voice, simulated voice and physical experience. Thus, to vary the conventions of quoted speech might suggest ways in which the meticulous observance of punctuation conventions (themselves a score for breathing) could be a way of managing pain. ('My laughter was unreal after all,' the narrator goes on to say, 'merely a gasp for air.') The point is that language, discourse and text are not simply descriptive or representational (let alone diagnostic), but, to use Murray Cox's terms, mutative or transformational. So we seek to apply to engagement with text what Cox and Theilgaard say of metaphor: 'Metaphor exerts its mutative effect by energizing alternative perspectival aspects of experience' (1987: 99 and throughout). Active engagement with text goes beyond description to articulate points for change.

What Did Maisie Know?

D.H. Lawrence sometimes luminously referred to the novel as a 'thought adventure'. Let's call this thought adventure after Henry James's novel *What Maisie Knew* (1897). Under whatever heading it were read, an English tutor would also hope that students would engage with the novel in terms of language, structure, context, nineteenth-century constructions of childhood, and so on. Those are important goals, and we would hope that the kinds of readings which are the subject of this chapter might themselves lead towards a deeper engagement with this novel or even with James's work at large. But the point here is slightly different. It is that the scenario of the novel might itself be used as a starting place for narrative construction within a group that was trying to understand more about its own professional role and relationships. Counter-intuitively, this would even be possible without them actually reading the whole novel. Let us think of a novel as a kind of software: equipment for carrying out certain sorts of thinking across the cognitive–affective border.

What, in this light, are the novel's key features? The narrative is written from the point of view of Maisie, a girl of six when the novel begins. (Let us leave aside tempting questions about a middle-aged male author posing, as it were, in the guise of Maisie: how could he possibly know what she feels? At what point might empathy become intrusive? Does the narrator collude in her parents' objectification of the child?) Nevertheless, the story vividly announces the problem of observation, and the reader's implication in what she observes. Maisie is the unwilling observer of her parents' adulterous affairs, and while often uneasy and troubled, she does not until late on in the story actually understand what it is she is witnessing, or the uses to which adults are putting her. We as readers (and the case is analogous to a contemporary success, Mark Haddon's *The Curious Incident of the Dog in the Night-time*, or, again, to Alan Bennett's *Talking Heads* monologues) are required to construct a parallel story through and behind what the protagonist is represented as thinking. The narrative – like Haddon's or Bennett's – necessitates the active construction of counter-narratives, an activation of the inner story inside the outer story, if it is to make any more than the most superficial sense. A constellation of generative foci emerges. These concern, among other things, the more or less subtle forms of abuse inherent in adult–child relations; the tension (among Maisie's various carers) between protection and exposure (or indifference); what it means to lack the symbolic resources to comprehend what is happening to you; and sexual knowledge as paradigm for relations between insiders and outsiders. Enigma, curiosity, knowing that one knows enough not to want to know any more, are all urgent features of Maisie's experience. Crucially (and true to James's aesthetic) we are not simply *told* about such matters. All these phenomena are layered in the unfolding reading experience as readers are manipulated between child and parent roles, the twists and turns of their own experience replicating those prefigured in the tale of Maisie.

An active reading engagement with *What Maisie Knew* could start from writing a short scene from a child's point of view, or describing as precisely as possible a moment in which an insight suddenly formed, or for that matter writing what Bleich calls a 'response statement' (Bleich 1978). Once the group had discussed its initial text, they could then move on to reconstructing the adult 'other' in the gaps of the child narrative. At each stage, participants could explore in small groups both the relation between textual management of subject matter and the affect released (in either writer or reader). All along we would be engaged with how the cognitive is carried along and enriched in a matrix of affect. The reading process (itself, to repeat, a form of re-writing) taps levels where knowledge is inflected by embarrassment, shame, rejection, exclusion, loneliness or stubborn adherence to a private inner world. Above all, as facilitators we would stress that engagement with the novel is not a matter of 'efferent' reading. We are not advocating raiding the novel for portable insights (*now* we know what it feels like to be the child of separating parents), but for engagement with the narrative and rhetorical means through which insight is achieved. Little Maisie's guesses, mistakes, her flashes of insight and stolid refusal of the role of victim prefigure the transferential adventure of reading. *Maisie* confronts the therapeutic trades with issues about the 'truth' of sudden intuitions, about betrayal, witness and guilt. Like Maisie, those who strive to witness may well experience feelings of irrational responsibility or complicity for what they have seen.[57]

As the discovery of the transference would complicate Freud's conception of narrative, so should it help us complicate, and refine,

> versions of narrative analysis that do not take account of the rela-
> tions of tellers and listeners. It is my premise that most narratives
> speak of their transferential condition – of their anxiety concerning
> their transmissibility, of their need to be heard, of their desire to
> become the story of the listener as much as of the teller ... (Brooks
> 1994: 50)

What we are describing here is akin to what Murray Cox and Alice
Theilgaard call 'the Aeolian Mode' in psychotherapy (Cox and Theilgaard
1987, Chapter 2 and throughout).[58] A summary of their argument is that
in the 'Aeolian Mode' the therapist activates verbal resonance to 'prompt'
the perspectival mutation of metaphor. This process involves an orientation of verbal attunement and creativity which they refer to as *poiesis*.
'The practice of *poiesis* is the pivot upon which the Aeolian Mode bal-
ances' (23). They are careful to distinguish their practice both from
'poetry therapy' and from the completed poem.

> For our purposes, it is poetic thinking, with its strongly hybrid
> cognitive-affective connotation, which is characteristic of *poiesis* as a
> dynamic component of the Aeolian Mode. (23)

> We are concerned NOT with the quotation of a 'known' poem. On the
> contrary, our concern is with the echoes evoked by the 'swarming
> shadows' of literary associations. This may energize the process of
> *poiesis* as we attune our response to the patient. Once again, it is the
> activity of *poiesis* which characterizes therapeutic space; such *poiesis*
> activates the growing awareness of creative possibilities in new options
> and the endorsement of a more coherent sense of self.

But, they go on to caution:

> mere awareness of earlier creative work. .. may have a restricting and
> obsessionally binding effect if it does not liberate the patient's own
> creativity. (25)

This meshes with our own case that the point of 'active reading' in
professional development is not to equip practitioners with obtrusive
literary knowledge any more than it is to equip them with a bolt-on kit
of verbal techniques. Rather that such activities – carried on individually
or, better still, in a group – convey their own 'aesthetic imperative' and
provide a model of linguistic creativity.

In attuning practitioners to the modalities of narrative and metaphor,
activities based on text alert them to those moments where meanings are
only glimpsed or not yet fully formed. In such situations we are

revisiting the evolutionary step of 'learning through the other' that humans made in learning to understand each other as intentional agents. The evolutionary anthropologist Michael Tomasello who explores the profound significance of 'joint attentional activities' (1999: 6), goes on to make a core point about the human invention of culture:

> As the child masters the linguistic symbols of her culture she thereby acquires the ability to adopt multiple perspectives simultaneously on one and the same perceptual situation. As perspectivally based cognitive representations, then, linguistic symbols are based not on the recording of direct sensory or motor experiences, as are the cognitive representations of other animal species or human infants, but rather on the ways in which individuals choose to construe things out of a number of other ways in which they might have construed them ... (1999: 9)

In short, cognition is collaborative. To which we would add that literary practice models and extends the processes of knowing. In all this we are making what amounts to a case against positivism. The tabular and instrumental form taken by much contemporary professional training (for teachers as much as for therapists) rests, we would argue, on a fairly naive referentialism which implies an uncomplicated equation between experience and description, intervention and outcome. The perspective we are borrowing here from Literary Studies suggests that symbolic performance rests on the aesthetic pleasure of form and verbal creativity. It is a mistake always to be trying to harvest an unmediated truth from representations. Even under stress and in extremity speakers and writers take aesthetic pleasure in form and making, in shaping words for their task which meld the iconic, the affective and the cognitive. The human situation has to become very dire for people to lose all pleasure in communication. So that the practice of literature is a lived reminder that form, metaphor, allusion, style, verbal play and rhetorical skill are not add-ons, or luxuries (let alone a decadent response to life's real pains and horrors). Literature is a symbolic environment, not a lexicon of truths. While his cultural constructionism is in many ways vulnerable to objectivist critique, we may cite Jerome Bruner's *Making Stories: Law, Literature, Life.*

> It is the conversion of private Trouble ... into public plight that makes well-wrought narrative so powerful, so comforting, so dangerous, so culturally essential. (2002: 35)

In fact, as Michael Holquist puts it in summarizing L.S. Vygotsky's idea of pedagogic dialogue, 'Literary texts ... serve as a prosthesis of mind'

(1990: 83). Even on a small and contained scale, experimental literary performance is a way of understanding the nature of symbolic and allusive discourse. Drafting and re-drafting are a cognitive process, but at the same time very much more than a tool for capturing discrete units of knowledge.

OTHER GROUPS

In this chapter we have concentrated on one particular tribe of listening readers. But since we believe that the literary activities which are our subject are applicable to the professional development of other groups as well, it remains to refer briefly to other areas. Over recent years, practices of storymaking and imaginative writing have extended beyond therapeutic applications into the domains of health and social care (see, for example, Gersie and King 1990). More recently, Richard Winter and colleagues at what is now Anglia Ruskin University have adopted methods of drafting and reflection which they refer to as the 'patchwork text' in the development of health and social care professionals (Winter *et al.* 1999).[59]

> Our argument ... is that the operation of the artistic imagination through the writing of fiction can be understood, precisely, as a mode of critical reflection upon, and re-interpretation of, experience.

There is a lot of common ground between their approach and that advocated in this book, not least in the authors' desire to build on 'the widespread (but curiously ignored) human capacity for understanding experience through *imaginative* representation'. In developing a format and protocols for the 'patchwork text', Winter and his colleagues, too, are drawing out the implications of a critique of the analytical essay. The major difference, however, concerns our recourse to already written texts (and forms of articulation drawn from literary discussion) as providing prompts for dialogue. In our project we see texts (in their very refusal always to fit in with what we want them to mean) as providing a formative distraction from formulaic thought.

Fired by some of the same preoccupations and as an offshoot of the 'Active Reading' project, we have ourselves experimented with writing workshops for higher education teachers. Our object in doing so was to supplement the frequently rather external and taxonomic approach of much staff development, and invite participants to make contact with the meaning of their own pedagogic experience. Teachers not only provide frameworks, but also they hold group anxiety, and become the subjects of emotions projected by student groups. As many writers in the Tavistock tradition have pointed out, this means that we cannot deny the emotional experience of teaching or helping other learners (Salzberger-Wittenberg *et al.* 1983, Knights 1992, Nano McCaughan in Evans 1995). But also that professionals, like everyone else, can learn from being prepared to contemplate their own experience of tolerating ambiguity.

We are not denying the value of other kinds of knowing, or research, qualitative or quantitative. But introspection and reflection on our own experience have value as equipment for learning – alongside such other kinds of equipment. To assist learning in others we have not only to be learners ourselves, but also to be critically aware of that process with all its pleasures and discomforts, and mistakes. But, once again, we cannot necessarily get at what we most need to know by the direct approach. To reiterate the earlier point, the value of literary activity is its indirection, its stimulus to processes of metaphor and parable. Writing and re-writing, we argue, enables the convergence of emotions and values in a way that is often brushed aside by more apparently rational, instrumental approaches.

Writing as professional development

While the project is based in the English discipline area, it has many wider implications for learning and teaching. Today I intend to touch briefly on some of those implications. Working from the assumption that 'student-centredness' does not oblige teachers to lose nourishing contact with their own subjective experience, we shall focus on the teacher's own reflective learning. The suggestion is that to carry out structured writing is to engage in a process of re-symbolization. Metaphor and parable offer us equipment for reflectivity. By making the familiar strange, metaphoric prompting can be a road to surprising insight.

Four theses about writing. It:

- is a form of communication that exceeds simple models of transfer of information;
- constitutes – with all its stylistic and syntactic choices – an experimental model for thought;
- involves the construction of hypothetical contexts for making meaning (words, like thoughts, acquire meaning in the context in which they are used);
- forms an inventive dialogue with self as well as with others.

The writing task

Please think about an encounter from your teaching life ... an encounter with a person, a group, an idea. An encounter that remains opaque or mysterious, something perhaps that won't go away.

Write down three or four lines summarizing that incident. Then jot down notes on as many of the following as you have time for.

1. What stays in your mind of the occasion, or the physical surroundings?
2. Note down some words for your mood or emotion ... the tone of the encounter.
3. Is there an image (an object, a colour, a light quality, a sound) you associate with the occasion?
4. If someone had taken a photograph of you at that moment what would you see in the picture?
5. Is there a body sensation associated with the event?
6. How you might describe the event to a colleague or friend later – seriously/jokily?
7. (Later) Write a paragraph from a campus novel in which your incident figures.

While our own workshops are more closely based in Literary Studies, such activities present parallels with the storytelling work of Maxine Alterio and Janice McDrury (2002). Individual and pair activity leads to developmental discussion at an individual level about perspectives and re-framing, and at a more general and theoretical level to an analysis of the narratives and metaphors of teaching. We look forward to developing the hypothesis that imaginative writing, generating its own kind of know-ledges, and always in dialogue with the already written, could give birth to forms of pedagogic research as well as of professional development.

CONCLUSION

At the end of his *Actual Minds, Possible Worlds* the great educationalist Jerome Bruner says:

> I have tried to make the case that the function of literature as art is to open us to dilemmas, to the hypothetical, to the range of possible worlds that a text can refer to. I have used the term 'to subjunctivize', to render the world less fixed, less banal, more susceptible to recre-ation. Literature subjunctivizes, makes strange, renders the obvious less so, the unknowable less so as well, matters of value more open to reason and intuition. Literature, in this spirit, is an instrument of freedom, lightness, imagination, and yes, reason ... (1986: 159)

In this chapter, we have been proposing literary reading as a form of *poiesis*, and literary practice as a formative environment for professional development. This argument is not restricted to the therapeutic encounter or to the domain of professional training. It represents one implication of a larger belief about the role of active textuality in lifelong learning. In engaging in writing out of and back into text, the learner re-activates the risk of textual activity. In a manner both exhilarating and disturbing one moves out of the safety of the achieved monument, safely bound between its covers, into the fraught world of process, of things potentially going wrong, the metaphorical voice breaking. It is a little like the difference between listening to music and attempting – however badly – to play or sing it. Imagination, disciplined through transform-ative writing, may be (to put it reductively) an implement of professional development. But if so, its power rests on the capacity of what we might call co-writing, or *writing alongside* the text to activate simultaneous levels of knowledge and of the self. To quote Cox and Theilgaard once more, this time on 'sunken images' in abstract art: 'In such art it is the very strangeness that suggests its inferential and evocative significance. And the aesthetic imperative is linked to its ability to disturb the spectator.' Resonantly, in their own context, they continue this 'is because subliminal vision is at work. And in the same way Kaufman . . . writes of *Troilus and Cressida*, "*as if we were writing the play* with Shake-speare", so the spectator may have the creative sensation "as if he were painting the picture"' (Cox and Theilgaard 1987:29). At the very least, the 'as if' activities we have discussed here may take us all back to the deeper creative roots of professional lives and relationships.

9 Towards the Autonomous Learner

English has a vital role to play in promoting the ideal of lifelong learning. (*English Subject Benchmark* 2.6)

It is axiomatic in the meliorist protocols of contemporary learning that the student experience of higher education moves seamlessly from a condition of relative dependency to the condition of the 'autonomous learner': confidently creative, a self-reliant researcher, someone equipped with generic skills which will enable a lifetime of flexible learning. Obligatory institutional Learning and Teaching Strategies, and documents such as the *Quality Assurance Agency Subject Benchmarks* (and at a more generic level the National Qualifications Framework) codify a narrative of growing independence leading to the capacity for lifelong learning. Yet there is much evidence that for all but a minority of students these admirable objectives remain largely aspirational. In this final chapter we would like to gather up the themes of both project and book in relation to the narrative of learner independence. Inevitably, what we have to say will in some ways question or at least complicate that narrative. While fully in favour of articulating, researching and enhancing the student experience, we believe that the subject matter of English Studies in itself presents obstacles to a technology of the self. These are important obstacles in that they compel attention to the roots of human self-imagining. The learning processes that are the subject of this book offer a way of thinking about the learning subject not as a success-bound individual locked in economic competition with others, but as an active participant in lifelong learning communities. In taking on the challenge of moving students towards inter-dependence in their active reading and transformative writing activities we will begin with an outline of our Level 3 independent study module 'Writing Back'. We then move on to speculate about the possible place of such modules in the wider world.

WRITING BACK

As expected, then, at Level 3, this is a more advanced negotiated learning module which allows for greater freedom and greater academic flexibility than the work produced in the second year. Again it is an optional module but it carries 'Writing for Reading' as its pre-requisite since nobody could be expected to dive straight into Level 3 work without proper active reading groundwork. The key features of the module are: first, its negotiated learning status; second, its lack of seminars and lectures; and third, its requirement for a writer's journal which counts for half of the final mark. The other half of the assessment is the production of a completed and autonomous writing project, a stand-alone crafted piece that has been developed and redrafted in response to one or more source texts chosen by the writer.

A number of important considerations arise in relation to the fostering of independence and personal, critical/creative development at Level 3, these are by no means specific to our own modules on this project but cut across much of the research and work that is inevitably produced by students in their final year. People at this last stage in their undergraduate career (semester six) are aware that this is the final chance to improve their marks and possibly move into a higher band if they can pull it off. There is an awareness that poor scores at this stage will have actual consequences in their overall classification (particularly true at our institution which weights Level 3 at 75 per cent). From the outset, then, we have a strange if not quite uncomfortable scenario: on the one hand there exists a greater freedom for students to explore and write back against texts of their own choosing, on the other a feeling grows that such freedom carries consequences and penalties. Add into the mix that this is also the writing-up stage for the English Dissertation Project and it becomes very clear that no small amount of self-organization and self-discipline will be necessary.

For the reasons mentioned above there is an added responsibility for the active reading tutor. He or she must be able to set clear goals, to suggest suitable directions for research and to frame carefully not only suggestions for how the work might proceed, but to draw realistic boundaries within which such explorations might fruitfully develop at the behest of the learner. This last is the area where things are apt to go wrong, or at least where such a danger certainly prowls. There are four main actions that can be taken in order to avoid potential pitfalls in this area and we have considered these in turn below.

Action number one involves the writing and signing of the negotiated learning contract. This is not a lengthy or demanding document in itself, partly because in the first half of the module it is subject to alteration by both parties and partly because a semi-structured approach has by its nature more give in the system than a tightly formulated document.

There is more to this, in truth, at a pedagogic, and even at an ideological level, and we must not underplay these deeper considerations: in order to encourage a smoother transition from the tutor-setting goals (at Level 2) to the student-setting goals (at Level 3), certain modes of linguistic and discursive engagement are appropriate to gradual induction and others are not. This is about confidence and about the individual learner's ability to re-tailor and renegotiate expectations in relation to specific aims and outcomes. It is wrong, for example, to believe that by semester six the candidates all know the rules of the game, the lie of the land on which they will be graded. This is simply not the case. From the educational point of view, we need a practical contract that is clear, accessible and relatively unthreatening, since it will actually form one of the criteria upon which the final writing is marked. From the ideological aspect, we need a contract that relates to the value systems and beliefs of both parties without wilfully importing ethical dilemmas which run counter to the stated aims of the project at hand. It needs to be a workable document grounded in the functions that the writer will actually perform – what areas are to be explored, what changes are to be made, what authors and source texts are to be addressed. We have seen learning contracts that run on for pages and pages, attempting to cover every possible eventuality in the learning or research experience. We resist such closed formulations as exactly the kind of impediment that turns learners into passive recipients of knowledge chunks instead of dynamic makers of their own enjoyable creations. Besides, the contract is ongoing, subject to uncertain swerves in direction, and amenable at all times to critical interaction and intervention. A page of A4 is long enough for these purposes, and an initial contract is shown below.

Example of a Level 3 'Writing Back'
negotiated learning contract

Name: Gemma Quinn

Initial writing contract (subject to alteration until week six):

Anticipated contact time with tutor: half an hour every fortnight?

- Series of 6 or so paintings by Edvard Munch
- Explore one main emotion per picture
- Expressionism exploration – theory/art history
- Different experimentation with genre/style
- Short story maybe (and/or poem)
- Parody of other authors?

- More contemporary chronology probably
- Change location/setting/space
- Development of multiple pieces to begin with
- Research Munch etc. – build in links (modernism)

I've found these paintings (a series really) by the Norwegian artist, Munch, and I want to write back against them. I'm not sure if I can relate them fully to modernist theory (Expressionism) but I'll try a few different styles and see how it goes. I'll bring in the paintings so you can have a look. Maybe I'll only use one or two in my final project but I'll see how the word limit goes. I might write a poem, but will try fiction too.

Tutor's comments

Gemma, I think you've chosen a fascinating topic here and I look forward to seeing how you develop it. I think you'll have to be careful, as you mention, not to take on too much material, but your idea, in principle, to build modernist theory into your response is a (potentially) strong one. What did you have in mind with change of location/setting? This might need to be handled rather carefully. Anyway, yes – it gets the green light. Let's amend it and sign it off together on Wednesday after I've seen the pictures.

signed (writer) _____ date:
signed (tutor) _____ date:

   Action number two: to help students develop their problem-framing and boundary-setting there is the writing journal itself, and this has a number of compulsory parts which we stipulate in the module handbook that it should include: weekly reflection on the process, including research; draft work and experimental writing itself; consideration of the negotiated learning structure of the module; and, at the end, a more formal critical appraisal of the completed writing project. It takes a few weeks for participants to actually get into their journals, and some are likely to require more guidance than others, but when they do it becomes a real and valuable tool for their own thoughts and output. Some liken it to the reading journal we ask them to keep at Level 1, while others see it more as a writer's notebook, a collection point for stray ideas, unanticipated details or noteworthy secondary material. Part scrap-book, part mnemonic device, it acts as an extension of the writer's hand in the important process of externalization that we have described elsewhere. It differs from the creative writer's notebook in that it is always responding to an already written text by another writer. This lends it a meta-functional and partly (though not always) meta-cognitive element since the student is constantly monitoring his or her outpourings in the context of an already written (you might call it parallel) text. This activity bears certain resemblances to the production or use of a hypertext site on the Internet. It contains active links to live ideas, cross-references to other sources of information, pictures and diagrams of the ongoing work and jottings which may or may not be revisited or mentally clicked upon. Indeed the ideas not used, the dead links, as it were, are often more telling as evidence of progress than the routes actually taken. As much as anything, the journal seems to operate as evidence of decisions made, evidence of the routes not taken, and as such it holds some valency or potential for the future as well as being a record of the immediate past. Above all, we believe, it holds something beyond its immediate purposes, something that is almost impossible to recover or reproduce by other means, and this is texture, the near-physical aura or affective essence of any handmade object. Set alongside the final writing project itself, these are often meaningful things in the sense of David Jones or D. H. Lawrence. They have word-object value as well as being simply assignments, and again this is why 'Writing Back' is a module that is remembered long after the individual has graduated.

Action number three, to help participants guard against poor projects is in fact an actual action, the organization of two meetings. Although we have stated that there are no actual seminars or lectures in the delivery, and that this is a significant signal in itself as to our expectations for autonomous learning, there are nevertheless two group meetings – one at the start and one in week 8 (of 15) – which seek to achieve specific objectives within the cohort. We book the rooms in advance of the module and I have bulleted the key features of Group Meeting One and Group Meeting Two here:

Meeting One (week one)

- Introduce and account for the different nature of this module
- Remind participants of the work they completed in Writing for Reading
- Share the portfolios submitted by previous participants (with permission)
- Talk through expectations of the negotiated aspects of the module
- Ask that individuals have a first stab at the initial learning contract
- Encourage support and mutual reinforcement regarding the tasks ahead
- Arrange dates for the first one-to-one meetings with the tutor

---

Meeting Two (week eight)

- Circulate a list of all the participants' projects that are underway
- Ask for a five-minute summary of each project by each person attending
- Provide time for open-forum feedback (questions and answers)
- Make consideration of marking criteria and ensure that projects meet these
- Identify and encourage future developmental meetings between similar topics
- Reassure participants that their work is valued and relevant to the module
- Address any matters arising as projects are taken into the final stage

---

Action number four: our final inoculation against ill framing and under-performance in 'Writing Back' might be labelled 'theory support'. In the selection of which text or texts to write back against, a selection which includes visual, musical and cultural texts as well as the conventionally literary, provision needs to be made for theoretical ballast or at the very least an informed contextual underpinning for the writing research. This, for us, is often the exciting part: one person may be engaged in a psychoanalytic project; another in a geographical mode; a third exploring gender-related questions; a fourth with therapeutic or healing overtones. Occasionally we will see work that is directly aimed at the kind of professional development discussed in the previous chapter, writing that tends towards journalism, freelancing, multi-media or reporting/reviewing. Finding the theory to underpin such projects is likely to be almost totally bespoke, and it is precisely such linguistic and epistemological tailoring that lends energy and originality to some of the high-scoring assignments we have experienced.

I (Chris Thurgar-Dawson) am going to end this first section of our final chapter not with two case studies, but with two writerly moments in order to illustrate the movement towards high achievement in transformative writing.

Writing Back: Moment One (Matt)

I meet Matt for a writing tutorial mid-week, mid-semester. He has been working with the history of *NME* (*New Musical Express*) while writing his own reviews of raves and gigs in the North East. His source texts, then, derive from the sub-genre of music journalism: articles from the 1970s onwards and, as ever, he comes into my room having had another all-nighter in Newcastle. He has reached that beyond-tiredness stage but is desperate to punch out his copy (which he'll be paid for) reviewing the band he's just seen. It is 9 am and he hasn't eaten. He shows me his work and the features of the *NME* piece he's based it on from several decades ago. I have to say I'm impressed. Matt is doing the double-outcome thing – crossing boundaries that would not normally be crossed in other modules. But this is OK. We've negotiated this from the start and it's all documented and signed off in our safety net, so actually we're completely on topic here. Matt leaves after we've had some coffee and set new goals for our next meeting. I'm not sure he'll actually make a music journalist when he graduates in a few months, but he's certainly an autonomous writer already, hitting the learning outcomes by reviewing the front-end of the music industry all night.

Writing Back: Moment Two (Bob)

At 84 years of age, Bob is a mature student. His project is something of a life review for him and he's writing back against a video (*A Century in Stone* by Craig Hornby). It is about mining in the Eston Ironstone Mines just South of Middlesbrough, near a pit village called California. Bob worked in the mining and engineering community there before he served in the Second World War. I'm learning a lot from Bob; in fact we all are. At the same time as finishing his degree, he's caring for his sick wife, Mary (who I later meet at graduation), as well as making a recording of his own about his experiences in Teesside before the university (technical college as was) was built. Bob coughs and splutters his way through our meeting and confesses he's fed up with all the '–isms' of theory. 'Spoil-sports,' he says. He tells me about his friends killed in the mine, about their attempts to defeat TB in the 1930s and about those other friends he knew, killed in action. All the time he's relating what he says to scenes in the video source text, fiddling with his hearing aid, and responding to my prompts in good grace. How can I help Bob to a better mark in his final few weeks, I'm thinking.

EQUIPMENT FOR LIVING[60]

Throughout this book we have sought to describe and advocate nego-tiation between communities. In the course of that negotiation, students develop greater control over their own curriculum and their own learn-ing. As indicated in the Introduction and in Chapter 1, we have no quarrel with the contemporary insistence on documenting and working with the grain of the student experience. Quite the reverse. At the same time we believe that nobody's interests are served (certainly not those of students themselves) if universities, in horror of losing custom, compel scholar teachers to abdicate their responsibilities to knowledge and culture. Students must indeed do their own learning. And in universities, as to some degree in most educational institutions, learning takes place to a greater or lesser degree under the auspices of teachers. But in turn that dialogic process takes place within the knowledge environment of disciplines. Each human element within this dynamic triangle owes respect to the other, just as both in turn owe respect to the community of knowledge. University teachers may inculcate respect for knowledge through their own respect for their students. But that respect need not mean capitulation to fads, cool or inter-generational derision. For responsibility to knowledge is not simply the product of a recondite, ivory-tower nostalgia, the displacement activity of sad people: it is a social and ethical responsibility. To leave knowledge and the struggle with knowledge out of the diagram would be to short-change a whole generation of learners.

All this prefaces a response to a charge to which we believe this book could be vulnerable. Briefly stated, that charge is that in advocating these kinds of learning activity we are betraying the scholarly study of literature and culture, replacing hard-won knowledge with word games, pastiche or parody, well-wrought, 'timeless' texts with ephemeral student effusion. We think we can deflect these charges, weighty though they are. Building on the performative, inferential nature of the reading process, we have attempted to carry out a process of pedagogic translation. It is not that we think that the study of Keats should be replaced with writing limericks, or *Pride and Prejudice* with the Level 1 equivalent of *Bridget Jones's Diary*. What we do think is that the realm of dedication and knowledge in which 'English people' believe has become more and more arcane, and that the protocols of 'reading English' inherited either from literary historical scholarship or from literary criticism now have a very limited currency. In any case, the total immersion model of being a student, dominant in the elite universities of the mid-twentieth century, is now residual. In these circumstances it behoves 'English' to key into the multiple identities, intelligences and aptitudes of its students. We are not going to lure students into the subject either by colluding with them in an 'information model' of knowledge, or by beating them over the head with all they do not know. But a love of culture, literature, varied and nuanced discourse, might take root in the kind of activities and within the learning environments which are the subject of this project and this book.

As university teachers, we should not fall into the trap of assuming that universities were, are now, or ever could be the sole home of knowledge. But a hyperactive, orally-fixated consumer society requires agencies (schools, museums, libraries, publishers, universities among them) which create, preserve and circulate knowledge and values on a longer-term basis than instantly consumable fashion. Schools and universities are themselves habitats, learning communities which promote satisfactions and fulfilments with an extended timescale, a shelf life which spans generations. This perception makes it, if anything, more incumbent on teachers to find ways of translating and making available their subject matter to the speakers of other discourses. The constructivist tradition that goes back to Vygotsky offers teachers the role of creating the conditions for leaps of insight or imagination. In this model they create and safeguard the collaborative contexts for making sense. This is ultimately an ethical relationship in that it concerns values and choices. In languages and cultures – as in any other disciplinary area – it requires us to pay vigilant attention to the creation of habitats for learning.

Gregory Bateson, anthropologist and communication theorist, was one of the first people to enquire into what difference impending environmental crisis must make to the nurture of human potential. In his important and teasing book of essays *Steps to an Ecology of Mind* (1972), he rested his theory of a healthy ecology of human civilization on the need for flexibility. He argued the importance of 'the distribution of flexibility among the many variables of a system'. To 'get out of the grooves of fatal destiny in which our civilization is now caught' would, he argued, require above all social flexibility (472). Responding to this argument, we suggest that both texts and learning groups may advantageously be seen as small-scale eco-systems: environments where every element impacts upon every other, yet where learners may practise symbolic action with a degree of safety. Literary reading performs symbolic communities into being, but literary academics should never underestimate the layered knowledges and skills required for successful function in this domain. If our students are to acquire the aptitudes we expect of them, then many of them will require guidance along the road. Students have not necessarily learned how to learn when they reach us – or, perhaps, panicked by the transfer from sixth form or Access course to university, they may revert to old stereotypes and abandoned habits. In all but a hardy or well-supported minority, intellectual and social stress (reinforced by public rhetorics about the 'value' of your degree) breed dependency. The 'Active Reading' project aims to create relatively safe learning spaces in which students can learn from teachers, from each other, and – above all – from themselves. In doing so they engage ever more fully with the exigencies of language and of verbal artefacts.

Within and beyond English Studies, many university teachers are commenting upon the embattled (and frequently defeated) relationship to written language exhibited by contemporary students. The subject is explored at length in *Writing Matters*, the recent Royal Literary Fund (RLF) report on its fellowship scheme.[61]

No optimistic gloss can be put upon it. No artfully crafted explanation will work. Large numbers of contemporary British undergraduates lack the basic ability to express themselves adequately in writing. Many students are simply not ready for the demands that higher education is making – or should be making – of them. The experience of the Royal Literary Fund Fellows has yielded an extraordinary consensus. From a wide variety of backgrounds, educational experiences, political and social starting points, all have reached the view that student writing is in need of urgent attention.

There may be debate about the causes, and about the prognosis, but there is unanimity about what the Fellows have seen. The single word that crops up most in describing what they have found in entering contemporary higher education institutions is 'shock'. None of them could have predicted that the writing ability of so many students would prove to be so inadequate. (2006: 7)

Central to the solutions offered by the RLF fellowship scheme is one-to-one tutorial attention from a writer. In a different way, and focusing on a single disciplinary group, our own project aims to inculcate in students some sense of belonging. Not in the sense of belonging to an elite or an exclusive community. We are talking about creating a space in which students feel that their insertion into language, their words, *matter* to someone else. Feeling that, they may acquire the confidence to treat difficult discourses as a habitat for which they too possess maps and in which they can learn to talk to the natives. The recovery of pleasure offers an enabling matrix for sophisticated writing and reading. Thus we advocate something akin to what Paul Dawson calls 'reading from the inside' (Dawson 2005: 49, 66–71). He is here engaged in a dialogue with Norman Foerster, one of the architects of the Iowa Writers Workshop, whom he quotes:

> One of the best ways of understanding imaginative literature is to write it, since the act of writing – the selection of materials, the shaping of them, the recasting and revising – enables the student to repeat what the makers of literature have done, to see the processes and problems of authorship from the inside. The time he spends in writing poems, stories, or plays ... will not be lost; pen, paper, and wastebasket are the apparatus of a laboratory second only in importance to the central laboratory of the literary scholar – the library ... (2005: 71)

Throughout, we understand insider status not in the sense of having a passport to enter the Ark, but of feeling licensed to take pleasure in the acquisition and practice of strange and difficult languages. Writing and reading, we have claimed throughout are symbiotic practices. We are addressing a context where, increasingly, university teachers are reporting a dispiritedness about reading among their students. So we would like to suggest the applicability – for a different level of the education system – of the words of the 2000 OECD Report *Reading for Change: Performance and Engagement Across Countries*:

> Struggling readers need both motivational and cognitive support. Motivational support is increased through real-world interaction, interesting texts, autonomy and collaboration (with peers) . . . There is evidence that cognitive strategy instruction is ineffective in isolation from a rich content domain . . . Cognitive and non-cognitive components of reading clearly go hand in hand. Cognition and motivation, proficiency and engagement in reading have an entangled relationship . . . Contemporary models of reading instruction aimed at fostering reading proficiency . . . stress that proficiency cannot be improved without taking into consideration the non-cognitive components of reading engagement: motivation and access to interesting and meaningful reading materials. (OECD Programme for International Student Assessment, 2000: 122, http://www1.oecd.org/publications/e-book/9602071E.PDF)

In our view, there is nothing sentimental or cosy about the programme of situated learning which is the subject of this book. We do not set out to offer 'active reading' practice (any more than literary languages) as a sheltered or utopian domain. Individually or in groups, students will still need to come to terms with writing as the representation and negotiation of 'things hard for thought': suffering, loneliness, guilt, exploitation, betrayal. Learning itself commonly involves the often painful loss of previous identities and communities. One frequent reaction can be passivity and dependence. Our invitation to teachers and students is to collaborate in developing forms of verbal and social activity that stimulate rather than dam energy and attentiveness. We certainly do not want to disable the capacity for critique, or for alert suspicion. But we have sought to make a case that a stark binary division between politicized critique and de-politicized expression is no longer (if it ever was) tenable. It has in fact been abandoned by many of its former proponents. Joy in the process of verbal making does not automatically entail uncritical submission to a narcissistic culture of self-expression. The confident, engaged writer can write against, as well as with, the grain of an unjust consumer society.

Finally, we want to make clear that we are not arguing that the kind of activities undertaken in modules such as these should be *all* that students of literature and culture do. An undergraduate programme made up solely of re-creative writing would have largely lost its point. We see the 'Active Reading' project as complementing other kinds of learning, encouraging synoptic insight and intellectual stamina across what in modular systems may often be experienced as discrete units. In the same way, drafting and portfolio work of the sort we recommend complements, but does not seek to replace, the traditional analytical essay. In the end, we hope that what students who have been involved in these modules take away with them into the increasingly labile communities of the globalized economy is a capacity for pleasure in written words and in the processes of knowledge. Active reading, in fact.

Appendix 1

SAMPLE ACTIVITIES

In the main body of the text we have tried from the outset to include examples of participant activities (in boxes). We hope that these might act as a kind of parallel text to the main content itself, forming part of a reciprocal narrative that seeks to move beyond ready answers or passive interpretation. However, for those who wish to try out some active reading in their own classes, we include here several hands-on exercises which can be altered to fit various academic contexts. For additional flexibility, we have ensured that the examples do not relate to specific source texts. As with other transformational tasks, our intention is to make explicit and enjoyable those inferential processes which, when recognized as such, act as triggers for personal development. Timings are for guidance only, depending on numbers and experience. Lastly, we include an encouraging reminder that such active reading exercises often work best when used not in bespoke writing modules, but in entirely conventional literature seminars. Here, we expect, lies their true contribution.

Exercise 1 (60 minutes)

1   Find a brief paragraph in a novel or short story that describes a specific event – not too long as this is your source text. (5 mins)
2   Now rewrite this event from a complete stranger's point of view, changing the location but not the time in which the event is set. (30 mins)
3   Share your version aloud with someone else in the room. (5 mins)
4   What difficulties did you face when completing this task? What choices did you make and why? Make a note of these. (10 mins)
5   Finally, how did your own rewrite change your interpretation of the original paragraph? Summarize your discussion/thoughts in the space below. (10 mins)

Exercise 2 (90 minutes)

1 Go out and find a poster or notice with some written text on it. This will be your source text. (10 mins)
2 Select your favourite eight words or phrases from it and build them into a short experimental poem on a topic of your choice. Give it a cunning title. (30 mins)
3 Now work out how best to perform or read your poem in front of others: which words to emphasize; how fast or slow certain bits might be; physical gestures to accompany the performance . . . and so on. Mark up your poem with prompts in the margin (perhaps use a highlighter pen?). (10 mins)
4 Return to the workshop and educate your neighbour about your new poem and your performance instructions. She or he will need to be quite clear about your prompts. Find some space and give it a dry run. Naturally, you will receive the same information and guidance from them on their poem. (20 mins)
5 Showtime! (c.20 mins)

Exercise 3 (90 minutes)

1 In the envelope on your desk you'll find a map. The map is your source text. Choose three places on it and circle them. Mark them A, B and C. (5 mins)
2 Write a piece of travel literature that takes you on your journey from A to C, via B. Look out for landmarks, imaginary scenery, evidence of old myths and monsters on the way. Perhaps you stop for a picnic or at a pub. Maybe you meet someone or something. You can be as creative as you like on this, but do remember to demonstrate clear links to the map. Mode of transport is up to you . . . possibly a mix? (45 mins)
3 You'll be given the opportunity to share your text with the rest of the group for feedback. If your content is sensitive or might cause offence, remember to give any warnings in advance (see group contract). (40 mins)

Exercise 4 (120 minutes)

1 DRAFTING: This week's short story from the anthology was highly detailed. Choose two minor characters from it and write a conversational dialogue about the events in the story from their perspective. Remember that your own rewriting of the story must

make suggestive and careful use of the source text itself. Feel free to
change the time/place/language as you wish. (50 mins)

2   EDITING: Re-read your first draft of the dialogue and edit it down
into a tighter, less wordy version. Change or delete any phrases or
clauses that do not contribute to the overall piece. Think about the
effects you are trying to achieve in your own version. Make a note of
them as you go. (30 mins)

3   REFLECTING: Get into a small group of three or four and share
your work. Ask other people for their constructive feedback on your
writing and do the same for them. Remember to help each group
member with any points you feel could be improved, or perhaps
done another way. Saying 'yeah great' is not much use to them!
Write down any constructive help you receive. (30 mins)

4   PLENARY: I'll make sure there's time to share one or two at the end
with everyone. (10 mins)

Exercise 5 (60 minutes)

1   In pairs, choose a short poem from your anthology and analyse it in
conventional critical terms. (20 mins)

2   Individually, write a passage (maybe a stanza or two) of your own
that you can smoothly insert into the middle of the poem with as
little disruption as possible to the kind of language, metre, rhythm
and imagery used by the writer. (20 mins)

3   Read your new whole poem to the other person and explain what you
were hoping to achieve. How did the insertion of your own text alter
your understanding of the original, unaltered source text? (20 mins)

Exercise 6 (120 minutes)

1   In small groups, define what you understand by the term 'parody'.
Make notes as you go along so that everyone is working to the same
brief. Refine these notes to a set of four agreed 'rules' for parody. (30
mins)

2   By yourself, select a text from one of our set anthologies and write
your own parody according to the four rules you outlined above. (60
mins)

3   Return to the group and share your output. Explain your use of the
rules and listen carefully to how others used them. Make a note of
any feedback you receive. (30 mins)

Exercise 7 (45 minutes)

1 Identify a paragraph or verse that focuses on one of the five senses (sight, touch, hearing, taste or smell). (10 mins)
2 Keeping as much of the general detail and context of the source text as you can, change only the sense through which the passage is experienced into one of the other four. If it was mainly sight, have a go at translating it into sound; if smell was primary, have a go at touch, and so on. (30 mins)
3 Even if you didn't get very far, be confident: read what you've written to your neighbour. (5 mins)

Exercise 8 (70 minutes)

1 Circle or highlight the 12 most suggestive keywords or phrases in today's text – the ones that stand out to you as an individual reader. (15 mins)
2 Make a list of these 12 words/phrases on a clean sheet of paper and form them into a short poem that is imaginatively related to your source text. (40 mins)
3 Now write a commentary on the strengths and weaknesses of this exercise as an exercise. What did it achieve and not achieve? What was it for? How could it be improved? (15 mins)

Exercise 9 (120 minutes)

1 In preparation for today's activity, we've all read the same short story. Spend a moment in groups of four reminding each other of its contents and broad themes. (10 mins)
2 Now, as a group, I'd like you to turn the story into a one-act play for performance on the radio. It's up to you how you go about this, but remember that you need at all times to make links and connections to the original story. Number of characters, setting, motivation, resolution and so on are all up to you as a group. You may wish to assign separate roles to each member of your writing team (e.g. stage directions; character development; final editing and so on). (100 mins)
3 Round-up. Keep working on this piece for next time and we'll hear them all then. Use the last ten minutes to sort out what still needs to be done and by whom. (10 mins)

Exercise 10 (80 minutes)

1   The poem we've just read together obviously offers several opportunities for a rewrite. Discuss with your neighbour whether you'd
like to write a prequel or a sequel to it. It can be in prose or poetry.
(10 mins)
2   Find your own space in the room and draft out your prequel or
sequel (but not both!). Make sure you pick up relevant images/links/
language and so on. (40 mins)
3   Find someone you haven't yet worked with and share what you've
written with them. Make detailed reflective notes on your drafts so
you can make a better redraft in the future. How does your added
text at the beginning or the end change the source text? Were you
successful? (30 mins)

Exercise 11 (120 minutes)

1   Our guest writer today is going to read her work. There's a copy of it
on your desk. The reading lasts about 15 minutes. Listen carefully.
As soon as she stops please don't talk but scribble all your thoughts
and reactions to it down on a clean sheet of paper. (15 mins)
2   And we're scribbling ... (15 mins)
3   Now please compare your own jottings with someone else's and
discuss what format or genre you might turn them into. (10 mins)
4   Now have a go at your chosen format. I've invited our guest to work
her way around the room and have a brief word with everyone while
you're doing this. (70 mins)
5   Final thoughts and tidy up ... keep working on this one for next
time. (10 mins)

Exercise 12 (60 minutes)

1   Last week I asked you to bring in a completed piece of work that you
now feel happy with. Please retrieve it and pass it to your left. Since
we're in a circle, you'll receive one from the right. (2 mins)
2   Read the text and make constructive comments on it. Don't be afraid
to say if there's something you think could be improved. (20 mins)
3   Now pass the original *and* your comments to the left again. Similarly, you'll get a set from the right. (2 mins)
4   Now please make your own comments on the original rewriting, but
also write your comments on the comments (if you follow...). (20
mins)

5   When you've finished all this constructive feedback, and when I give
      the signal, please pass your bundle of papers back to the original
      person (i.e. two to the right). You'll get your own back too, of
      course. Please spend the remaining time reflecting on the feedback *in
      writing*. Did you agree with them? Did anything strike you as odd or
      unfair? Did reader one agree with reader two? Ask them if you can't
      follow their comments. (16 mins)

Exercise 13 (120 minutes)

1   We're all at different stages with our various active reading pieces. I
      want to spend today's workshop doing some consolidation work.
      Please simply use the next hour to progress your draft-work, and to
      return to previous unfinished pieces. Do feel free (quietly) to ask
      others' advice, but please respect those who are obviously engaged in
      writing themselves. We'll use the second hour for reading our work
      out and for reflecting on the important commentary element of the
      assessment. (70 mins)
2   Readings and reflection, taking time to enjoy and dwell on the work
      that is being produced by the group. Discussion on how to improve
      the commentary that will accompany every written piece that is
      submitted. (50 mins)

Exercise 14 (90 minutes)

1   Last week I asked you to bring in a short text from another module
      you are studying. Please do a quick 'show and tell' with your
      neighbour. (5 mins)
2   Using what you've brought as your source text, I'd like you to reduce
      it first into a haiku (17 syllables, as per the examples and rules on the
      handout) and then into a tanka (31 syllables, ditto). Make sure you
      get the syllable count and format right in each case. (45 mins)
3   Editing time. Make these two short poems as good as you can by
      altering individual words, punctuation, pacing and images. Think
      about the sound of your poems and their relation to the original
      source text. (10 mins)
4   Group reading/sharing of work produced. (30 mins)

Appendix 2

TEXTUAL EXAMPLES

1. Throughout the project, we have sought to break down the
    assumption that there can be one box labelled 'texts' and another
    labelled 'criticism' or 'critical contexts'. We seek to accustom stu-
    dents to the idea that – alongside critical resources – texts reflect
    upon and write back to each other. As a way of explaining and
    defining the kind of activity we are talking about, we often draw
    students' attention to published examples of literary texts which
    build directly upon another text. It is frequently illuminating to
    tease out the 'active reading' principle in relation to texts they may
    have studied elsewhere in their programme: Jean Rhys's *Wide Sar-
    gasso Sea*,[62] for instance, or Tom Stoppard's *Rosencrantz and Guil-
    denstern Are Dead*, or J.M. Coetzee's *Foe*. Zadie Smith's recent *On
    Beauty* may not have entered the teaching canon yet, but its pretext,
    E.M. Forster's *Howards End* has, and could well be illuminated by
    attention to Smith's appropriation. There are first-year modules
    which are employing Peter Carey's *Jack Maggs* in dialogue with
    Dickens' *Great Expectations*: see, for example http://www.qub.ac.uk/
    en/imperial/austral/Dickens-Carey.htm
        Or again, Angela Carter's story 'Overture and Incidental Music for
    A Midsummer Night's Dream' could suggestively reframe the play for
    those who studied it at school. A workshop combining the energies
    of writing and criticism could be modelled upon a reading of
    Coleridge's 'Kubla Khan' through the lens of Stevie Smith's
    'Thoughts About The Person From Porlock'. We see such texts as
    hubs for further experimentation.
2. Clearly, there is a continuum here. All texts exhibit a propensity to
    quotation, allusion, or even plain old-fashioned susceptibility to
    influence. All teachers of literature take for granted that much of
    their subject matter is literally or metaphorically a translation from
    identifiable sources – Classical myth and the Bible being out-
    standing and almost inescapable examples. Theories of inter-
    textuality, as we noted in Chapter 4, are closely connected to the
    thesis of this book. Further, the awareness of metafiction and the

reflexive nature of texts that became prominent in English Studies in
the early 1980s have major practical and pedagogic implications.
Metafictional texts may themselves be seen as contributions to
creative criticism: the interrogative text questioning, as it does, the
assumed boundaries between fiction and criticism. Thus, a novel
which holds up to attention its own fictive status (say by offering the
reader a choice of more than one ending) not only provokes
engagement, but also offers itself as a starting place for transformative re-creation. We recall a DUET session led by Susan Bassnett,
which took as its basis the Cuban novelist Alejo Carpentier's short
story 'Journey Back to the Source', which tells its story in reverse
chronological order. In doing so, it provides a powerful stimulus to
the re-imagining of other narratives. Again, Julian Barnes' *Flaubert's
Parrot* exemplifies a mixed genre where critical (and biographical)
commentary is interwoven with its own narrative. (And could
profitably lead students back to *Un Coeur Simple*.) In their very
nature, such texts provoke responses which are themselves forms of
re-making.

3. The field is potentially limitless. In the face of this abundance, we
    limit ourselves to talking about texts which patently represent the
    re-writing of a prior text. Teachers of 'active reading' are likely to
    build up their own collection of examples – the contemporary
    publishing success of prequels and sequels constitute another,
    abundant source. And that, of course, is without going further into
    the adjacent domain of film and TV adaptation. This appendix could
    not pretend to be systematic or inclusive. These notes are intended
    simply as a suggestive starting place. Thus, an alternative suggestion
    would be to draw on the apocrypha surrounding a particular text.
    Again, teachers are likely to want to assemble their own lists. But, to
    take a specific example (one suggested by reference to Stoppard), one
    strand in work around *Hamlet* would be an examination (through
    different and more or less 'creative' modes of writing) of the muta-
    tions the play has undergone in parallel with its perpetual reincar-
    nation on stage. Thanks to the British Library's Quarto Digitization
    Project (www.bl.uk/treasures/shakespeare/homepage.html), active
    textual work could well begin from an examination of the con-
    temporary para-text represented by Q1, the so-called 'Bad Quarto'.
    (Without entering into the argument about the status of the text, we
    could invite students to re-invent an actor or reader's garbled
    memory of any play on which they are working as a fore-text for
    discussion. Students would then be invited to identify what themes
    or personal or cultural interferences had governed the fragments of
    memory.) The interplay of criticism and creative re-appropriation is
    instantiated in Graham Holderness's novel *The Prince of Denmark*

(University of Hertfordshire Press 2002), itself in turn illuminated by his *Textual Shakespeare: Writing and the Word* (University of Hertfordshire Press 2003) – on *Hamlet* see specifically Chapter 7. Indeed, the argument of *Textual Shakespeare* resonates in many ways with our own procedures. Over the years we have used both Zbigniew Herbert's 'Elegy of Fortinbras' and Ursula Fanthorpe's 'Mother-in-Law' (in the group of Shakespeare poems 'Only Here for the Bier') as starting places for the re-orientation of point of view. Or again, Ophelia's madness – apart from being the subject of Elaine Showalter's luminous and much-anthologized essay 'Representing Ophelia: Women, Madness, and the Responsibilities of Feminist Criticism' – has resurfaced in transmutations as various as the paintings of John Everett Millais and John W. Waterhouse (easily accessible on the Internet), and more recently in Angela Carter's *Wise Children*.

4. While, as readers will be aware, we are uneasy about the identification of 'active reading' simply with pastiche or parody, there is of course a mass of suggestive material to be found in anthologies of parody such as William Zaranka's *Brand-X Anthology of Poetry* (Applewood 1981), the *Faber Book of Parody*, or in individual collections such as Wendy Cope's *Making Cocoa for Kingsley Amis* (1986). Enrichment ideas for our narratological starting activity of asking students to summarize novels in 60- or 100-word 'mini-sagas' might be derived from E.O. Parrott's *How to Become Ridiculously Well Read in One Evening* (Penguin 1986). (Or David Bader's *One Hundred Great Books in Haiku*, Viking Penguin 2005.) Colleagues may well have to hand over their own favourite examples of parody. These might include classic parodies such as Henry Reed's 'Chard Whitlow' ('As we get older we do not get any younger'), or Lewis Carroll's 'Aged, aged Man' ('I'll tell thee everything I can; There's little to relate . . .') embedded as he is in the White Knight's own elaborate metafiction.

5. We implied earlier that the translation and re-appropriation of Classical myth was adjacent to, but lay beyond, our immediate purview. We would like to make one exception and briefly take up an example we have used in recent workshops with teachers. These workshops were designed to explore 'active reading' by taking up the idea of 'echo' as a metaphor which resonates with both intertextuality and teaching. For these workshops we made available (or requested participants to read) a group of texts. These began with the Latin text of Ovid's story of Echo and Narcissus from the *Metamorphoses*, a prose translation (Penguin or Loeb), Arthur Golding's 1567 translation of the relevant section, and Ted Hughes' *Tales from Ovid*. (We also at different times used examples of poems – from

Christina Rossetti and Tennyson to Ken Smith – which simultaneously meditate upon and employ the sound properties of 'echo'. So a starting place for using Tennyson's 'The splendour falls on castle walls' can be a playing of the setting from Benjamin Britten's 'Serenade for Tenor, Horn and Strings'.) The workshops were themselves self-referential in giving participants the opportunity to reflect upon their own experience as teachers-temporarily-become-students, and on the 'echoes' set up with other learning experiences. As early stages for a workshop, which became a dialogue on textuality and on teaching, we offered various activities, all of which participants were invited to modify or abandon according to their own inclinations or the direction in which the writing itself led: the collection of 'found' images as the starting places for their own poems; the selection of lines to build into their own macaronic poem, or a set form, e.g. villanelle; re-writing a key moment from a different point of view; straight or free 'translation' from the original or from one of the subsequent versions; 'editing down': to what basic metaphors or narrative could you reduce this text and still preserve a germ of meaning? We preface this workshop by inviting a group collection and consideration of myths and cultural memories which still have widespread currency: Faust, Robin Hood, Don Juan, Frankenstein, 'fairy tales' (Red Riding Hood), the Flood. This can lead to re-workings of these stories – an activity which can also be stimulated through a reading of, for example, Liz Lochhead's early poems (*Dreaming Frankenstein*), or Angela Carter's variations on Bluebeard or wolf stories.

6. Another area in which students might be interested to build and annotate their own anthologies has to do with the overlay of textual re-appropriation upon forms of homage to the author. For reasons which may have a lot to do with Harold Bloom's 'anxiety of influence', there are strong traditions of such homage between male poets, and students can be invited to trace out the implications of poems like Ezra Pound's 'A Pact' ('I make a pact with you, Walt Whitman/I have detested you long enough'). Students' own parallel texts could be threaded around readings of Pound and Whitman himself. In critical terms, such activity can then lead on to a dynamic consideration of the relations between influence and revolt, or the nature of the imagined community to which a writer feels the need to belong. We would like to conclude this appendix by taking the example of the recent flurry of novels which – obliquely or directly – take Henry James as their subject.[63] While these novels do not attempt a stylistic approximation to James, we suggest that extracts such as those below might be used with students alongside excerpts of critical writing to exemplify the making and re-making of the

figure of the author. All are novels which seek and demonstrate proximity to the writing process and the springs of creativity. The pursuit through writing or traditional criticism of the haunting of Henry James might lead students to a reading in and of James that deepened and went beyond a passing Level 1 acquaintance with 'The Turn of the Screw'. Alternatively, it might provide a starting place for 'conversations' with other authors.

Echoes of the Master: A Starting Place

The Anglo-American novelist Henry James (1843–1916) has enjoyed an extensive after-life. Staple ingredients of university English programmes, his many novels and stories are constantly being republished. He is the subject of a vast critical industry, and in recent years many of his novels (e.g. *The Portrait of a Lady*, *The Europeans*, *The Wings of the Dove*) have been the subject of film adaptations. More recently still, James himself has become the subject of several novels and fictive biographies. In this session we would like to broach questions about the meaning of this phenomenon of male novelists writing about a male novelist.

'I'm starting at UCL next month; doing graduate work in English.'
'Ah ... yes ...' Lord Kessler's faint smile and tucked-in chin suggested an easily mastered disappointment. 'And what is your chosen field?'
'Mm. I want to have a look at *style*,' Nick said. This flashing emphasis on something surely ubiquitous had impressed the admissions board, though Lord Kessler appeared uncertain. A man who owned Mme de Pompadour's escritoire could hardly be indifferent to style, Nick felt; but his reply seemed to have in mind some old wisdom about style and substance.
'Style *tout court*?'
'Well, style at the turn of the century – Conrad, and Meredith, and Henry James of course.' It all sounded perfectly pointless, or at least a way of wasting two years, and Nick blushed because he really was interested in it and didn't yet know – not having done the research – what he was going to prove.
'Ah,' said Lord Kessler intelligently: 'style as an obstacle.'
Nick smiled. 'Exactly ... Or perhaps style that hides things and reveals things at the same time.' For some reason this seemed rather near the knuckle, as though he were suggesting Lord Kessler had a secret. 'James is a great interest of mine, I must say.'
'Yes, you're a James man, I see it now.'
'Oh absolutely!' – and Nick grinned with pleasure and defiance, it

was a kind of coming out, which revealed belatedly why he wasn't
and never would be married to Trollope.

'Henry James stayed here, of course. I'm afraid he found us rather
vulgar,' Lord Kessler said, as if it had only been last week. (Alan
Hollinghurst, *The Line of Beauty*, Picador, 2004: 54–5).

'It's very interesting to hear you speak of yourself; but I don't know
what you mean by your allusions to your having fallen off,' Paul
Overt observed with pardonable hypocrisy. He liked his companion
so much now that the fact of any decline of talent or of care had
ceased for the moment to be vivid to him.

'Don't say that – don't say that,' St. George returned gravely, his
head resting on the sofa-back and his eyes on the ceiling. 'You know
perfectly what I mean. I haven't read twenty pages of your book
without seeing that you can't help it.'

'You make me very miserable,' Paul ecstatically breathed.

'I'm glad of that, for it may serve as a kind of warning. Shocking
enough it must be, especially to a young fresh mind, full of faith –
the spectacle of a man meant for better things sunk at my age in
such dishonour.' St. George, in the same contemplative attitude,
spoke softly but deliberately, and without perceptible emotion. His
tone indeed suggested an impersonal lucidity that was practically
cruel – cruel to himself – and made his young friend lay an argu-
mentative hand on his arm. But he went on while his eyes seemed to
follow the graces of the eighteenth-century ceiling: 'Look at me
well, take my lesson to heart – for it *is* a lesson. Let that good come
of it at least that you shudder with your pitiful impression, and that
this may help to keep you straight in the future. Don't become in
your old age what I have in mine – the depressing, the deplorable
illustration of the worship of false gods!' (From James's own story
'The Lesson of the Master', 1888)

Over the years he had learned something about the English which
he had quietly and firmly adapted to his own uses. He had watched
how men in England generally respected their own habits until
those around them learned to follow suit ... His habits, of course,
were sociable and, in the main, easy; his inclinations were civil and
his idiosyncrasies mild. Thus it had become convenient to himself,
and simple to explain to others that he should turn down invita-
tions, confess himself busy, overworked, engaged both day and
night in his art. His time as an inveterate dinner guest at the great
London houses had, he hoped, come to an end.

He loved the glorious silence a morning brought, knowing that
he had no appointments that afternoon and no engagements that

evening. He had grown fat on solitude, he thought, and had learned to expect nothing from the day but at best a dull contentment. Sometimes the dullness came to the fore with a strange and insistent ache which he would entertain briefly, but learnt to keep at bay. Mostly, however, it was the contentment he entertained; the slow ease and the silence could, once night had fallen, fill him with a happiness that nothing, no society nor the company of any individual, no glamour or glitter, could equal. (Colm Tóibín, *The Master*, Picador, 2004: 48–9)

Browsing through the pages of his notebook, that precious mine of unworked, richly-veined deposits of raw story-stuff, he was particularly taken with two ideas for novels – one about a widowed father and his daughter, greatly attached to each other, who both married at the same time, then discovered that their respective spouses were in fact lovers, but managed to redeem the ugly situation by nobility of soul and social cunning; the other – over which the spirit of Minnie Temple hovered – about a beautiful rich young woman who contracted a fatal illness which threatened to deprive her of the experience of love, and was exploited by friends poorer and less scrupulous than herself. But the possible narrative development of these ideas remained vague and amorphous ... If you made up a story as you went along, there was always a danger that it would go in too many directions, inhabit the consciousnesses of too many characters, touch on too many themes, to achieve unity and concentration of effect ... But this reflection prompted another. Suppose one were to apply to prose narrative the method he had used in developing his ideas for plays, namely the scenario ...? And then, he thought, with gathering excitement, might not the dramatic principle itself, of presenting experience scenically – 'showing' rather than 'telling' the story. .. might this not give prose fiction the kind of structural strength and elegance it so often lacked, while the narrative artist remained free to *add* the priceless resource, denied to the dramatist, of being able to reveal the secret workings of consciousness in all its dense and delicate detail? (David Lodge, *Author, Author*, Secker and Warburg, 2004: 282–3)

St. George's forty volumes are, at the last, papier-maché. He has sold out. He has betrayed 'the great thing'. He cannot muster the conviction 'the sense of the having done the best – the sense which is the real life of the artist and the absence of which is his death, of having drawn from his intellectual instrument the finest music that nature had hidden in it, of having played on it as it should be played.' Marriage is the impediment: 'Women don't have a conception of such things' (Nietzsche, again). Had the disciple contrived the Master's too many books, 'you'd put a pistol ball in your brains.' The authentic writer must 'be able to be poor.' The coda is merciless: 'I wish you had left me alone,' says the Master to his acolyte.

At stake is the axiom of Yeats's 'The Choice': 'perfection of the life or of the work.' James falters at the noveletish dénouement. The title of the Master's magnum, *Shadowmere* is facile. To Paul Overt he has become 'the mocking fiend'. As often in classic American fiction, the Faust theme lies to hand. (George Steiner, *Lessons of the Masters*, Harvard, 2003: 126)

Appendix 3

EXTRACT FROM NATIONAL TEACHING FELLOWSHIP
PROJECT APPLICATION 2001

Active Reading is a structured process of imitation, variation and experiment: students learn and understand cultural discourses by practising them. This project is addressed to an urgent situation in English Studies. The discipline faces a number of challenges: the increasingly plural and diverse cultures of the student body, the rise of A-level English Language, and the soon to be apparent effects of Curriculum 2000. The subject confronts the loss of a taken-for-granted 'common core' of reading, and the narrowing of the band of 'high' readers during a simultaneous explosion of powerful cultural industries: 'English' now takes place in a highly mediated society. In HE, English is in danger of splitting between 'high status' critical knowledge and theory and 'low status' practice. Alongside the current expansion of creative writing programmes, there is a real need to foster dialogue between writing as expression (or as pragmatic communication) and writing as medium for analysing and historicizing texts. This project seeks to circumvent such divisions by working across the implied boundaries.

 . . . By building on my existing work with structured re-writing, I will research with students ways in which they might through the transformation of texts attain deep knowledge of cultural diversity and the resources of the cultural past. The project seeks to overcome the stark dichotomy between 'critical' and 'creative' activity, or between 'self expression' and impersonal knowledge. It does not concern creative writing as such: rather its originality lies in enhancing linguistic inventiveness. It supplements – rather than supplants – conventional forms (analytical prose: essay, dissertation) with the portfolio of re-writings and creative 'translations'. It examines the sharing and constructive criticism of students' drafts as a basis for developmental dialogue in what Robert Scholes calls the 'craft of reading'.

Aims

Through the Active Reading project I hope to:

- enable understanding of texts and theory through production (re-writing, translation)
- develop bridges between A-level/Access and HE as Curriculum 2000 unrolls
- promote an understanding of culture as dialogue including dialogue between generations
- support students during exposure to unfamiliar or threatening cultural materials
- challenge a widespread perception of HE as purely instrumental
- evolve the reflective portfolio as simultaneously a method of students identifying their own learning needs *and* as a mode of assessment
- involve students in implementation and evaluation
- build pedagogic bridges between English/Literary study and other cognate disciplines
- explore the European dimension of intellectual mobility between cultures.

Notes

1   See, for example, the unjustly neglected 1999 report of the National Advisory
    Committee on Creative and Cultural Education: *All Our Futures: Creativity, Culture
    and Education* (www.dfes.gov.uk/naccce/index1.shtml). See also Rob Pope's recent
    Creativity: Theory, History, Practice (2005).
2   We argue that our approach enables us to meet directly the Benchmark objectives
    excerpted below:

    An undergraduate education in English should

    *   enable students to develop independent critical thinking and judgement;
    *   engage students imaginatively in the process of reading and analysing
        complex and sophisticated literary and non-literary texts;
    *   help students to understand and appreciate the expressive resources of
        language;
    *   problematize the act of reading so that students can reflect critically upon
        textual reception both in history and in their own practice;
    *   promote an understanding of verbal creativity and the formal and aesthetic
        dimensions of literary texts;
    *   develop a range of subject specific and transferable skills, including high-
        order conceptual, literacy and communication skills of value in graduate
        employment;
    *   provide a basis for further study in English or related disciplines and for
        teachers of English at all levels;
    *   provide an intellectually stimulating and satisfying experience of learning
        and studying, within the distinctive framework of English;
    *   encourage in students a sense of enthusiasm for the subject and an
        appreciation of its continuing social and cultural importance.

    (Quality Assurance Agency for Higher Education: English Subject
    Benchmark 1.3)

3   Edited extracts from this chapter were used as a briefing paper for the British
    Council Video Conference 'Higher Education Pedagogy in Literary Studies', 23
    February 2006.
4   There are some parallels between our argument and that of Tim Mayers' *(Re)Writing
    Craft* (2005). Yet his attempt to reconcile Composition and Creative Writing in
    outflanking the dominance of Literature is set in a very different context to that of
    the UK. And Mayers only gives transformative writing an oblique mention (2005:
    149, 154).
5   A vivid example is Ken Jones, *et al.* (2005), 'Investigating the Production of

University English in Mass Higher Education: Towards an alternative methodology', *Arts and Humanities in Higher Education*, 4, 247–64.

6   My use of the term 'tribes' here represents a loose appropriation of the work of Tony Becher (Becher and Trowler 2001).

7   See the English Subject Benchmark Statement (QAA 2000). www.qaa.ac.uk/academicinfrastructure/benchmark/honours/english.pdf

8   I remember being ruefully told by a mature student in one of my own first writing classes that my ideal of a story would be 'In the beginning, the end'. (Cf. Knights 1991).

9   Some of these issues are discussed on the English Subject Centre website at www.english.heacademy.ac.uk/explore/resources/scholarship/index.php

10 See throughout the English Subject Centre website, *Survey of the English Curriculum and Teaching in UK Higher Education*, eds Jane Gawthrope and Philip Martin (Halcrow 2003).

11 See, for example, Evans 1993: 170–3. Note that the language curriculum and the teaching of language have been subject to changes which parallel and perhaps even exceed those in the literature curriculum.

12 A crucial stage in the movement away from stylistics towards post-structuralist theory can be glimpsed in Coward and Ellis 1977.

13 For a retrospect, see Richard Gooder (2005), 'What English Was', *Cambridge Quarterly*, 34, (3).

14 See the English Subject Benchmark 4.1.4 on the essay: 'English students should be required to write essays as a fundamental part of their learning experience'.

15 We draw here on Benedict Anderson's term (Anderson 1983). The signs of strangeness for many of our students go beyond the obvious language differences, or some knowledge of the Bible, Classical Mythology, or the history of art, of classical music or of Europe. They extend, too, to the imaginative lexicon drawn from the natural world and the agrarian presuppositions of the subject as it came to be practised in the mid-twentieth century.

16 The subject criteria and assessment objectives may be accessed on the website of the Qualifications and Curriculum Authority: www.qca.org.uk/2982.html

17 See for example Michelene Wandor, Graeme Harper and Steve May in Siobhan Holland (ed.) 2003, and O'Rourke 2005. The dialogue between creative writing and English is the subject of Paul Dawson's recent *Creative Writing and the New Humanities* (Routledge 2005). Unfortunately, this illuminating book came to hand too late for us to engage fully with its arguments.

18 It is perhaps worth reminding the reader that Raymond Williams was himself a practising novelist.

19 The critical theory literature is full of references to criticism as 'a practice of collusion with the very ambition the text sets itself', of the tendency of the text to 'slip and slide from alibi to alibi' (Musselwhite 1978: 221).

20 For a judicious account of the prolonged tussle over the 'death of the author' see Burke 1992.

21 In the English, Welsh and Northern Irish system, the General Certificate of Education A (advanced) level is the highest academic qualification taken at secondary school, and provides the conventional qualification for university entry. Students normally take it in school years 12 and 13, traditionally known as 'the sixth form'. Since 2000, the A-level (see the previous chapter) has been modularized and divided into AS (advanced subsidiary) and A2.

22 This is now best known for identifying the phenomena which came to be known as 'deep' and 'surface' learning. These approaches became fundamental to those later

developed by Paul Ramsden and others (e.g. Ramsden 2003). A useful summary can be found at www.learning.ox.ac.uk/iaul/IAUL+1+2+2+main.asp

23 For example David Fuller's *Blake's Heroic Argument*. London: Croom Helm (1988).

24 The phrase is Q.D. Leavis's (1932: 270). See also Knights 1978; Baldick 1983; Doyle 1989.

25 'Future Developments of Literary Criticism', Essay submitted for the Members' English Essay Prize, 1929. Unpublished.

26 Lubbock was to take his own programme literally. In 1925 he published his novel *The Region Cloud* (London: Jonathan Cape), the earliest instance known to me of the James apocrypha on which we shall touch in Appendix 2. This is an extensive intertext with a number of James's 'author' stories, like 'The Lesson of the Master', 'The Figure in the Carpet' or 'The Author of Beltraffio'. Fascinatingly, it too is a study in disillusionment. The narrative turns upon the betrayal of the follower by the author to whom he is both reader and disciple.

27 A useful example of a critic turning to creative writing in order to tease out a theoretical point is David Lodge's 'Oedipuss: or, the practice and Theory of Narrative' in Lodge 1981. Here Lodge decided to use the drafts of a story he had recently written 'as an illustrative case, combining authorial introspection with formal analysis in the hope that this bifocal view of a narrative text might throw some light on the laws of narrative in general and literary narrative in particular' (1981: 48).

28 A British example of feminist subversion of theory genres is Diana Collecott's 'A Double Matrix: Re-Reading H.D.' in Sue Roe (ed.), *Women Reading Women's Writing*, Brighton: Harvester Press, 1987. A good example of transaction across the theory–writing border would be the work of Cixous' British advocate, Susan Sellers. See Sellers 1989 and 1991.

29 It was in her dual role as poet and critic that Veronica Forrest-Thomson played a significant part in the early mediation of 'theory' in Britain. Her dialogue with William Empson (not to mention her Ph.D. thesis on Wittgenstein) also suggest links back into the alternative traditions of linguistic criticism touched on in the previous chapter. See also Mark 2001.

30 The metamorphosis of Julia Kristeva or Jacqueline Rose into novelists is highly germane to the argument of this chapter, as was, some years before, that of Umberto Eco.

31 Jean 'Binta' Breeze, 'Verbal Arts in Education: Teaching as Performance', unpublished paper delivered at the 'Verbal Arts Conference: "Next in Text"' at The National Centre for Popular Music, Sheffield, 18 May 2002.

32 See, for example, John Vorhaus, *Creativity Rules: A Writer's Workbook* (Los Angeles: Silman-James, 2000) and Robert Wolf, *Jump-Start: How to Write from Everyday Life* (Oxford and New York: OUP, 2001).

33 Christian McEwen, 'Artists' notebooks: poetry, drawing and creative journaling,' unpublished paper given at the 'National Association for Writers in Education Conference on Writers and Location', St. Mary's College, University of Surrey, 1 May 2004; and Colin Evans, Writing Event 2, 'Annual DUET Workshop: 1999', Stephenson Hall, University of Sheffield, 9 July 1999.

34 Here please refer to our bibliography for useful texts by Murray Cox and Gillie Bolton.

35 See, in particular, 'Calypso', Book Five of *The Odyssey* (London: Penguin, 1981: 89), beginning 'The cave was sheltered by a verdant copse of alders, aspens, and fragrant cypresses ...'

36 For a brief outline relating specifically to English delivery, see Colin Evans (ed.) *Developing University English Teaching* (1995: 1–16).

37   In 2004, the whole cohort of 32 participants gave formal, signed permission to have their week 6 tutorials transcribed and used in this publication. These became known as the 'Active Reading Project Interviews' and we are particularly grateful to all those who took part.

38   See, for example, the informative research by John McLeod, *Narrative and Psychotherapy* (London: Sage, 1997).

39   Norman Holland, *Five Readers Reading* (1975a: 209–10).

40   Martin Heidegger's 'dwelling' argument in *Being and Time* (trans. John Macquarrie and Edward Robinson, Oxford: Blackwell, 1962) is an intertext for Jeff Derksen's underrated long poem, *Dwell* (Vancouver: Talon, 1993).

41   Almost any page of Stevie Smith's *Novel on Yellow Wallpaper* (London: Virago, 1980) seems to me a lesson in condensed clarity, 'Oh flood of tears' flow. Oh sweetest scent of death. Oh disarray, dismay, and dudgeon.' (206). Olson's *The Maximus Poems* (Berkeley and Los Angeles: University of California Press, 1983) may of course appear sprawling but is in fact anything but. Pound's *ABC of Reading* (London: Faber, 1951) famously steals its compression advice from Basil Bunting, 'dichten = condensare' (92), but really all of Chapter 8 can be revisited.

42   I owe my use of triolets to the North-East poet, Bob Beagrie, who has devised powerful creative exercises around this reiterating eight-line form. Our Polish workshop in Warsaw 2005 coped incredibly well with this form in a second language.

43   John Turner, 'The Arbourthorne Project' unpublished paper, 'VAA Conference: "Next in Text," ' 18 May 2002.

44   Turner, 2002.

45   This is Jonathan Tulloch, author of six novels including *The Season Ticket* (2000), which gained popular success as the film *Purely Belter*. Like many RLF Fellows across the country, Jonathan provides professional writing support and guidance to our students.

46   Matthew Arnold, 'The Function of Criticism at the Present Time', *Essays in Criticism: First Series* (1864; 1895: 18–19); and, less well known, perhaps, Dorothy Livesay, 'The Documentary Poem: A Canadian Genre' in Eli Mandel (ed.), *Contexts of Canadian Criticism* (1971: 267–81).

47   On this topic we have found the work of Martin Nystrand and Steven Mailloux useful. The former's *The Structure of Written Communication: Studies in Reciprocity between Writers and Readers* (Academic Press, 1986) is matched by the latter's *Rhetorical Power* (Cornell, 1989). Both are texts that move beyond obvious theorization of negotiation and meaning-making.

48   We recognize that this is a contentious issue and that it is unfair to lump all 'traditional assessment' together. For further general discussion of HE assessment see Entwistle *et al.* (1992), G. Brown *et al.* (1997), Brown and Glasner (1999) and Wakeford (2001).

49   Leafing through Eysenck and Keane (2005) put me on to this, but to get a proper sense of the educational impact of analogical reasoning and related ideas it's best to read the research itself: John E. Hummel and Keith J. Holyoak (2003), 'A symbolic-connectionist theory of relational inference and generalization', *Psychological Review*, 110: 220–64.

50   This remarkable poem, translated from the Serbo-Croat by Francis R. Jones, often paves the way for some very accomplished rewrites. It is available in Neil Astley, (ed.) *Staying Alive: Real Poems for Unreal Times* (2002). In addition, it raises questions about the nature of translation *as itself* a version of active reading.

51   For recent examples of non-academic sociality of reading see Jenny Hartley's *Reading Groups* (2001).

52 I would like to acknowledge here the encouragement of Tim Bond and Malcolm Sweeting, and the support of students on the former Durham MA in Counselling, and on 'Healing Texts' courses, who at a time when these activities were far from conventional, lent encouragement and enthusiasm. For a study of the ways in which literary reading may feed into therapeutic training, see Knights 1995.

53 See Hillis Miller on re-reading *Wuthering Heights*: 'If in Lockwood's dream the air swarms with Catherines, so does this book swarm with ghosts who walk the Yorkshire moors inside the covers of any copy of *Wuthering Heights*, waiting to be brought back from the grave by anyone who chances to open the book and read.' (*Fiction and Repetition* 1982: 72).

54 Perhaps, indeed, as Daniel Gunn and others have argued, Freud should himself be seen as a writer (Gunn 1988: 58).

55 Hunt and Sampson in particular give insight into the MA/PGDip programme in 'Creative Writing and Personal Development' at the University of Sussex. See, throughout, the bibliography provided by LAPIDUS, the society for Literary Arts in Personal Development (www.lapidus.org.uk/resources/index.shtml).

56 As well as Katherine Mansfield, short-story writers we have used in professional development sessions have included Bobbie Ann Mason, Grace Paley, Alice Walker, Eudora Welty and Tillie Olsen. Elizabeth Bowen or Alice Munro, though we haven't actually used their work in this context, would also be good choices.

57 The idea of the thought adventure or thought experiment is deeply germane to the whole process of teaching fiction in professional development. Therapists, after all, seek to persuade clients to frame alternative narratives. Perceptual estrangement arises from invented worlds under conditions of narrative pleasure. This is perhaps particularly vivid in the case of certain kinds of futurist or speculative fiction where the fictive scenario estranges and reframes familiar subjects and dilemmas. In the kind of workshops described we could use, for example, novels like Doris Lessing's *The Marriages between Zones Three, Four and Five*, Ursula Le Guin's *The Left Hand of Darkness*, or dystopian fictions like Margaret Atwood's *The Handmaid's Tale* or Kazuo Ishiguro's *Never Let Me Go*.

58 The thesis is spelled out at considerably greater length in the same authors' *Shakespeare as Prompter* (1994), and in Cox (ed.) *Shakespeare Comes to Broadmoor*, 1992.

59 There is an easily accessible selection of Richard Winter's writings at http:// web.apu.ac.uk/richardwinter/publications.html. He and his colleagues are developing an implication of the 'reflective practitioner' tradition: that 'reflection' itself requires genre, formal scaffolding and linguistic vitality. To make 'connections across more than one mental space' (Turner 1996) we sometimes need more prompting from other imaginations.

60 Here, as elsewhere, we would like to acknowledge the influence of Kenneth Burke. The specific reference here is to his essay 'Literature as Equipment for Living' (1937) in Davis and Finke 1989.

61 *Writing Matters: The Royal Literary Fund Report on Student Writing in Higher Education*, London, 2006. A further observation from the same report is directly relevant to our argument. 'Anxiety is at the heart of many of the problems students experience with their writing ... Unfamiliar with academic writing styles, they seek to emulate, [sic] but without guidance, their writing often only worsens. The result is that many of them feel insecure and see that insecurity as evidence that they don't belong in higher education ...' (2006: 10) We should make clear that the RLF Report applies to all disciplines, not just English Studies.

62 Students may be incited, too, to follow up the doubling back of this trail represented by Derek Walcott's poem 'Jean Rhys' (in *The Fortunate Traveller*), or again his reflections on the meaning of cultural Englishness in Sonnet XXIII of *Midsummer*.

Carrying out 'writing back' and re-appropriation of their own provide students with a luminous route into considerations of the post-colonial. Such consideration, it should perhaps go without saying, would enable them to do something positive with their own sense of being strangers within the culture they have elected to study.

63   Though, as noted in Chapter 3, novels in this vein go back as far as Percy Lubbock's *The Region Cloud* (1925). Which in turn might be seen as re-echoing James' own 'Coleridge' story 'The Coxon Fund'. Parodies of James have a long history, too. See for example Max Beerbohm's classic 'The Mote in the Middle Distance' – available on Project Gutenberg at www.gutenberg.org/files/14667/14667-h/14667-h.htm #mote

Bibliography

Abbs, Peter. 1982. *English Within the Arts: A Radical Alternative for English and the Arts in the Curriculum.* London: Hodder and Stoughton.

Allen, Roberta. 2002. *The Playful Way to Serious Writing.* Boston and New York: Houghton Mifflin.

Anderson, Benedict. 1983. *Imagined Communities: Reflections on the Origin and Spread of Nationalism.* London: Verso.

Armstrong, Isobel. 2000. *The Radical Aesthetic.* Oxford: Blackwell.

Arnold, Matthew. (1865). 'The Function of Criticism at the Present Time', *Essays in Criticism: First Series.* London and New York: Macmillan. Also in Super, R.H. (ed.) 1962. *The Complete Prose Works III Lectures and Essays in Criticism.* Ann Arbor: University of Michigan Press.

Astley, Neil (ed.) 2002. *Staying Alive: Real Poems for Unreal Times.* Newcastle: Bloodaxe.

Attridge, Derek. 2003. *The Singularity of Literature.* London: Routledge.

Baldick, Chris. 1983. *The Social Mission of English Criticism.* Oxford: Oxford University Press.

Barnett, R. 2000. *Realizing the University in an Age of Supercomplexity.* Buckingham: Open University Press.

Barthes, Roland. 1975. *S/Z.* Trans. Richard Miller. London: Cape.

—— [1971] 1986. 'From Work to Text'. Trans. Richard Howard. Rpt. in *The Rustle of Language.* Oxford: Blackwell.

—— 1975. *The Pleasure of the Text.* Trans. Richard Miller. New York: Hill and Wang.

Bateson, Gregory. 1972. *Steps To An Ecology of Mind: Collected Essays in Anthropology, Psychiatry, Evolution, and Epistemology.* London: Intertext.

Becher, Tony and Paul Trowler. 2001. *Academic Tribes and Territories: Intellectual Enquiry and the Cultures of Disciplines.* Buckingham: Open University Press.

Bennett, Andrew (ed.) 1995. *Readers and Reading* (Longman Critical Readers). Harlow: Longman.

Berger, Arthur Asa. 1997. *Narratives in Popular Culture, Media and Everyday Life.* London: Sage.

Bleich, David. 1978. *Subjective Criticism.* Baltimore MD: Johns Hopkins University Press.

—— 1988. *The Double Perspective: Language, Literacy and Social Relations.* New York: Oxford University Press.

—— 2001. 'The Materiality of Language and the Pedagogy of Exchange', *Pedagogy: Critical Approaches to Teaching Literature, Language, Composition, and Culture* 1(1).

Bleiman, Barbara. 1991. *Activities for A-level English.* Harlow: Longman.

Bolton, Gillie. 1998. *The Therapeutic Potential of Creative Writing: Writing Myself.* London: Kingsley.

Brantlinger, Patrick. 2001. *Who Killed Shakespeare? What's Happened to English Since the Radical 60s?* New York: Routledge.

Breeze, Jean 'Binta'. 2002. 'Verbal Arts in Education: Teaching as Performance' (unpublished paper), Verbal Arts Conference: 'Next in Text'. The National Centre for Popular Music, Sheffield, 18 May.

Brooks, Peter. 1994. *Psychoanalysis and Storytelling*. Oxford: Blackwell.

Brown, G., J. Bull and M. Pendlebury. 1997. *Assessing Student Learning in Higher Education*. London: Routledge.

Brown, S., and S. Glasner (eds). 1999. *Assessment Matters in Higher Education*. Buckingham: SRHE and Open University Press.

Bruner, Jerome. 1986. *Actual Minds, Possible Worlds*. Cambridge, MA: Harvard University Press.

—— 1987. 'Life as Narrative'. *Social Research* 54: 11–32.

—— 2002. *Making Stories: Law, Literature, Life*. Cambridge, MA: Harvard University Press.

Bruton, Anthony and Angeles Broca. 1993. *Active Reading: Problem-solving Activities for Developing Reading Skills*. Edinburgh: Nelson.

Burke, Kenneth. 1966. *Language as Symbolic Action: Essays on Life, Literature, and Method*. Berkeley, CA: University of California Press.

—— 1989. 'Literature as Equipment for Living'. Reprinted in (eds.) Robert Con Davies and Laurie Finke. *Literary Criticism and Theory*. London: Longman.

Burke, Sean. 1992. *The Death and Return of the Author: Criticism and Subjectivity in Barthes, Foucault and Derrida*. Edinburgh: Edinburgh University Press.

Carter, Ron. 2004. *Language and Creativity: The Art of Common Talk*. London: Routledge.

Charlwood, W. B. 1951. *Active Reading*. London: Pearson.

Cochrane, James (ed.). 1969. *The Penguin Book of American Short Stories*. London: Penguin.

Coward, Rosalind and John Ellis. 1977. *Language and Materialism: Developments in Semiology and the Theory of the Subject*. London: Routledge.

Cox, Brian. 1991. *Cox on Cox: an English Curriculum for the 1990s*. London: Hodder and Stoughton.

—— 1995. *Cox on the Battle for the National Curriculum*. London: Hodder and Stoughton.

Cox, Murray. 1992. *Shakespeare Comes to Broadmoor: 'The Actors are Come Hither': The Performance of Tragedy in a Secure Psychiatric Hospital*. London: Kingsley.

Cox, Murray and Alice Theilgaard. 1987. *Mutative Metaphors in Psychotherapy: The Aeolian Mode*. London: Tavistock.

—— 1994. *Shakespeare as Prompter: The Amending Imagination and the Therapeutic Process*. London: Kingsley.

Crystal, David. 1998. *Language Play*. Harmondsworth: Penguin.

Davis, Philip (ed.). 1997. *Real Voices: On Reading*. Basingstoke, Macmillan.

Davis, Philip. 2002. *The Oxford English Literary History: Volume 8, 1830–1880, The Victorians*. Oxford: Oxford University Press.

Davis, Robert Con and Laurie Finke (eds). 1989. *Literary Criticism and Theory: From the Greeks to the Present*. London: Longman.

Dawson, Paul. 2005. *Creative Writing and the New Humanities*. London: Routledge.

Derksen, Jeff. 1993. *Dwell*. Vancouver: Talon.

Dixon, John. 1969. *Growth Through English*. Oxford: Oxford University Press for the National Association for the Teaching of English.

Donoghue, Denis. 1998. *The Practice of Reading*. New Haven: Yale University Press.

Doyle, Brian. 1989. *English and Englishness*. London: Routledge.

Eakin, Paul John. 1999. *How Our Lives Become Stories: Making Selves*. Ithaca, NY: Cornell University Press.

Ediger, Anne, Roberta Alexander and Krystyna Srutwa. 1989. *Reading for Meaning: Skills Development for Active Reading*. New York: Longman.

Ehrenzweig, Anton. 1967. *The Hidden Order of Art*. London: Paladin.

Ellmann, Maud. 1994. *Psychoanalytic Literary Criticism*. Harlow: Longman.

Emerson, Ralph Waldo. 1971. 'The American Scholar', in *The Collected Works of Ralph Waldo Emerson I*. Cambridge, MA: Harvard University Press.

Empson, William. [1930] 1961. *Seven Types of Ambiguity*. Peregrine edition. Harmondsworth: Penguin.

Entwistle, Noel, S. Thompson and H. Tait. 1992. *Guidelines for Promoting Effective Learning in Higher Education*. Edinburgh: University of Edinburgh.

Eraut, Michael. 2001. *Theories of Professional Expertise*. London: Chapman.

Eubanks, Philip. 1999. 'Conceptual metaphor as rhetorical response: A reconsideration of metaphor'. *Written Communication* 16 (2): 171–99.

Evans, Colin. 1993. *English People: The Experience of Teaching and Learning English in British Universities*. Buckingham: Open University Press.

—— 1999. 'Writing Event 2' (seminar notes), Annual DUET Workshop. Stephenson Hall, University of Sheffield, 9 July.

—— 1995. (ed.) *Developing University English Teaching: An Interdisciplinary Approach to Humanities Teaching at University Level*. Lampeter: Mellen.

Everett, Nick. 2005. 'Creative Writing and English', *Cambridge Quarterly*, 34 (3).

Eysenck, Michael W. and Mark Keane. 2005. *Cognitive Psychology: A Student's Handbook*. 5th edition. Hove and New York: Taylor and Francis.

Felman, Shoshana. 1982. 'Teaching Terminable and Interminable', *Yale French Studies* 63: 94–207.

Fish, Stanley. 1980. *Is There a Text in This Class? The Authority of Interpretive Communities*. Cambridge, MA: Harvard University Press.

Fry, Heather, Steve Ketteridge and Stephanie Marshall (eds) 2001. *A Handbook for Teaching and Learning in Higher Education: Enhancing Academic Practice*. London: Kogan Page.

Fullbrook, Kate, Ian MacKillop, Fred Price, *et al.* 1996. 'English and the Assessment Challenge', *Cambridge Quarterly*, 25 (3) 266–84.

Fuller, David. 1988. *Blake's Heroic Argument*. London: Croom Helm.

Gawthrope, Jane and Philip Martin. 2003. *Survey of the English Curriculum and Teaching in UK Higher Education*. (English Subject Centre Report No. 8.). London: Halcrow.

Gersie, Alida and Nancy King. 1990. *Storymaking in Education and Therapy*. London: Kingsley.

Giroux, Henry A. 1988. *Teachers as Intellectuals: Toward a Critical Pedagogy of Learning*. Westport, CT: Bergin and Garvey.

Gooder, Richard. 2005. 'What English Was', *Cambridge Quarterly*, 34 (3).

Green, Andrew. 2005. *Four Perspectives on Transition: English Literature from Sixth Form to University*. (English Subject Centre Report No. 10). London: Halcrow.

Greenblatt, Stephen. 1980. *Renaissance Self-Fashioning from More to Shakespeare*. Chicago: Chicago University Press.

Gunn, Daniel. 1988. *Psychoanalysis and Fiction: An Exploration of Literary and Psychoanalytic Borders*. Cambridge: Cambridge University Press.

Hackman, Susan. 1987. *Responding in Writing: The Use of Explorating Writing in the Literature Classroom*. NATE.

Harding, Denys, W. [1963] 1974. *Experience into Words*. Harmondsworth: Penguin.

Hartley, Jenny. 2001. *Reading Groups*. Oxford: Oxford University Press.

Haswell, Richard H. *et al.* 1999. 'Context and rhetorical reading strategies: Haas and Flower (1988) revisited'. *Written Communication* 16 (1).

Heidegger, Martin. 1962. *Being and Time*. Trans. John Macquarrie and Edward Robinson. Oxford: Blackwell.

Hilgers, Thomas L. *et al.* 1999. 'As you're writing you have these epiphanies'. *Written Communication* 16 (3).

Himley, Margaret. 1986. 'Genre as generative: one perspective on one child's early writing growth'. Ed. Martin Nystrand. *The Structure of Written Communication: Studies in Reciprocity between Writers and Readers*. Orlando, FL: Academic.

Hodgson A. and Spours K. 2003. *Beyond A-levels: Curriculum 2000 and the Reform of 14–19 Qualifications*. London: Kogan Page.

Holderness, Graham. 2003. *Textual Shakespeare: Writing and the Word*. Hatfield: University of Hertfordshire Press.

Holland, Norman. 1975b. *The Dynamics of Literary Response*. New York: Norton.

—— 1975a. *Five Readers Reading*. New Haven and London: Yale University Press.

Holland, Siobhan (ed.). 2003. *Creative Writing, a Good Practice Guide*. (English Subject Centre Report No. 6.) London: Halcrow.

Hollinghurst, Alan. 2004. *The Line of Beauty*. London: Picador.

Holquist, Michael. 1990. *Dialogism: Bakhtin and His World*. London: Methuen.

Homer. *The Odyssey*. 1981. Trans. E.V. Rieu. London: Penguin.

Hughes, Ted. 1967. *Poetry in the Making*. London: Faber.

Hughes, Ted. 1997. *Tales from Ovid*. Farrar Straus Giroux.

Hummel, John E. and Keith J. Holyoak. 2003. 'A symbolic-connectionist theory of relational inference and generalization'. *Psychological Review*, 110: 220–64.

Hunt, Celia. 2000. *Therapeutic Dimensions of Autobiography in Creative Writing*. London: Kingsley.

Hunt, Celia and Fiona Sampson. 2006. *Writing: Self and Reflexivity*. Basingstoke: Palgrave.

Iser, Wolfgang. 1978. *The Act of Reading*. Baltimore: Johns Hopkins University Press.

Jones, Ken, Monica McLean, David Amigoni and Margaret Kinsman. 2005. 'Investigating the Production of University English in Mass Higher Education: Towards an alternative methodology'. *Arts and Humanities in Higher Education* 4: 247–64.

Knights, Ben. 1978. *The Idea of the Clerisy in the Nineteenth Century*. London: Cambridge University Press.

—— 1991. 'Writing Relations in a Men's Prison', *Free Associations Psychoanalysis, Groups, Politics, Culture*, 2 (21): 65–85.

—— 1992. *From Reader to Reader: Theory, Text and Practice in the Study Group*. Hemel Hempstead: Harvester Wheatsheaf.

—— 1995. *The Listening Reader: Fiction and Poetry for Counsellors and Psychotherapists*. London: Kingsley.

—— 1995. 'Creative Reading' in (ed.) Peter Preston, *Literature in Adult Education: Reflections on Practice*. Nottingham: Department of Adult Education.

—— 2005. 'Intelligence and Interrogation: The Identity of the English Student', *Arts and Humanities in Higher Education*, 4 (1): 33–52.

Lakoff, George and Mark Johnson. 1980. *Metaphors We Live By*. Chicago: University of Chicago Press.

Lakoff, George and Mark Turner. 1989. *More Than Cool Reason: A Field Guide to Poetic Metaphor*. Chicago: University of Chicago Press.

Lalić, Ivan V. 1996. *A Rusty Needle*. Trans. Francis R. Jones. London: Anvil.

Lave, Jean and Etienne Wenger. 1991. *Situated Learning: Legitimate Peripheral Participation*. Cambridge: Cambridge University Press.

Leavis F.R. 1932. *How to Teach Reading: A Primer for Ezra Pound*. Cambridge: Cambridge.

—— [1932] 1963. *New Bearings in English Poetry: A Study of the Contemporary Situation*. Harmondsworth: Penguin.

Leavis, Queenie D. 1932. *Fiction and the Reading Public*. London: Chatto and Windus.

Lee, Hermione (ed.). 1985. *The Secret Self 1: Short Stories by Women*. London: Dent.

Lee, Vernon. [1923] 1927. *The Handling of Words and Other Studies in Literary Psychology*. London: Bodley Head.

Livesay, Dorothy. 1971. 'The Documentary Poem: A Canadian Genre' in Eli Mandel (ed.), *Contexts of Canadian Criticism*. Chicago: Chicago University Press. 267–81.

Lodge, David. 1966. *The Language of Fiction: Essays in Criticism and Verbal Analysis of the English Novel*. London: Routledge.

—— 1981. *Working with Structuralism: Essays and Reviews on Nineteenth- and Twentieth-Century Literature*. London: Routledge.

—— 1996. *The Practice of Writing*. London: Secker and Warburg.

Lubbock, Percy. [1921] 1926. *The Craft of Fiction*. London: Cape.

Macherey, Pierre. 1978. *A Theory of Literary Production*. Trans. Geoffrey Wall. London: Routledge.

Machor, James L. and Philip Goldstein (eds). 2001. *Reception Study: From Literary Theory to Cultural Studies*. New York: Routledge.

Mailloux, Steven. 1982. *Interpretive Conventions: The Reader in the Study of American Fiction*. Ithaca, NY: Cornell University Press.

—— 1989. *Rhetorical Power*. Ithaca, NY: Cornell University Press.

Maker, Janet and Minette Lenier. 1996. *Academic Reading with Active Critical Thinking* Belmont, CA: Wadsworth.

Mark, Alison. 2001. *Veronica Forrest-Thomson and Language Poetry*. Tavistock: Northcote.

Marton, Ference and Roger Säljö. 1976. 'On qualitative differences in learning: Outcome and Process', *British Journal of Educational Psychology*, 46: 4–11.

Mayers, Tim. 2005. *(Re)Writing Craft: Composition, Creative Writing, and the Future of English Studies*. Pittsburgh: University of Pittsburgh Press.

McCurrie, M. and M. Kilian. 2004. 'From the Edges to the Center: Pedagogy's Role in Redefining English Departments', *Pedagogy* 4 (1): 43–64.

McDrury, Janice and Maxine Alterio. 2002. *Learning Through Storytelling in Higher Education*. London: Kogan Page.

McEwen, Christian. 2004. 'Artists' notebooks: poetry, drawing and creative journaling', (unpublished paper). National Association for Writers in Education Conference on Writers and Location, St. Mary's College, University of Surrey, 1 May.

McGregor, Graham and R. S. White (eds). 1990. *Reception and Response: Hearer Creativity and the Analysis of Spoken and Written Texts*. London: Routledge.

McLeod, John. 1997. *Narrative and Psychotherapy*. London: Sage.

Mieszkowski, Sylvia. 2005. 'Vernon Lee – Gen(i)us Loci of the Academic Periphery', in (eds.) Miriam Kauko, Sylvia Mieszkowski and Alexandra Tischel, *Gendered Academia: Wissenschaft und Geschlechterdifferenz 1890–1945*. Göttingen: Wallstein.

Miller, Hillis. 1982. *Fiction and Repetition: Seven English Novels*. Oxford: Blackwell.

Mills, Paul. 1996. *Writing in Action*. London: Routledge.

Moi, Toril. 1986. *The Kristeva Reader*. Oxford: Balckwell.

Monteith, Moira and Robert Miles (eds). 1992. *Teaching Creative Writing: Theory and Practice*. Buckingham: Open University Press.

Morris, Pam (ed.). 1994. *The Bakhtin Reader: Selected Writings of Bakhtin, Medvedev, Voloshinov*. London: Arnold.

Mulhern, Francis. 1978. *The Moment of Scrutiny*. London: New Left Books.

Musselwhite, David. 1978. 'The Novel as Narcotic', in Francis Baker *et al*. (eds). 1848: *The Sociology of Literature*. Colchester: University of Essex.

Newlyn, Lucy. 2003. *Synergies: Creative Writing in Academic Practice* (Two volumes). Oxford: Chough.

Nystrand, Martin. 1982. *What Writers Know: The Language, Process and Structure of Written Discourse*. New York: Academic.

—— 1986. *The Structure of Written Communication: Studies in Reciprocity between Writers and Readers*. Orlando: Academic.

Olson, Charles. 1983. *The Maximus Poems*. Berkeley and Los Angeles: University of California Press.

O'Rourke, Rebecca. 2005. *Creative Writing: Culture, Education and Community*. Leicester: National Institute of Adult Continuing Education.

Ortony, A. 1993. *Metaphor and Thought*. Cambridge: Cambridge University Press.

Parker, Ian and The Bolton Discourse Network. 1999. *Critical Textwork: An Introduction to Varieties of Discourse and Analysis*. Buckingham: Open University Press.

The Pelican Guide to English Literature. Volume 2: The Age of Shakespeare. 1955. London: Penguin.

Pater, Walter. 1905. 'Henri-Frédéric Amiel', *Essays from the Guardian*. London: Macmillan.

Poe, Edgar Allan. 1994. *The Complete Illustrated Stories and Poems*. London: Chancellor.

Pope, Rob. 1995. *Textual Intervention: Critical and Creative Strategies for Literary Studies*. London: Routledge.

——. 2005. *Creativity: Theory, History, Practice*. London: Routledge.

Pound, Ezra. 1951. *ABC of Reading*. London: Faber.

Protherough, Robert. 1989. *Students of English*. London: Routledge.

Ramsden, Paul. 2003. *Learning to Teach in Higher Education*. 2nd edition. London: Routledge Falmer.

Readings, Bill. 1996. *The University in Ruins*. Cambridge, MA: Harvard University Press.

Ricoeur, Paul. 1986. *The Rule of Metaphor*. London: Routledge and Kegan Paul.

Richards, I.A. [1929] 1964. *Practical Criticism: A study of Literary Judgment*. London: Routledge and Kegan Paul.

Rodrigues, Dawn, and Myron C. Tuman. 1998. *Writing Essentials*. 2nd edition. New York: Norton.

Roe, Sue (ed.). 1987. *Women Reading Women's Writing*. Brighton: Harvester Press.

Rommetveit, R. and R. M. Blakar. 1979. *Studies of Language, Thought and Verbal Communication*. London: Academic.

Rosenblatt, Louise. 1978. *The Reader, The Text, The Poem: The Transactional Theory of The Literary Work*. Carbondale, ILL: Southern Illinois University Press.

Rossiter, A.P. 1961. *Angel with Horns: Fifteen Lectures on Shakespeare*, Ed. Graham Storey. London: Longman.

Salzberger-Wittenberg, Isca, Gianna Henry and Elsie Osborne. 1983. *The Emotional Experience of Teaching and Learning*. London: Routledge.

Sanders, Wilbur. 1968. *The Dramatist and the Received Idea*. Cambridge: Cambridge University Press.

Sarbin, T. R. (ed.) 1986. *Narrative Psychology: The Storied Nature of Human Conduct*. New York: Praeger.

Scholes, Robert. 1985. *Textual Power: Literary Theory and the Teaching of English*. New Haven, CT: Yale University Press.

—— 1998. *The Rise and Fall of English; Reconstructing English as a Discipline*. New Haven, CT: Yale University Press.

—— *The Crafty Reader*. New Haven, CT: Yale UP, 2001.

Sellers, Susan. 1989. *Delighting the Heart: A Notebook by Women Writers*. London: Women's Press.

—— 1991. *Taking Reality by Surprise: Writing for Pleasure and Publication*. London: Women's Press.

Sennett, Richard. 1998. *The Corrosion of Character: The Personal Consequences of Work in the New Capitalism*. New York: Norton.

Shotter, John. 1993. *Cultural Politics of Everyday Life*. Buckingham: Open University Press.

Shotter, John and Kenneth J. Gergen (eds). 1989. *Texts of Identity*. London: Sage.

Showalter, Elaine. 2003. *Teaching Literature*. Oxford: Blackwell.

Smallwood, Philip. 2002. 'More Creative than Creation: On the Idea of Criticism and the Student Critic', *Arts and Humanities in Higher Education*, 1 (1).

Smith, Stevie. 1980. *Novel on Yellow Wallpaper*. London: Virago.

Spivey, Nancy Nelson. 1997. *The Constructivist Metaphor: Reading, Writing and the Making of Meaning*. San Diego, CA: Academic.

Suleiman, Susan and Inge Crossman (eds). 1980. *The Reader in the Text: Essays on Audience and Interpretation*. Princeton, NJ: Princeton University Press.

Tannen, Deborah (ed.). 1993. *Framing in Discourse*. New York: Oxford University Press.

The Teaching of English in England, Being the Report of the Departmental Committee Appointed by the President of the Board of Education to Inquire into the Position of English in the Educational System of England [The Newbolt Report, 1921 and 1924]. 1924. London: HMSO.

Tóibín, Colm. 2004. *The Master*. London: Picador. 48–9.

Todorov, Tzvetan. 1984. *Mikhail Bakhtin: The Dialogical Principle*. Trans. Wlad Godzich. Manchester: Manchester University Press.

Tomasello, Michael. 1999. *The Cultural Origins of Human Cognition*. Cambridge, MA: Harvard Univesity Press.

Travis, Molly Abel. 1998. *Reading Cultures: The Construction of Readers in the Twentieth Century*. Carbondale, ILL: Southern Illinois University Press.

Tulloch, Jonathan. 2000. *The Season Ticket*. London: Cape.

Tuman, Myron C. (ed.). 1992. *Literacy Online: The Promise (and Peril) of Reading and Writing with Computers*. Pittsburgh: University of Pittsburgh Press.

Turner, John. 2002. 'The Arbourthorne Project' (unpublished paper). Verbal Arts Association Conference: 'Next in Text'. The National Centre for Popular Music, 18 May.

Turner, Mark. 1996. *The Literary Mind: The Origins of Thought and Language*. New York: Oxford University Press.

Veer, Rene Van de, and Jaan Valsiner (eds). 1994. *The Vygotsky Reader*. Oxford: Blackwell.

Vorhaus, John. 2000. *Creativity Rules: A Writer's Workbook*. Los Angeles: Silman-James.

Vygotsky, L.S. 1978. *Mind and Society: The Development of Higher Psychological Processes*, eds. Michael Cole, Vera John-Steiner, Sylvia Scribner and Ellen Souberman. Cambridge, MA: Harvard University Press.

Wakeford, Richard. 2001. 'Principles of Assessment', eds. Heather Fry, Steve Ketteridge and Stephanie Marshall. *A Handbook for Teaching and Learning in Higher Education: Enhancing Academic Practice*. London: Kogan Page.

Wetherell, Margaret, Stephanie Taylor and Simeon J. Yates (eds). 2001. *Discourse Theory and Practice: A Reader*. London: Sage.

Wilde, Oscar. 1930. 'The Critic as Artist.' *Plays, Prose Writings and Poems*. Everyman's Library.

Wilder, Laura. 2002. 'Get Comfortable with Uncertainty: A Study of the Conventional Values of Literary Analysis in an Undergraduate Literature Course', *Written Communication* 19 (1): 175–221.

Williams, Raymond. 1977. 'Literature in Society' in (ed.) Hilda Schiff, *Contemporary Approaches to English Studies*. London: Heinemann for the English Association.

Williams, Sadie. 2002. *Admissions Trends in Undergraduate English: Statistics and Attitudes*. English Subject Centre.

Winnicott, D.W. 1971. *Playing and Reality*. London: Tavistock.

Winter, Richard, Alyson Buck and Paula Sobiecheska. 1999. *Professional Experience and The Investigative Imagination: The Art of Reflective Writing*. London: Routledge.

Wold, Astri Heen (ed.). 1992. *The Dialogical Alternative: Toward a Theory of Language and Mind.* Oslo: Scandinavian University Press.

Wolf, Robert. 2001. *Jump-Start: How to Write from Everyday Life.* Oxford and New York: Oxford University Press.

Young, Katherine G. 1987. *Taleworlds and Storyrealms: the Phenomenology of Narrative.* Dordrecht, Netherlands: Nijhoff.

WEB ARCHIVES

We would like finally to note two website archives both of which contain a large amount of relevant and provocative material. In the project area of the website of the Higher Education English Subject Centre *www.english. heacademy.ac.uk/explore/projects/index.php* can be found a number of valuable project reports. Those most directly relevant include Graeme Harper's Reading to Write, Writing to be Read', Robert Sheppard's 'Supplementary Discourses in Creative Writing Teaching' and Steve May's 'Teaching Creative Writing at Undergraduate Level; How, Why, How, and Does it Work?'

Writing in Education, the journal of the National Association for Writing in Education (NAWE), has published a number of relevant articles. The complete archive can be accessed (by members of NAWE) through the website at *www.nawe.co.uk*. We would particularly draw attention to articles by Jane Bluett on 'Critical and Creative Writing in the A-level Classroom' (2006), by Graeme Harper 'Creative Writing and Literature Development on UK Campuses' (2002), Robyn Bolam's 'Creativity and Criticism: a Current Debate' (2002), Rob Pope's 'Critical-Creative Re-Writing: a Briefing' (2002), and Neil Rutledge, 'Helping Learners Link the Critical and the Creative' (2006).

Index

Jones, David 155
journalism 15

Kafka, Franz 67
keyword task 97–100
Knight, Wilson 52
knowledge 16, 17, 21, 61, 158, 162
Kristeva, Julia 68, 100

Lacan, Jacques 25
launch-pad activities 93–6
Lawrence, D. H. 143, 155
learners
  autonomous 10, 151–62
  identity as fluid construct 9
learning
  deep 2
  forms of 56
  lifelong 16, 150, 151
  opportunities for 2
  outcomes 61, 114, 120
  situated 161
  strategic 2
  styles 34, 54
  temporality 63–4
learning communities 2, 159
Learning/Teaching/Politics (LTP)
    Conferences 56
Leavis, F. R. 43, 46, 47
Leavis, Q. D. 43, 46
lectures 63, 152, 155
Lee, Vernon 47, 48
lexis 119, 123
liberal humanism 24, 53
liberalism 10
lifelong education 16
lifelong learning 16, 150, 151
linguistic corpora 9
linguistics 11, 15, 22
listening tasks 84
listing 94, 100
literary practice 28
Literary Practice Book, The 28
literary studies 1, 27, 146, 149
literary theory 69
literature
  as an object 23

as work of co-operation 48
  goals of 20
  imagined community of 14
  in adult education 135
  postcolonial approach to 15
  relationship to writing 21
  social reach of 15
  trends in 12–13
Lodge, David 47, 49, 65
LTP, *see* Learning/Teaching/Politics
Lubbock, Percy 48
Lurie, Alison 49

Macbeth 52–3
Macherey, Pierre 57, 61
Making Sense module 60–1, 71
marketization 16
marking 111, 131; *see also* assessment
Martin, Graham 23
Marton, Ference 34
Marxism 24, 61
masculinities 58
maturity 53
McDrury, Janice 140
McEwen, Christian 81
media studies 15
meetings 155–7
message/noise contrast 67
meta-cognitive breaks 95
meta-cognitive reflection 96
meta-cognitive writing 107
meta-critical breaks 95
metafiction 58, 169
meta-languages 71
metaphor 141, 143, 148
Miles, Robert 59–60
mime 84
modality 123
modelling 76
monologue performance 84
morality 21
motivation 161
Mulhern, Francis 53
myths 171, 172

naming 67
narrative 86, 141